Dictators at War and Peace

D1072864

A volume in the series

CORNELL STUDIES IN SECURITY AFFAIRS

edited by Robert J. Art, Robert Jervis, and Stephen M. Walt

A list of titles in this series is available at www.cornellpress.cornell.edu.

Dictators at War and Peace

JESSICA L. P. WEEKS

Cornell University Press

ITHACA AND LONDON

Cornell University Press gratefully acknowledges the receipt of funds from the Smith Richardson Foundation, which aided in the publication of this book.

First published 2014 by Cornell University Press
First printing, Cornell Paperbacks, 2014

Printed in the United States of America

Library of Congress Cataloging-in-Publication Data

Weeks, Jessica L. P., author.
  Dictators at war and peace / Jessica L. P. Weeks.
    pages cm
  Includes bibliographical references and index.
  ISBN 978-0-8014-5296-3 (cloth : alk. paper)
  ISBN 978-0-8014-7982-3 (pbk. : alk. paper)
  1. Dictators. 2. Authoritarianism. 3. Military policy—Decision making.
4. War—Political aspects. I. Title.
  JC495.W44   2014
  321.9092'2—dc23   2014021002

Cloth printing   10 9 8 7 6 5 4 3 2 1
Paperback printing   10 9 8 7 6 5 4 3 2 1

For Jon

Contents

[vii]

Tables and Figures

Acknowledgments

This book owes its existence to the help and support of a large number of advisors, colleagues, friends, and members of my family.

I am greatly indebted to my advisors at Stanford University for their advice on the first incarnation of this book. Ken Schultz was incredibly generous with his time and ideas. At many points, he suggested a crucial reframing, and I am deeply grateful for his open door. Scott Sagan repeatedly helped me distill the most important insights, package the ideas in a way that was understandable to others, and make connections to other scholarship and to real-world problems. Jim Fearon provided invaluable feedback, and talked me off the ledge when I was tempted to ditch the project (as we all want to do sometimes). Finally, Mike Tomz has been a true mentor, and now friend. His support and feedback have been central to my growth as a scholar.

Many other people at Stanford left their stamp on the project. David Laitin's research seminar led to the first ideas, and I still remember when David first said that the project "had legs." Early on, Steve Haber also provided both theoretical insights and enthusiastic support of the project and encouraged me to send out the first article. Jonathan Wand and Simon Jackman were very supportive in my training in quantitative methods, and having a spot on the third floor of Encina Hall not only spurred me to work harder but also allowed me to interact with professors and students in different subfields. Paul Sniderman took me under his wing during my fourth year and helped me define the project much more clearly. Steve Krasner, Beatriz Magaloni, and Jeremy Weinstein all taught outstanding classes that influenced the project either directly or indirectly. I am grateful to all of them. I was also lucky to study with a superb group: Claire Adida, Ed Bruera, Dara Kay Cohen, Luke Condra,

[xi]

Ashley Conner, Desha Girod, Oliver Kaplan, Alex Kuo, Bethany Lacina, Neil Malhotra, Kenneth McElwain, Victor Menaldo, James Morrison, and Maggie Peters all deserve special thanks for both friendship and feedback on the project in its early stages.

Outside Stanford, other individuals gave me helpful comments or shared data that shaped the project early on. First among these is Barbara Geddes, who generously shared the raw data that inform important parts of the empirical analysis. I also thank Hein Goemans, who shared helpful data early in the process and was an important source of advice and encouragement throughout.

While the seeds of the project were sown at Stanford, the book took its current form during my time at Cornell University and was profoundly influenced by my interactions with colleagues there. Peter Katzenstein, Jonathan Kirshner, Matt Evangelista, Thomas Pepinsky, Allen Carlson, and Andrew Mertha all read an early version of the manuscript and gave me feedback that fundamentally transformed the project. Of course, their advice meant that it took several more years for me to finish the book, but I believe that the project is much richer for it. I thank Peter Katzenstein in particular for many illuminating conversations. I am also grateful to Sarah Kreps, Kevin Morrison, David Patel, Val Bunce, Peter Enns, Gustavo Flores-Macias, Elizabeth Sanders, Christopher Anderson, Ron Herring, Mary Katzenstein, Ken Roberts, Nic van de Walle, Anna Bautista, and Katrina Browne for providing extremely helpful feedback.

Some very talented undergraduate students at Cornell were also invaluable to the project. I thank Judah Bellin, Nathan Cohen, Melissa Frankford, Dia Rasinariu, Jonathan Panter, Anna Collins, Jimmy Crowell, Charlotte Deng, Laura Jakli, Tracey Hsu, Kailin Koch, Andres O'Hara-Plotnick, Jennifer Pinsof, Olivia Pora, Aaron Glickman, Katherine McCulloh, Tracy Robinton, Marissa Esthimer, Elena Moreno, Carrie Bronsther, and Skyler Schain for their outstanding work.

Outside colleagues also provided extremely helpful feedback throughout the advanced stages. I am particularly grateful to Rice University for hosting me during the 2011–2012 academic year. Songying Fang, Ashley Leeds, Cliff Morgan, and Ric Stoll not only were welcoming but also gave excellent feedback on the project. I am indebted to each of them for their friendship and insights. I thank Christopher Way and Jeff Colgan for their support and scholarly collaboration on related projects that helped shed new light on the material in this book. I am very grateful to Sarah Croco for her help and support balancing work and life in the final stages of this project and to Michael Horowitz for his support and many conversations about data. I am also grateful to Dan Reiter, Alex Debs, Hein Goemans, Giacomo Chiozza, Joe Wright, Rena Seltzer, Leslie Simon, and Julia Gray for help and feedback at various stages, and to Dean Robbins for superb editing. Robert Jervis and Bruce Russett both deserve special thanks for providing comments that greatly improved the book. I also thank Roger Haydon for shepherding the book through the process and for his good-humored guidance.

I put the finishing touches on the final draft at the University of Wisconsin–Madison and am grateful to several graduate students for reading and commenting on the penultimate draft: Ryan Powers, Patrick Kearney, Roseanne McManus, Mark Toukan, and Susanne Mueller. Special thanks go to Kira Mochal for checking every page of the manuscript numerous times.

Several institutions provided generous financial support. The Center for International Security and Cooperation gave me a very generous pre-doctoral fellowship. The National Science Foundation awarded me Doctoral Dissertation Improvement Grant #SES-0720414, "Leaders, Accountability, and Foreign Policy in Non-Democracies," facilitating some of the early data collection. The Smith Richardson Foundation provided a generous grant that freed up my teaching time. Cornell University also provided generous funding at various stages of the project.

As anyone who has written a book knows, it is impossible to do without friends and family. I am indebted to Dara Cohen and Sarah Kreps for many years of friendship and both personal and professional guidance. I am also grateful to Ed Bruera for years of support and encouragement. My parents Steve and Ursula and sister Stephanie have also rooted me on at all stages; I am particularly grateful to them for knowing when *not* to ask how the book was going.

And finally, I thank my four loves: Jon, Claire, Ava, and Carl. While much of the thinking and research on this book was done before you came into my life, I could not have completed it without you. Claire and Ava, you were so patient when I had to work, and I can't tell you how much I appreciated your tiptoeing into the basement office with snacks and hot chocolate. Carl, though you were still in utero as I finished writing, it was your anticipated entry into the world that at long last gave me a credible deadline. And more than anyone, Jon, you supported me in the (long) final stretch. You had the impossible task of giving me feedback on the manuscript when I was only a couple of months away from my deadline—a feat you handled with impressive diplomacy. More important, you took care of me and buoyed my spirits every day. Jon, thank you. This book is for you.

Dictators at War and Peace

Introduction

In August of 1990, Saddam Hussein sent Iraqi tanks rumbling into neighboring Kuwait, announcing that Iraq had regained its nineteenth province and sparking a conflict with the United States and its allies. In April of 1982, General Leopoldo Galtieri, the military dictator of Argentina, sent his forces to occupy the Falkland/Malvinas Islands, a forlorn piece of British territory that had long inspired acrimony between the two nations, and declared that the Malvinas had been restored to its rightful owners. Through the early 1960s, the communist dictatorship in North Vietnam intensified its campaign to reunify North and South, pulling the United States deeper into what would become a full-fledged international war.

The three countries that provoked these conflicts had much in common. Each was ruled by a highly repressive dictatorship that denied its citizens civil and political rights and ruthlessly suppressed domestic opposition to the regime. Each placed control over decisions about war and peace in the hands of a small coterie of elites. And each instigated a costly war against a vastly more powerful democratic foe with the goal of enlarging its own territory.

How did these wars turn out for the authoritarian side? Judging from existing scholarship, one might guess that the outcomes would be determined by the hard constraints of military power and the idiosyncrasies of history. Alternatively, one might look to domestic politics, as more recent research has done, and expect the more sober and accountable democratic target to rout the nondemocratic aggressor, whose dictator would nevertheless remain in power.

Neither of these expectations, however, fits all three cases. The Iraqi experience seems to confirm the stereotype of the belligerent and unaccountable dictator. Saddam Hussein refused to back down, and a large coalition of

[1]

Western and Middle Eastern countries intervened in Kuwait. Their armies handed Iraqi forces a decisive defeat, but Saddam Hussein nonetheless survived as the undisputed ruler of Iraq for more than another decade.

The Argentine case, however, departs from this mold. On the one hand, as in the Iraqi case, the nondemocratic aggressor suffered a humiliating reversal. Argentine expectations that Britain would not respond with force turned out to be terribly wrong. Britain quickly dispatched portions of its navy and air force to the South Atlantic and soon beat Argentina into surrender. Unlike Saddam Hussein, however, Galtieri was unable to shrug off defeat. Instead, four short days after the Argentine capitulation, his peers in the military forced him out and replaced him with another general.

The Vietnamese case differs from both of the above templates. Unlike the leaders of Iraq or Argentina, Vietnamese leaders Ho Chi Minh and Le Duan made decisions cautiously and shrewdly, using force only after lengthy internal debate. Their approach paid off: the United States withdrew in 1973, and Vietnam was reunified in 1975. It was a stunning defeat for the democratic side, and Le Duan's reward for the victory was a long career as ruler of a united Vietnam.

What explains these divergent paths? Why do some dictators make such risky, and in some eyes foolhardy, decisions about the use of force, whereas others are much more cautious in their decisions to exercise military power? Why do some authoritarian leaders limit themselves to winnable wars, whereas others embroil their countries in defeats that could surely have been avoided? And why do some dictators weather defeat, whereas others are ousted within days of losing a war?

Existing scholarship, which tends to focus on differences *between* democracies and dictatorships rather than variation *among* dictatorships, provides relatively few answers. It is widely accepted that democratic leaders use force more cautiously than authoritarian leaders because for democrats, policy failures or unpopular campaigns can lead to punishment at the hands of the *demos*.[1] In contrast, because dictators are much less accountable to ordinary citizens, they are typically seen as willing to undertake much riskier uses of force. However, the domestic factors scholars usually invoke to explain differences between democracies and dictatorships—such as free and fair elections or the strength of democratic norms—do not vary greatly *among* authoritarian regimes. Existing scholarship cannot therefore provide direct insight into differences among the Husseins, Galtieris, and Le Duans of the world.

WHY CARE ABOUT DIFFERENCES AMONG DICTATORSHIPS?

Autocracies are surprisingly resilient in the modern era. Despite a trend toward political and economic liberalization, many of the most important actors in contemporary world politics remain nondemocratic. Among their ranks are countries with massive economic and military power, such as China and Russia; countries with important natural resources, such as Iran and some Arab nations; and economically fragile countries that have nonetheless managed to develop potent weapons, such as North Korea.

Yet scholars and policymakers have a poor understanding of the domestic political incentives of leaders of different types of authoritarian regimes when it comes to decisions about national security. Why are some dictatorships conflict-prone, others relatively pacific? What are the prospects for peace when countries are led by unconstrained dictators rather than by leaders who must answer to a powerful collective, such as the highest ranks of a political party in a single-party dictatorship? Does it matter whether the primary decision-makers are civilians, or do military officers make similar choices about war?

Answering these questions is important for those tasked with understanding the behavior of authoritarian regimes. Yet current scholarship provides few systematic answers. As a result, scholars and policymakers have several competing but incorrect views of how domestic politics affect the foreign policy behavior of dictatorships.

The first is the idea that all authoritarian regimes are similar in that their leaders face few domestic constraints when making decisions about war and peace. This perspective, which typically concludes that democracies as a group are less warlike than dictatorships, dominates the existing international relations scholarship on regime type and foreign policy. The core of this view, introduced by Immanuel Kant, is that nondemocratic leaders are freer to choose war than leaders who must answer to the public.[2] This assessment rests in part on the assumption that citizens find it difficult to punish dictators who subject them to the ravages of war.[3] Dictators internalize fewer of the costs of war and are therefore more likely to use military force, whereas democratic leaders have incentives to choose less costly, and hence more peaceful, options.

Drawing on these insights, scholars have explored many differences between democracies and autocracies on questions related to national security. With few exceptions, however, that literature has failed to differentiate among different kinds of authoritarian regimes, and it has concluded that because dictators are not directly accountable to the public, domestic political factors must play little role in their policy decisions.

An alternative view holds that domestic politics do play an important role in dictatorships, but that the relationship between domestic politics and foreign policy is unique to each country. For example, some have argued that in modern China, public nationalism plays a major role in foreign policy decisions.[4] Others have argued that Iranian attempts to pursue nuclear weapons are driven in part by domestic political concerns. Countless country specialists have studied the foreign policies of individual authoritarian states and have provided valuable insights about the specific policies of particular countries.[5] However, most country-specific analyses treat individual countries as *sui generis* cases rather than seeking to develop more general insights. Research that focuses on individual countries such as China or Iran is not usually designed to detect patterns in the relationship between domestic politics and foreign policy across different authoritarian regimes. In fact, partly as a result of focusing on individual countries, observers sometimes conclude that the domestic politics of war are mostly idiosyncratic. They dismiss the notion that domestic regime type might systematically shape how states behave.

Together, these existing approaches have resulted in misconceptions about how and why dictatorships make decisions about war and peace. This book, instead, exposes predictable patterns across different types of regimes, with important payoffs. Patterns of foreign policy decisionmaking are different in different kinds of autocracies, and the strategies policymakers use when confronting different types of leaders must therefore be tailored appropriately.

The insights of this book thus have important implications for both theory and policy. For example, the findings suggest that conventional views of the relationship between regime type and war, including the argument that democracies are more selective than any other kind of regime about initiating international conflict, are either incomplete or wrong. I show that by obscuring differences among dictatorships, the usual dichotomy between democracy and authoritarianism leads to faulty conclusions about the effects of democracy on foreign relations. Surprisingly, many autocratic leaders face a realistic possibility of punishment by a civilian domestic audience; they confront many of the same domestic pressures as democratic leaders, only in a different guise. Similarly, leaders of military juntas face a form of domestic "accountability"—but due to the preferences of the audience, this does not lead to peace. Only some extraordinarily centralized regimes behave in a way that resembles the conventional view of dictatorships.

DOMESTIC POLITICS AND THE USE OF FORCE IN AUTHORITARIAN REGIMES

In order to shed light on how and why authoritarian regimes make decisions about war and peace, this book synthesizes insights from the study of comparative authoritarianism with those about the causes of war. The resulting framework draws attention to three crucial questions.

[4]

First, does the leader face a domestic audience able to punish him or her for decisions about international conflict? Second, what are the preferences and perceptions of that audience when it comes to the use of force? Third, what are the preferences and perceptions of the leader himself?[6]

To answer these questions, I blend insights from different theoretical traditions in international relations. The argument partially draws on the "rationalist" assumption that leaders carefully weigh the effects of foreign policy decisions on their survival in office and, broadly speaking, seek to maximize their chances of staying in power. Like much of the modern literature on war, I assume that political institutions shape actors' personal interests and therefore inform their decisions in important ways. However, the nature of international politics means that there are limits on the extent to which objective external circumstances determine how individuals will perceive particular situations. Foreign policy decisions are made under conditions of enormous uncertainty and often duress, and it is difficult for individuals to anticipate the consequences of specific decisions. In the words of Robert McNamara, when it comes to making decisions about war, "Time is short. Information is sparse or inconsistent."[7] As a consequence, policymakers must often turn to shortcuts and rules of thumb to help them navigate international politics. Therefore, I draw on ideational, psychological, and sociological arguments about how decision-makers' personal backgrounds affect their interpretations of external events, their views of military force, and their perceptions of their own interests. In sum, I highlight the role of political institutions, but also the individuals within them. Institutions shape incentives and disincentives, but individuals' preferences and perceptions are an important part of the picture.

It is also worth noting that despite my focus on domestic politics, in this book I recognize that leaders make decisions under conditions of international anarchy and that external or "structural" factors such as relative power are very important. My argument shows how domestic politics and the individual backgrounds of leaders and domestic audiences filter perceptions of the international system, making certain types of leaders more likely to behave like prudent realists than others. Rather than viewing the contributions of different paradigms as competitive or mutually exclusive, the argument merges these insights to explain why some domestic political contexts are more likely to generate incautious or aggressive international behavior than others.

To develop the argument, I begin by laying out a simple framework that highlights the potential domestic costs and benefits of using—or not using—military force abroad. Although authoritarian leaders are not directly accountable to the public like democratically elected leaders, they nonetheless rely on the support of important domestic audiences. The

[5]

intensity and source of this "accountability" vary across autocracies and affect leaders' costs of using force. These insights lead me to distinguish regimes along two core dimensions: (1) whether the leader faces a powerful domestic audience, and (2) whether the leader or audience stems from the civilian or military ranks. These two dimensions produce four kinds of regimes: nonpersonalist *machines*, in which the leader faces a powerful domestic audience composed primarily of civilian regime insiders; nonpersonalist *juntas*, in which the leader faces a domestic audience composed primarily of military officers; and two kinds of personalist regimes without meaningful audiences—personalist regimes led by relatively unfettered civilian *bosses* and personalist regimes led by military *strongmen*.[8]

Each of these core regime types creates a different set of incentives and opportunities for leaders' foreign policy decisions. Leaders of nonpersonalist civilian machines, such as modern China or the post-Stalin Soviet Union, face a surprising amount of domestic accountability for decisions to use force. Moreover, the civilians who exercise power in these regimes tend to take a prudent and cautious attitude toward the use of force, much like voters and politicians in democracies. This causes leaders of machines to initiate military conflicts relatively infrequently, to prevail in the conflicts they do initiate, and to face punishment when they miscalculate. Indeed, I show that machines are virtually indistinguishable from democracies in terms of these three behavioral patterns.

Like the leaders of machines, the leaders of juntas, such as the infamous Argentine military junta of the late 1970s and early 1980s, face much greater domestic accountability than is commonly assumed. But in contrast to machines, the core domestic audience in juntas is composed of other military officers, often those at the junior and middle level. These military officers tend to have substantially more hawkish preferences than the civilian audiences in machines. Why? Career military service tends to select for certain types of individuals and then further socialize them into a "military mindset" in which force is seen as a necessary, effective, and appropriate policy option. Often, militaries also have narrow parochial interests that cause them to prioritize force over diplomacy. Leaders of juntas therefore initiate more conflicts than leaders of machines and enjoy somewhat less successful outcomes. Yet, because they are ultimately accountable to other regime insiders, they tend to be punished domestically after military defeat.

Finally, personalist bosses and strongmen such as Saddam Hussein, Muammar Gaddafi, Kim Jong Il, Idi Amin, or (some argue) Vladimir Putin do not face powerful, organized domestic audiences. Instead, these are regimes in which the leader personally controls the state and military apparatuses and can use that control to thwart potential rivals.[9] Given

[6]

these leaders' personal supremacy in matters of foreign policy, we must inquire into the preferences of the leaders themselves. I draw on research from psychology, history, and political science to argue that the challenges of attaining and maintaining absolute power mean that personalist boss and strongman regimes tend to feature leaders who are particularly drawn to the use of military force and often have far-ranging international ambitions. Moreover, the sycophants who surround these leaders have few incentives to rein in their patrons' impulses, to correct any misperceptions they may have about the likely outcome of a war, or to try to oust them if things go poorly. Compared to leaders of other kinds of regimes, then, leaders of personalist boss and strongman regimes initiate conflict more frequently, lose a higher proportion of the wars they start, and yet survive in office at a remarkable rate even in the wake of defeat.

EXISTING INSIGHTS ABOUT AUTOCRACIES AND WAR

Although the literature on the conflict behavior of autocracies remains sparse, a small number of studies have started to explore some of the questions raised here. One strand of research, a series of papers by Mark Peceny and colleagues, concludes that personalist dictatorships, in which the leader depends on only a small coterie of supporters, are more likely to initiate conflicts than both democracies and other authoritarian regime types.[10] Peceny and Butler (2004) argue that this pattern is consistent with selectorate theory, which focuses on two groups: the "winning coalition," or the group of regime insiders whose support is necessary to sustain the leader in office, and the "selectorate," the group of individuals who have a role in selecting the leader (Bueno de Mesquita et al. 2003). According to selectorate theory, when the winning coalition is small relative to the selectorate, members of the winning coalition have strong incentives to stay loyal to the leader regardless of his or her performance in providing public goods such as national security. In contrast, when the winning coalition is large relative to the selectorate, as it is in democracies, members of the winning coalition have greater incentives to evaluate leaders based on their ability to provide public goods, because they are more likely to survive the turnover of the incumbent. As a consequence, selectorate theory suggests, leaders with large winning coalitions have incentives to initiate only those military disputes that they are likely to win at a low cost, which depresses their rates of dispute initiation. According to Peceny et al., personalist regimes become involved in disputes at high rates because they tend to have very small winning coalitions.

[7]

However, there are problems with using selectorate theory to explain why some autocracies are more belligerent than others.[11] First, while a key assumption of selectorate theory is that small-coalition regime insiders believe that they will lose their privileged positions under a new ruler, this assumption is inaccurate for many small-coalition regimes.[12] In some nondemocracies, elites have independent bases of power, and their political survival does not depend on the whims of the incumbent. When leaders lack the power to determine who is inside the winning coalition, regime insiders can survive under a new leader even when the winning coalition is small. Elites inside the winning coalition therefore have fewer incentives to remain loyal than selectorate theory supposes.

Many real-world examples support this alternative view. In nonpersonalistic small-coalition regimes such as post-Stalin USSR, modern China, and Argentina and Brazil under their military juntas, individuals gained their positions of privilege because of seniority or competence, not the favor of the sitting leader. Because regime insiders' political power did not depend entirely on the favor of the incumbent, they believed they could jettison an incompetent or reckless leader and survive politically, just as most of the members of Khrushchev's Presidium did when they ousted him as premier. In fact, members of the winning coalition often coordinate to establish and maintain norms against arbitrarily dismissing top officials precisely because such rules give them power vis-à-vis the leader.[13] Thus, selectorate theory relies on a key assumption that holds only in some small-coalition authoritarian regimes. In many dictatorships, leaders are *not* so insulated by loyalty, casting doubt on the conclusion that they need not care about foreign policy outcomes.

A second problem with using selectorate theory to explain differences among authoritarian regimes is its assumption that, conditional on coalition size, all actors perceive the world in the same way.[14] This assumption overlooks the great uncertainty that exists in decisions about international relations. If different types of regimes systematically empower actors with different perceptions of the costs and benefits of war, this could affect international bargaining in ways not explained by selectorate theory.

Finally, selectorate theory assumes that some disagreement already exists between two countries; it does not explain how such disputes develop but rather how domestic institutions affect the decision to use force to settle disputes once they have arisen. There is no room in the theory for regime type to affect the extent to which conflicting interests, and thus disputes, come about in the first place. If some kinds of regimes are more likely to have revisionist preferences or to view other countries as more threatening, conflicts of interest with other countries could arise

[8]

more frequently in the first place. Understanding variation in those underlying preferences is therefore crucial.

A second strand of the emerging literature on authoritarianism and war argues that it is not insulation from punishment that leads to war but the opposite—dictators' relative vulnerability. One view is that domestic institutions affect authoritarian regimes' levels of "infrastructural power" or "capacity to enforce the leadership's decisions throughout the national territory."[15] Lai and Slater assume that military-led regimes have less infrastructural power than party-based regimes and that an important way to deflect attention from domestic troubles is to start an international conflict. Combining these assumptions, they argue that military regimes are more likely to use force because doing so makes up for low levels of infrastructural power and meets their need for domestic support and legitimacy. Thus, Lai and Slater offer an argument about variation in the conflict behavior of dictatorships based on the logic of diversionary war.

However, even if diversion is common enough to explain variation in conflict behavior, it is not clear that infrastructural power as envisioned by Lai and Slater would cause military regimes to engage in diversion more frequently than other types of regimes. Democracies and civilian autocracies also suffer the crises of legitimacy that supposedly motivate diversion, particularly in tough economic times. In fact, some argue that because democratic leaders lack other options for stabilizing their rule, diversionary war is most common in democracies.[16] Given these issues, it is unsurprising that studies have failed to find evidence that military regimes engage in more diversionary force than civilian regimes. Indeed, recent empirical work on diversion in authoritarian regimes finds that it occurs most frequently in single-party regimes.[17]

In a similar vein, Debs and Goemans (2010) suggest that what leaders really care about is avoiding severe punishment such as exile, imprisonment, or death.[18] They argue that leaders of authoritarian regimes are particularly likely to be ousted for making concessions in international bargaining, and that ousted leaders of *military* regimes are especially likely to meet a violent end. Because striking a peaceful deal can be so costly, these leaders have incentives to gamble on war rather than accept the deal on the table. In other words, the desire to save their own skin causes leaders of military regimes to resort to war more often than leaders of other regime types.

There are reasons to doubt this argument as well. First, gambles for resurrection typically only make sense when the leader is already relatively certain to lose office.[19] This is probably not the case often enough to drive overall levels of dispute initiation, even if it can explain isolated cases. Moreover, Debs and Goemans do not show evidence that

[9]

nondemocratic leaders really are more sensitive to the outcomes of peaceful negotiations than democratic leaders, leaving this key assumption unsubstantiated even though one might expect the opposite pattern to hold.[20]

A final issue is that while these studies have proposed several important hypotheses about autocracies and war, they have focused primarily on the initiation of conflict and assessed their conclusions using quantitative cross-national data. While this is an important start, we are lacking research into other implications of these arguments (such as patterns of war outcomes), and the hypotheses have not been carefully assessed using qualitative evidence. In sum, while scholars have begun to study differences in the conflict behavior of autocracies, so far they have only scratched the surface.

THE PLAN OF THE BOOK

Why are some authoritarian regimes more belligerent than others? Why do some lose most of the wars in which they become involved, while others are much more selective about choosing wars they can win? This book combines theory, cross-national quantitative evidence, and historical case study analysis in order to answer these questions.

The first chapter presents the core of the argument. Rather than focusing only on whether or not the leader faces institutional constraints, as much of the existing literature has, I also consider the preferences of the groups that can impose those constraints and, in the absence of constraints, the characteristics of the individual leader. The theory thus combines insights from a diverse set of literatures and from different levels of theoretical analysis. The chapter closes by discussing implications of the argument and strategies for assessing those implications empirically.

Chapters 2 and 3 turn to assessing three predictions of the theory using cross-national data. Chapter 2 evaluates the argument that juntas and personalistic regimes are more likely to initiate military disputes than civilian, nonpersonalist machines. After introducing a new measure of authoritarian regime type, I carry out an extensive analysis of patterns of dispute initiation and show that personalist bosses and strongmen and nonpersonalist military juntas are substantially more likely to initiate conflicts than civilian nonpersonalist machines, which are about as likely to initiate militarized disputes as democracies. The results dispel the notion that all autocracies are equally belligerent. In actuality, differences among autocracies are as large as differences between democracies and some autocracies, and some dictatorships—specifically, civilian nonpersonalist machines—initiate no more conflict than democracies.

[10]

Chapter 3 explores a second empirical domain: defeat in war and punishment in its aftermath. Using an original dataset of all major combatants in wars started between 1920 and 2007, I show that civilian nonpersonalist machines fare as well in war as democracies, followed by juntas. Bosses and strongmen, in contrast, fare much worse. As in the case of conflict initiation, the differences among authoritarian regimes are as important as or more important than the differences between democracies and dictatorships in general. I then analyze the fortunes of leaders *after* wars and show that personalist bosses and strongmen survive in office at high rates even after military defeat. When leaders of juntas or machines lose wars, in contrast, they tend to lose office. This chapter therefore also shows that while personalist bosses and strongmen can usually survive all but the most catastrophic military defeats, other autocrats are not nearly as insulated from domestic punishment as is commonly assumed.

The subsequent three chapters further probe the argument and causal mechanisms through a series of historical case studies. Each chapter focuses on a different type of regime, analyzing two historical cases for a combination of depth and breadth. Of course, like all approaches, qualitative methods provide certain challenges for causal inference, particularly when the relationships are probabilistic rather than deterministic.[21] Moreover, the historical record can rarely provide smoking-gun evidence of the causes of a specific historical event, particularly when actors have incentives to conceal their motivations. An additional problem emerges when trying to study how constraints bind; according to my argument, constrained leaders have incentives to refrain from initiating conflict in the first place, but it is difficult to study "non-events" such as decisions to remain at peace. Nonetheless, the case studies allow me to demonstrate that the arguments and mechanisms I propose are evident in multiple important historical contexts.

Chapter 4 begins that exercise by focusing on two personalist bosses—Saddam Hussein and Joseph Stalin—and showing how a combination of personal characteristics and lack of constraints cause personalist leaders to take much greater foreign policy risks than other kinds of leaders.[22] While the conclusions in this chapter are consistent with some of the conventional wisdom about foreign policy in autocracies, the chapter establishes a baseline against which the more surprising dynamics of juntas and machines can be evaluated. The chapter also shows that it is not only an absence of constraints that encourages the reckless behavior of personalist dictators. Rather, these leaders have a tendency to be highly ambitious and to view violence as a legitimate and effective way to fulfill those ambitions. The first part of the chapter focuses on Saddam Hussein, tracing his decision to initiate the Gulf War and his political survival

[11]

in the aftermath of defeat. This is a particularly interesting case because of new evidence about the inner workings of Saddam's regime that emerged during the recent U.S. occupation. The chapter then turns briefly to Joseph Stalin of the Soviet Union, showing how a relative lack of domestic accountability allowed Stalin to take risky and aggressive actions that a more constrained leader would probably have eschewed. This analysis also sets the stage for chapter 6, in which I return to the USSR and show how the foreign policy process changed once Stalin's successors became more inhibited by collective decision-making.

Chapter 5 focuses on two nonpersonalist military regimes: Argentina in the Falklands War[23] and Japan in the prelude to World War II. The Argentine case provides a canonical example of aggression by a military junta. I show that the common diversionary interpretation of the Falklands War is incomplete unless one understands the particular perceptions, biases, and preferences of the military leaders and their domestic audience. The case also illustrates that the leaders of military juntas can be punished by their audience of high- and mid-level officers. I then turn to Japan in the 1930s and early 1940s, where the military's seizure of political power and the bellicose preferences of its officers helped push the country into a series of tragic decisions. This case demonstrates vividly how the preferences of a military audience can drive leaders of juntas to initiate war in situations where leaders faced with a civilian audience likely would not.

Finally, chapter 6 turns to nonpersonalist civilian machines, showing how the domestic politics of these regimes generate much greater selectivity about using military force. Studying how constraints restrain leaders from war does present certain challenges. Historians tend not to focus in detail on low-drama events such as why a leader chose to pursue peaceful relations with another country, and for this reason it is difficult to know where to look for evidence that constraints encouraged peace. On the other hand, studying a constrained leader's decision to initiate a war turns our attention, by definition, to situations in which the hawks ultimately prevailed. If domestically constrained leaders have incentives to fight only wars that enjoy broad support, we will not find as much evidence of domestic debate and consensus-seeking. Such cases provide a harder test of the argument that machines take fewer risks than personalists, are less influenced by innately hawkish views, and seek consensus before initiating a conflict.

Keeping these challenges in mind, chapter 6 focuses on two machines that ultimately chose war. Much of the chapter explores the surprising case of North Vietnam. Quite counter to common portrayals of the Vietnamese communists as expansionist and war-hungry, I demonstrate the caution and prudence they displayed in their wars against the United

States and other countries. North Vietnamese leaders were clearly responsive to a primarily civilian audience of powerful Politburo and Central Committee members; this encouraged calculation, caution, and consensus-seeking before major foreign policy decisions and ultimately helped the North Vietnamese to drive out a superpower. I then return to the Soviet Union after the death of Stalin. Party officials reacted to Stalin's reign of terror by greatly curtailing the power of the general secretary, with important implications for post-Stalin foreign policy decisions. When Nikita Khrushchev proved to be less competent and prudent than was desired, his colleagues ousted him and replaced him with the cautious and consensual Leonid Brezhnev, illustrating the vulnerability of nonpersonalist leaders.

The concluding chapter explains the book's implications for both theory and policy. Most generally, the findings suggest that the conventional view of the relationship between regime type and foreign policy, including the argument that democracies are uniquely selective about initiating international conflict, is either incomplete or wrong. By masking variation among authoritarian regimes, the usual dichotomy between democracy and authoritarianism can foster mistaken conclusions about the effects of democracy on foreign relations. In the process of exposing these differences among dictatorships, the book also provides valuable lessons for policymakers confronting authoritarian regimes in international politics.

[1]

Authoritarian Regimes and the Domestic Politics of War and Peace

The historical record is littered with the names of brutal tyrants who not only abused their own citizens but also terrorized neighboring countries. Perhaps for this reason, many have concluded that authoritarian regimes are generally less discriminating than democracies when it comes to using military force. But not all authoritarian regimes share the aggressive tendencies so commonly attributed to them. Why do some initiate so much more military conflict than others? Why do some lose the majority of wars they start, whereas others are more successful? Why do some autocratic leaders survive embarrassing wartime defeats, while others find themselves ejected from power?

To answer these questions, this book focuses on state leaders and the domestic political environments that can constrain them. Domestic political constraints can take two general forms. First, *ex ante* constraints could prevent leaders from choosing and implementing certain policies at all.[1] However, because excessive *ex ante* constraints could hamstring leaders in times of danger, even leaders of well-institutionalized democracies usually enjoy substantial latitude over decisions to mobilize troops and deploy military force. Many scholars have therefore focused on a second type of constraint: *ex post* accountability, which can deter leaders from choosing unpopular or risky policies. Countries vary, however, in the extent to which a domestic audience can and will pass judgment on specific policies, either rewarding or punishing the leader after the fact.[2]

In order to explain why some countries are more prone to fighting wars than others, we must answer several questions. First, does the leader face a powerful domestic audience with the ability to remove or otherwise punish him? Second, if the leader faces a strong domestic audience, how does that audience view the costs and benefits of using force

[14]

and thus the wisdom of military action? Third, in regimes in which the lack of a powerful domestic audience gives the leader greater latitude, what are the leader's preferences and perceptions about the use of force?[3]

The first question focuses on whether the regime features a domestic audience whose continued support is necessary for the leader to survive in office. In democracies, domestic audiences are powerful and typically consist of voters, who can turn against the leader and his political party. In autocracies, as I argue in greater detail below, audiences often exist as well, though they consist of a much smaller group of elites whose positions inside the regime give them leverage over the leader.[4] In fact, there is much greater variation in the power of domestic audiences among authoritarian regimes than is commonly assumed.[5]

Second, how do those audiences perceive the costs and benefits of war? Simply knowing whether leaders can be punished for their decisions tells us only part of the story: we must also know something about the audience's perceptions and preferences about the use of force compared to other possible actions.[6] Some audiences view the use of military force as routine and low-cost, whereas others are more skeptical about resorting to violence. Similarly, some audiences have characteristics that make them particularly skittish about diplomacy, while others have more faith in nonmilitary options.

Third, we must know something about how the individual leader views the use of force. This is particularly important when no powerful audience exists and the leader is relatively unfettered, both during the policymaking process and in its aftermath. Of course, knowledge of the leader's perceptions and preferences could be important even when the leader does face *ex post* punishment, if secrecy and urgency force him to make a decision before he has the opportunity to sound out the domestic audience.

The discussion so far leads us to ask: What kinds of perceptions and preferences about the use of force matter most for audiences and leaders? From the myriad potential factors that leaders and audiences could weigh, I focus on four: the benefits of winning a war relative to the peaceful status quo, the costs of fighting, the costs of defeat, and the likelihood of winning.

First, actors form views about the *benefits of winning* compared to continuing on a nonmilitary pathway. Some actors find sticking with the status quo unattractive because they greedily desire a greater share of the international pie.[7] Others, however, fear the status quo because they believe the international environment to be threatening; leaders or audiences may fear that failure to act today will invite danger in the future. Actors who view nonmilitary options such as diplomacy as hopeless are less likely to be satisfied with the current state of affairs. Whatever the

[15]

specific reason, actors who desire the benefits of victory, or are unhappy with the status quo, are more likely to wish to change it.

Second, actors form perceptions of the *costs of fighting*, regardless of the outcome of the conflict. Audiences and leaders could be averse to using force because it is either materially costly or because it is morally undesirable. For example, drawing on Kant's early insight, many scholars have argued that voters (the audience in democracies) are more sensitive to the material or moral costs of military conflict than are leaders or, as I will discuss later, the elites who can sometimes constrain the leader in autocracies. Leaders and audiences may also perceive low net costs of using military force because it furthers parochial interests.

Third, in addition to generic views about force, audiences and leaders have perceptions of the *costs of defeat* in a military challenge. In fact, many scholars have argued that defeat in international disputes is one of the cardinal sins of international politics.[8] The costs of defeat could be either direct, in the form of lost military and economic resources, or more indirect; for example, defeat could invite future attacks by revealing military weakness.

Finally, actors form estimates of the *likelihood of winning* a military contest. War is fraught with uncertainty, and actors need to form judgments about the likely success of military action based on limited information. For various reasons, some actors may be more optimistic about their chances than others.

Knowing all this about leaders and audiences allows us to make predictions about the conflict behavior of different kinds of regimes. For example, holding constant all other factors, those who view the use of military force as low cost would be more willing to resort to armed conflict. Greedy leaders who wish to attain international goods, fearful leaders who perceive the status quo as dangerous, and optimistic leaders who believe that a military struggle will be successful—or leaders facing audiences with those characteristics—would also be more willing to resort to force.

It is worth noting that these conjectures fit easily with theories viewing war as a bargaining process between two states. According to that literature, estimates of the value of the goods to be attained relative to the status quo, the costs of fighting, the costs of defeat, and the likelihood of winning each affect the bargaining range between two countries.[9] Leaders who view the value of winning relative to the status quo as high, the costs of fighting or defeat as low, or the likelihood of victory as high will find a much narrower range of settlements acceptable compared to leaders who do not value the benefits of victory as greatly, who view war and defeat as costly, or who believe that their opponent will prevail. These factors therefore can affect the probability that a country will seek to revise the status quo in its favor, giving rise to disputes in the first place.[10] In the presence of a dispute, additional factors like secrecy, commitment problems, and indivisible issues may then prevent countries from locating solutions short of war.[11] The following section examines how these parameters vary among authoritarian regimes and what this variation means for regime type and international conflict.

Audiences, Preferences, and Decisions about War

Above, I suggested that in order to explain why some countries are more war-prone than others, we must focus on whether the leader is constrained by a domestic audience, and the perceptions and preferences that audiences and leaders have about the use of military force. Below, I explain why this approach leads us to focus on two key dimensions: the extent to which the regime is "personalist," and whether the regime is led by civilians or by members of the military.[12] Because regimes can have any combination of these two characteristics, the two dimensions combine to form four ideal types, shown in table 1.1.[13] I adopt Slater's (2003) labels, distinguishing among nonpersonalist civilian regimes (*machines*), nonpersonalist military regimes (*juntas*), personalist regimes led by civilians (*bosses*), and personalist regimes led by military officers (*strongmen*).[14]

Domestic Audiences: Personalist versus Elite-Constrained Dictators

The first issue is what types of authoritarian regimes face a powerful domestic audience that can punish or, in the extreme, remove leaders who do not represent their interests. Scholars have shown empirically that most authoritarian leaders lose power at the hands of regime insiders rather than mass uprisings.[15] Yet dictatorships vary enormously in the extent to which regime insiders have the opportunity and incentives to oust their leader.

At one end of the spectrum are despotic, sultanistic, or, here, "personalist" regimes in which one individual controls instruments of state such as the military forces, any ruling party, and the state bureaucracy.[16] Crucial

TABLE 1.1 Typology of authoritarian regimes

	Civilian audience or leader	Military audience or leader
Nonpersonalist (Elite-constrained leader)	Machine	Junta
Personalist (Unconstrained leader)	Boss	Strongman

to the leader's hold on power is his ability to appoint friends, relatives, and cronies to important offices, and arbitrarily dismiss those who have outlived their usefulness. These handpicked regime insiders have strong incentives to remain loyal to and uncritical of the leader, lest they risk their own political demise either at the hands of the incumbent, or a successor government.[17] Therefore, a defining feature of personalist regimes such as North Korea under the Kims, Iraq under Saddam Hussein, the Soviet Union under Stalin, Syria under the Assads, and Libya under Gaddafi is that their leaders do not face a strong, organized domestic audience able to exert *ex ante* or *ex post* constraints on their policy choices.[18]

This lack of an influential domestic audience in personalist dictatorships contrasts greatly with the powerful domestic audiences found in nonpersonalist autocracies. Unlike their counterparts in personalist dictatorships, government insiders in nonpersonalist autocracies often have both the will and the means to punish their leader. In nonpersonalist party-based machines such as contemporary China and the post-Stalin Soviet Union, government insiders rise through the ranks based in significant part on merit and seniority rather than personal or family relationships to the paramount leader. Moreover, in these regimes the leaders cannot typically spy on subordinates and dispose of them if they detect disloyalty. In turn, since regime elites expect that they can retain their positions even if a new leader comes to power, their loyalty to the incumbent is much more tenuous.

The ability to punish or oust the leader is not limited to civilian single-party regimes. In many military dictatorships—in places as varied as Latin America, Algeria, South Korea, and Thailand—members of the junta and the officer corps do not depend on the incumbent for their own political survival. Just as the Argentine junta ousted Galtieri after the Falklands debacle, high-ranking officers in nonpersonalist military dictatorships can often punish or even remove the leader for policy failures. Officers in the Argentine military acted as a "constituency to which the junta remained attentive . . . much evidence exists to support the notion that a very real form of political constraint was exercised on Argentina's putative rulers."[19] Government insiders serve as a powerful domestic audience in nonpersonalist regimes.

It is important to consider why any audience, whether in a democratic or authoritarian regime, would be motivated to dole out rewards and mete out punishment for foreign policy decisions that have already run their course. One possibility is that the audience could wish to encourage good behavior in the future.[20] Another is that the audience could want to rehabilitate the country's international reputation by removing an offending leader.[21] Yet another is that foreign policy decisions reveal important information about the leader's competence or preferences;

[18]

audiences may glean information by comparing the outcome of a dispute to the audience's expectations had the leader acted differently.[22] Faced with the rotten fruits of a leader's decision, audiences may conclude that the leader is unable or unwilling to further their policy interests and that a new leader would improve their well-being. The question then becomes whether other concerns, such as the fear of losing insider status, overwhelm audience members' desire for a competent leader who does not make poor foreign policy choices. The argument here is that, since audience members in nonpersonalist autocracies can usually assure themselves that they can hold on to their positions even under a new leader, they should wish to replace leaders who make unwelcome foreign policy decisions. This is what distinguishes nonpersonalist autocracies from personalist regimes, where there is no effective audience because the cronies surrounding the leader have neither the means nor the will to remove their patron.[23]

Thus, one way to think of the first dimension—whether the leader faces a powerful domestic audience with the ability to punish or depose him—is to consider whether or not a regime is personalist. Personalist regimes are particularly unlikely to feature effective domestic audiences. In contrast, in nonpersonalist regimes leaders must reckon with powerful domestic audiences, and their fear of removal at the hands of those audiences affects their behavior.[24] The preferences of domestic audiences in nonpersonalist dictatorships are therefore important.

The Content of Constraints: Audience and Leader Preferences over the Use of Force

We now must turn to audience and leader preferences about using military force abroad. These preferences derive from actors' evaluations of the relative costs and benefits of war outlined earlier: the value of the stakes to be won relative to the status quo, the costs of fighting, the costs of defeat, and the likelihood of winning.[25] I argue that evaluations of these factors vary according to the background of the relevant decision-maker and audience, with important differences between military and civilian actors. In personalist regimes without an effective domestic audience (boss and strongman regimes), I focus mainly on the preferences of the dictator.

Peaceful Machines: Elite-Constrained Dictatorships with Civilian Audiences

What are the preferences of the civilian leaders and elites who govern nonpersonalist civilian machines, and how do they compare to those of

[19]

voters in democracies? Regime insiders in machines are typically officials in a dominant party, as in contemporary China, though they could also potentially be family members in a nonpersonalist monarchy or high-level officials in an autocracy with limited multiparty competition. As I argued in the introductory chapter, regime insiders in nonpersonalist autocracies are not, as some scholars maintain, necessarily dependent on the leader for their own survival.[26] Thus, even though the winning coalition in machines is relatively small, these elites are not so bound to the leader by loyalty that they will overlook foreign policy failures. By revisiting the costs and benefits of war through the eyes of civilian regime insiders in nonpersonalist regimes, it becomes clear that they are not categorically more enthusiastic about war than voters or leaders in democracies.

A first possibility is that perhaps autocratic audiences are eager to revise the status quo because they have a greater desire for the potential benefits of victory. Some have argued that authoritarian elites can keep the spoils of war rather than sharing them with the population, making military conquest seem more attractive.[27] But this would only be the case where the spoils of war are excludable—for example, proceeds from a new oil field or similar rent-providing resource. In many cases—such as securing strategically or symbolically important territory or protecting state borders—it is not clear that elites would benefit disproportionately. A related possibility is that authoritarian elites are more fearful of, and hence less likely to be satisfied with, the status quo. Although I return to this issue in the discussion of military regimes, it is not clear why civilian authoritarian elites would, all else equal, be more skeptical of nonmilitary options such as diplomacy or view other states as more threatening than voters in democracies. The value of winning compared to sticking with the nonmilitarized status quo should not therefore be substantially higher for typical civilian autocratic elites than for democratic audiences.

Second, many scholars have argued that the (perceived) costs of fighting are lower for autocratic leaders and audiences than for democratic leaders and audiences. Following the logic of Immanuel Kant, for example, one might believe that elites, particularly in authoritarian regimes, are more insulated from the physical dangers of war than ordinary citizens. Yet there are reasons to doubt this argument. Except in the most serious conflicts, most wars involve the mobilization of only a very small proportion of the population, so the probability of physical harm to any individual citizen is usually low.[28] Moreover, enemy governments often target regime elites directly, and unlike the paramount leader, most regime insiders do not enjoy personal security details or have access to networks of secret underground bunkers to protect their families. Their land and property also remain vulnerable. In fact, the expectation that war will destabilize the leadership is common enough that many belligerents fight wars with this express goal in mind.[29]

Of course, other costs of war accrue to citizens off the battlefield, for example economic disruptions. Most scholars assume that ordinary citizens bear the brunt of these costs, but regime insiders have much to lose themselves.[30] Elites' economic interests are especially likely to be hard hit by a conflict, which can destroy infrastructure and disrupt trade. Indeed, some scholars have argued that business elites are especially averse to war because of its economic effects.[31] In addition, elites may find it difficult to simply compensate themselves by taxing the public at a higher rate. As Wintrobe (2000) argues, most autocratic regimes stay in power through a combination of repression and loyalty. Taxing the citizens at higher rates to compensate for wartime losses is likely to reduce the loyalty of the public. That is particularly problematic in the aftermath of war when the military—a key instrument of repression—has been exhausted by fighting. For all of these reasons it is not clear that autocratic elites are substantially more insulated from the direct or indirect material costs of fighting than are ordinary citizens.

Beyond physical and economic factors, normative or moral concerns can raise the perceived costs of fighting.[32] Perhaps elites in autocracies are socialized to view military force as a more appropriate way to settle disputes than are leaders or citizens in democracies. Although I revisit this issue in the discussion of military officers, there is little evidence that *civilian* elites in dictatorships are more likely than their democratic counterparts to see war as legitimate. Most literature suggests that democracies apply pacific norms only when the opponent is also a democracy; in fact, many scholars have commented on democracies' willingness to use force even against innocent civilians.[33] Even when scholars have found differences in the willingness of democracies to refrain from certain practices, such as abusing enemy combatants, they have attributed those differences to strategic rather than normative factors.[34] Thus, available evidence suggests that civilian autocratic audiences view the costs of fighting similarly as democratic audiences.

A third possibility is that officials in autocratic regimes are less concerned with the possible costs of defeat. Yet, even absent outright military occupation, authoritarian regime insiders are likely to view defeat in war with extreme disfavor. One issue is that defeat can weaken domestic support for the regime by providing a focal point for citizen discontent. Defeated soldiers might even turn against their own regime, as many Arab soldiers did in the aftermath of the humiliating defeat to Israel in 1948. Given the drastic consequences of regime change, autocratic audiences would be wary of leaders who take what seem to be foolish or selfish risks in this regard. Defeat can also reveal or even increase a country's military vulnerability and make it more open to future invasion. Because of their greater understanding of international affairs, political and military elites might be especially attuned to the perils of exposing their military weaknesses or losing strategic territory. Finally, defeat may reveal information about the leader's caution or skill more generally, both to citizens and the audience. Unlike the mass public, authoritarian elites have their own access to information about the details of the war outcome and are not as vulnerable to favorable framing by the leader. For all these reasons, the consequences of possible defeat should loom as large in the minds of autocratic audiences as in democratic audiences.

Finally, both the leader and the domestic audience form judgments about the likelihood that a military venture would be successful. Again, it is not clear why decision-makers in machines would be systematically predisposed to over-optimism. Since leaders of machines know that they can be punished for defeat or other policy failures, they have strong incentives to encourage elite debate about the merits of a military venture and to solicit a variety of perspectives on the likely success of a mission, both from high-level civilians and from military experts. Moreover, elites in machines are likely to be well informed about potential outcomes. By virtue of their high-level positions, they have access to detailed information and are sophisticated in matters of foreign policy. While the "marketplace of ideas" is restricted to the higher echelons of the regime, the atmosphere at the top can be quite open. The discussions of the Soviet Union and North Vietnam in chapter 6 demonstrate just how heated elite-level debates can become in these kinds of regimes. As we shall see, this contrasts sharply with the atmosphere in more centralized personalist regimes.

We can thus conclude that civilian authoritarian actors—even when they are not representative of the broader public—should tend to view military conflict with similar trepidation as democratic domestic audiences. Although these autocratic audiences may approve of using force if the benefits outweigh the costs, they are no less wary of the possibility of defeat than their democratic counterparts and do not see systematically greater gains from fighting.

How do these factors affect the leader's decision to initiate military conflict? While the leader may have the ability to deploy military force without the formal consent of his domestic audience, the fact that he serves at the pleasure of regime elites means he has incentives to consider whether they support his decision—whether in their view, the anticipated benefits of using military force outweigh the likely costs. If the leader initiates a war that drains the treasury with few returns, his domestic audience may turn against him. That fear of *ex post* loss of support induces the leaders of machines to pay attention to the audience's perceptions and preferences in the first place.

This conclusion is at odds with much of the conventional wisdom. One might expect that it is much easier for a leader to convince a small coalition of elites to forgive him for launching a foolish war than it would be to assuage, for example, Congress or voters and that even nonpersonalist autocrats would therefore feel less constrained by the views of their audiences. However, for the reasons provided earlier, the conventional wisdom underestimates the vulnerability of nonpersonalist autocrats. First, leaders of machines typically lack the control over resources needed to buy off potential opponents; and the tools to intimidate them. Their audiences know that they can probably survive the leader's ouster. Second, leaders of machines may find it much more difficult to massage domestic opinion when the audience consists of high-level officials—themselves often active in foreign policy—than a "rationally ignorant" mass public.[35] Even long after the fall of Baghdad, the U.S. public had substantial misconceptions about basic facts concerning the threat that Iraq had posed at the time of the invasion, and judged Bush's decision accordingly.[36] It is difficult to imagine the same being true of a cohort of elite policymakers composing a dictator's audience.

This discussion leads to a series of testable hypotheses about the conflict behavior of machines compared to democracies as well as the behavior of machines compared to other types of authoritarian regimes. Machines should not be appreciably more likely to *initiate* military conflicts than democracies, holding all other factors constant.[37] Machines and democracies should also win a comparable proportion of the wars in which they become involved.[38] And, when leaders of machines do miscalculate and lose armed conflicts, they should, like democratic leaders, be punished at higher rates than leaders who are not domestically accountable for defeat in war.[39] These three implications will each be tested in chapters 2 and 3 using cross-national data on the initiation, outcome, and aftermath of wars.

The argument also has a series of more fine-grained implications for the processes by which individual leaders have decided to use force historically. If leaders of machines know that they are accountable to a domestic audience, they should consult extensively with that audience in advance to gauge their support, pursue diplomatic alternatives rather than reflexively turning to violence, and generally behave as though the audience's opinion matters. To assess these claims, chapter 6 investigates North Vietnamese decision-making in the 1960s and 1970s as well as the decision-making of post-Stalin Soviet leaders to see whether these important cases conform to the logic laid out here.

Juntas and the Military Mindset: Military Regimes
with Elite Constraints

While the discussion above focused on nonpersonalist regimes led by civilians, many nonpersonalist dictatorships are better characterized as military juntas in which the leader faces an audience composed primarily of military officers.[40] Some of the arguments about elite audiences in nonpersonalist civilian autocracies apply to military regimes as well. For example, as in machines, elites and leaders in military juntas are not insulated from the costs of defeat, and are likely to view defeat with great concern. And, given their military expertise, they would not be more likely to overestimate the likelihood of victory (though in some cases, military officers' ignorance of diplomacy is problematic).[41] Predictable differences do exist, however, with regard to military officers' perceptions of dangers of the status quo and the costs of fighting. I will argue that military officers have been selected for, and socialized to hold, specific beliefs about military force as an instrument of politics, with implications for their decisions about war.

Scholars of public opinion would find it uncontroversial to argue that different individuals view the same events through quite different lenses. For example, beliefs about the use of force vary greatly by gender and education, even when there is no tangible link to the individual's personal well-being.[42] A burgeoning literature on how the backgrounds of leaders affect their decisions reaches a similar conclusion.[43]

Many scholars have used the word *culture* to describe collections of beliefs that are specific to particular groups. Such beliefs, in turn, have important consequences for an actor's choices because beliefs define what an actor values, what information an actor sees as salient, his or her expectations about cause and effect, his or her expectations about the values and intentions of other actors, and more.[44] Preexisting beliefs are particularly likely to influence perceptions and preferences when individuals operate under significant uncertainty, as in decisions to use military force abroad.

In turn, a large literature emphasizes that professional military officers tend to hold deeply engrained beliefs about the role of military force in international affairs.[45] Certain kinds of individuals tend to choose military service, and once there, they are further socialized into a culture that reifies particular ways of seeing the world and prioritizes certain types of policy responses.[46] Several specific beliefs contribute to a bias in favor of military over diplomatic options: military officers are more likely than civilians to form ominous views of the status quo, less likely to see value in diplomacy, and less likely to view military force as costly.[47] For both military leaders and their military audiences, these views raise the perceived net benefits and lower the anticipated costs of war.

[24]

To begin, military officers are particularly likely to view the international environment—and hence the status quo—as threatening. In his seminal work on the beliefs of military officers, Huntington (1957) argues that there is a "military ethic" that "views conflict as a universal pattern throughout nature and sees violence rooted in the permanent biological and psychological nature of men."[48] Soldiers are socialized to believe that "human nature being what it is, a stronger state should never be trusted even if it proclaims the friendliest intentions" (66), and to "view with alarm the potency and immediacy of the security threats to the state" (66). Building on this view, Levy argues that "By professional training, [military officers] are more sensitive to military threats to their country's security, more predisposed to worst-case analysis, more concerned about a long-term decline in military assets, and perhaps more willing to resort to extreme solutions in order to avert any further decline in military strength."[49] Or, as Vagts (1956) puts it, "The military are the closest, most expert, and often the most suspecting observers of dangers threatening their country from an enemy growing superior." In contrast, civilians believe that threats "may decrease in due time with the help of diplomacy and counter-alliances and additional armaments on one's own part [and] that too much additional armament may even unleash a preventive war by the opponent in his determination to prevent an over-balancing" (263). A common theme in this work is that while civilians believe that diplomacy can keep the country safe, military officers trust only military power. In fact, professional officers become so "functionally specialized" in using force that they "forget that other means can also be used toward the same end."[50] Because they tend to be less satisfied with the peaceful status quo and its weak diplomatic tools, military officers perceive higher relative benefits of military conflict.

Moreover, military officers tend to view using military force as less costly than their civilian counterparts. The military's parochial interests can support beliefs that force is not costly because military conflict increases institutional prestige and requires larger budgets; in fact, war can bring about net gains to the military as an organization.[51] As Vagts (1956) writes, "As individuals, diplomats seek their triumphs through peace-keeping and peace-making, soldiers through martial deeds in war" (8). In the officers' Hobbesian worldview, resorting to force is unavoidable. It is therefore also morally acceptable, which further reduces its perceived costs. As Brecher (1996) puts it, "Violence is normal behavior for the military in power," which sees violence as "legitimate and effective" (220).

Finally, while it is not clear that military officers categorically overestimate the likelihood of victory, they are nonetheless trained to believe in the advantages of offensive action and first strikes. Once they see war as the only available option, military officers may advocate in favor of seizing the initiative because acting first can decrease uncertainty, which is anathema to militaries.[52] In other words, military officers believe that they can improve the probability of victory by striking first. This, of course, can heighten the danger of conflict initiation even further.[53]

Not all scholars subscribe to the view that military officers are biased in favor of using force; some have argued that officers have conservative tendencies that offset their hawkish leanings.[54] For example, although Huntington sees military leaders as prone to exaggerating external threats, he ultimately argues that professional soldiers favor war only rarely, because "war at any time is an intensification of the threats to the military security of the state" (69).[55] And in an influential book, Richard Betts (1977) finds that in the context of Cold War crises, U.S. military officers did not uniformly advocate more aggressive policies than civilian officials.[56]

Who is right? Given that most of the data informing the "military conservatism" hypothesis stem from the U.S., it is worth revisiting that case. In one of the only studies of its kind, Feaver and Gelpi (2004) carried out an extensive survey of U.S. military and civilian elites' views on foreign policy and military force. Do military officers exhibit the belief patterns outlined above? More specifically, are officers more likely to perceive other countries as militarily threatening, less likely to see diplomacy as effective, and more likely to view military force as low-cost? Given that the most famous proponents of the military conservatism hypothesis have based their conclusions in large part on the American case, it is worth analyzing the Feaver and Gelpi survey data in some detail.

Table 1.2 compares the beliefs of military officers to those of civilian elites.[57] Two items addressed "military threats": whether the emergence of China as a military power and the proliferation of weapons of mass destruction to less-developed countries posed threats to U.S. security.[58] The first rows of table 1.2 indicate that in both cases, military officers were more likely to perceive a very serious threat than civilian elites by a significant margin.[59] Moving down the table, military officers were also more likely to express skepticism with diplomacy compared to military tools. For example, officers were more likely to say that military tools are as effective as or more effective than nonmilitary tools in coping with the emergence of China as a military power and the threat of WMD. They were also significantly more skeptical about the value of engaging with international organizations such as the UN. Finally, military officers repeatedly expressed the belief that military force was a legitimate response in a wide array of situations, including terrorist strikes and preventing aggression by an expansionist power. They were much more likely to say that it is very important to maintain superior military power worldwide

[26]

TABLE 1.2 The beliefs of military officers and civilian elites

	Civilian elites	Military officers	Diff
Threat perception			
The emergence of China as a military power is very seriously threatening to U.S. national security.	28.7	34.8	6.1**
The proliferation of WMDs to less-developed countries is very seriously threatening to U.S. national security.	73.8	81.3	7.5***
Diplomacy and international organizations versus military tools			
Military tools are as or more effective than nonmilitary tools in coping with the emergence of China as a great military power.	58.7	66.6	7.9***
Military tools are as or more effective than nonmilitary tools in coping with WMD proliferation to less-developed countries.	68.6	75.5	6.9**
Very important to strengthen the UN.	27.9	19.1	−8.7***
Very important to foster international cooperation to solve problems such as food, inflation, and energy.	58.0	42.7	−15.2***
Agree strongly that it is vital to enlist UN cooperation in settling international disputes.	32.7	25.8	−6.9**
U.S. national security depends more on international trade and a strong domestic economy than on our military strength.	57.0	39.6	−17.4***
Legitimacy of using military force			
The American missile strikes against suspected terrorist sites in Afghanistan and Sudan were a legitimate response to the bombing of U.S. embassies in Kenya and Tanzania.	67.5	77.4	9.9***
The United States should take all steps including the use of force to prevent aggression by any expansionist power.	60.9	76.9	16.0***
Very important to maintain superior military power worldwide.	51.3	74.3	23.0***
The military is a very important instrument of foreign policy, even if that means engaging in operations other than war.	29.5	52.1	22.6***

*** $p<0.001$, ** $p<0.01$, * $p<0.05$

and that the military is an important instrument of foreign policy. All of these differences were highly statistically significant in *t*-tests.

In sum, the Feaver and Gelpi surveys indicate a strong tendency of U.S. military officers to favor military over diplomatic means for confronting a variety of traditional security issues. It is notable that this is true even in the United States, a country with an extremely professionalized military that is recruited from wide segments of society. This is especially important since some have concluded from the American experience that military officers are more conservative about using military force.

Of course, ideally, one would study the perceptions of military officers in various nondemocracies to see whether they are more hawkish than civilians. While such studies appear to be virtually nonexistent, a fascinating recent study by Stewart and Zhukov (2009) shows evidence on this question from (a decidedly nondemocratic) Russia under Putin. Stewart and Zhukov carry out a content analysis of the speeches of Russian military and civilian elites, and find that military leaders are significantly more likely to articulate support for the use of force, confirming the hypotheses about military officers laid out here. New cross-national evidence further supports the claim that military officers have systematically different views about the costs and benefits of war. Horowitz and Stam (2014) find that leaders with military training are significantly more likely to initiate armed conflict, even when controlling for a host of confounding factors. While this evidence is indirect (focusing on behavior rather than underlying preferences and beliefs), Horowitz and Stam explicitly attribute the behavior of military officers to their beliefs as military officers.

Thus, there is compelling evidence from a variety of contexts that military officers have systematically different beliefs about military force than civilians. These beliefs, in turn, have important consequences for states' behavior. As in machines, leaders of military juntas have incentives to heed the preferences of the audience and to get feedback on the likelihood of defeat. Greater dissatisfaction with the peaceful status quo (because of threat perception and a lack of faith in diplomacy) and lower perceived costs of fighting mean that juntas should be more likely to initiate military conflicts than machines and democracies, all else being equal. Moreover, because audiences in juntas perceive high threat and view force as necessary, they will select into wars with somewhat lower objective chances of victory and therefore lose a higher proportion of their wars. Still, this tendency should be muted compared to the personalist leaders discussed below, since leaders of juntas believe that they may be held accountable by their domestic constituency for abject failures. Because military officers are more likely to believe that force is necessary, however, they should be somewhat more forgiving of a failed gamble than audiences in machines. Thus, leaders of juntas who lose armed conflicts should be punished at rates that are higher than those of personalist bosses and strongmen but lower than those in democracies and machines.[60]

When it comes to historical cases, additional implications should be evident. Because leaders of juntas are accountable to military officers, they should initiate conflicts only when they enjoy the support of the officer corps. Compared to machines and democracies, they should be more likely to perceive high costs of inaction and evince reflexive skepticism about the value of diplomacy. To assess whether this is the case, chapter 5 explores the decision-making of two military-led regimes: Argentina in the decision to invade the Falklands in 1982 and Japan as military officers took over from civilians in the 1930s, culminating in the Japanese decision to attack Pearl Harbor.

Personalist Dictators: Ambitious and Unconstrained

What are the preferences of decision-makers in personalist regimes—civilian bosses and military strongmen? Personalist leaders are remarkably insulated from punishment at the hands of a domestic audience compared to nonpersonalist leaders. We must therefore not only consider the effects of low accountability, but also focus in some detail on personalist leaders' *personal* views about the costs and benefits of using force.[61] After discussing personalist regimes generically, I comment on how military strongmen may differ from civilian bosses.

First, personalist leaders are more likely to have revisionist preferences—to be less satisfied with the status quo and see higher relative benefits from winning a war—than typical leaders or audience members in a democracy, machine, or junta. One reason is that in the rare cases where the benefits of war can be kept from the public, for example when a country seizes territory rich in natural resources, personalist leaders have greater discretion over potential spoils than their more constrained counterparts. This could make victory in a conflict more attractive. A potentially more important reason, however, has to do with the personal characteristics of these leaders. Personalist regimes tend to be led by individuals who are particularly prone to grand international ambitions. One way to think of personalist leaders is as individuals with unusually "tyrannical" personalities who managed, through force and luck, to create domestic political conditions that feed their desire to dominate others. Psychological studies of tyrants (that is, the types of individuals who are particularly likely to become personalist dictators) consistently highlight their need for domination and the grandiose ambitions that ensue.[62] Rosen (2005) draws on classical works by Xenophon and others to argue that tyrants are particularly likely to crave supremacy over others, and Glad (2002) argues that many tyrants are narcissists who attempt to "buttress [their] exalted self-image" by placing themselves above others.[63] One of Saddam Hussein's many aspirations, for example, was to establish a pan-Arab caliphate—with himself, of course, as caliph. As the heir of Nebuchadnezzar and Saladin, Saddam would naturally order the construction of an ostentatious palace in Babylon with his own initials inscribed on each brick.[64] Muammar Gaddafi of Libya dubbed himself the "King of Kings" in 2008, gathering more than two hundred African tribal rulers and monarchs and declaring his hope for a single African government over which he would presumably preside. Similarly, Adolf Hitler is infamous for his unlimited aims, which included not only abolishing the Treaty of Versailles and destroying communism, but creating a vast German empire in Central and Eastern Europe.[65]

Next, personalist dictators are, like military officers, less likely to perceive high costs of using military force or high costs of defeat compared to democratic voters or civilian officials in nonpersonalist regimes. On the one hand, as previously discussed, authoritarian elites are not shielded from all of the costs of war. War results in economic disruption, and even personalist dictators are typically better off when the pie, so to speak, is larger and the public is happier. On the other hand, compared to typical elites, personalist dictators have extraordinary resources at their disposal to protect themselves from harm during wartime, with access to safe houses and secret bunkers, such as the nuclear bunker Saddam Hussein built for himself in Baghdad. They can also squirrel away vast sums of money, cushioning the effects of war on their own personal consumption. Even more important is that leaders of personalist regimes only internalize their *own* costs. Leaders of machines and juntas, in contrast, bear the brunt of their audience's anger in *addition* to their personal suffering. Personalist dictators' insulation from domestic punishment thus means that the costs of war affect them less than both typical regime insiders and leaders of nonpersonalist regimes.

Finally, there are reasons to believe that personalist dictators are prone to overestimating the likelihood of victory. Many personalist dictators, such as Stalin, Mao Zedong, Saddam Hussein, and Idi Amin, attained their station through violent means such as revolution, civil war, or a violent coup. These types of leaders have learned that force is an effective means of dispute resolution.[66] Fueling this confidence in the efficacy of violence is the exaggerated sense that personalist dictators often have of expertise, competence, and control. On an individual level, psychologists have found that normal human beings tend to harbor "positive illusions" in that they view themselves more positively, believe they have greater control over events, and see the future more optimistically than is warranted by objective facts. Johnson (2004) argues that the competitive nature of politics means that leaders and other politicians are more prone to positive illusions than ordinary individuals; the hazards of trying to attain high office ensure that the politicians who do succeed have been selected for their overconfidence and perseverance (Taylor and Brown 1988). The career path of personalist dictators is particularly likely to result in leaders of this mold: men who took great risks to pursue power and were also lucky enough to survive. Accordingly, many assessments of individual tyrants have pointed to the leaders' inflated sense of prowess or competence.[67]

While leaders of other kinds of regimes may also be prone to positive illusions, the problem is that in personalist dictatorships, the sycophants surrounding the dictator are especially unwilling to dispel the leader's false beliefs and may even have incentives to encourage them. In the Kremlin under Stalin, "There was a clear etiquette: it was deadly to disagree too much. . . . Silence was often a virtue and veterans advised neophytes on how to behave and survive" (Montefiore 2004, 341). Once surrounded by such an entourage, personalist leaders may become habituated toward seeing their own views as infallible. What is more, the harsh strategies that personalist dictators use to discourage disloyalty may encourage subordinates to inflate information about the country's military capacity. Hitler's generals, for example, were famously reluctant to deliver bad news. Interviews with high-level Iraqi officials after the 2003 U.S. invasion indicate that Saddam Hussein's subordinates were afraid to pass on anything other than glowing reports about Iraq's military effectiveness because it would reflect poorly on their own performance and expose them to Saddam's wrath (Woods et al. 2006). While similar pathologies may occur in all regimes, these tendencies are exacerbated in personalist autocracies in which the leader is so unusually powerful.

To summarize, the logic leads to a series of testable implications about the international behavior of personalist leaders. The path toward becoming a personalist dictator selects for leaders who have grand international ambitions and view force as an effective strategy, raising the anticipated benefits of war while reducing its expected costs. Moreover, personalist dictators are less vulnerable to the costs of defeat than leaders and audiences in nonpersonalist regimes and they tend to overestimate the likelihood of victory. We should therefore observe several related patterns. First, personalist dictators should initiate conflicts more frequently than leaders of democracies or machines and somewhat more often than leaders of juntas. Second, because they are more willing to become involved in conflicts even when success is not assured, they should lose a higher proportion of the conflicts that they fight. Third, they should be less likely to lose office even in the aftermath of defeat, compared to leaders of machines, democracies, and juntas.

In the case studies, we should also observe a series of predictable patterns. Personalist leaders will have fewer incentives to plan carefully for military operations and will be less likely to solicit honest feedback from civilian or military officials in their regimes, who will in turn face pressure to greenlight even poorly thought-out plans. Personalist leaders should also exhibit a consistent tendency to employ violence when facing political threats, whether domestic or international. I assess these conjectures by studying Saddam Hussein's decision to invade Kuwait in 1990 and subsequently stand firm in the face of Western intervention as well as Stalin's foreign policy decision-making after he had consolidated power in the 1930s.

Strongmen: More Belligerent than Bosses or Juntas?

Are personalist strongmen—personalist leaders with a professional military background—more likely to initiate conflict than nonpersonalist juntas? Are strongmen more likely to embrace international conflict than (civilian) bosses? I consider each comparison—strongmen vs. juntas and strongmen vs. bosses—in turn.

First, are strongmen more belligerent than juntas? The argument about juntas was that even though their leaders must satisfy a domestic audience, military officers are more likely than members of a civilian audience to view force as a sound long-term strategy and to perceive the status quo ominously. These perceptions raise the anticipated net benefits of using force. Much like military officers, personalist leaders often believe that military force is necessary, effective, and superior to diplomacy. However, unlike personalist dictators, leaders of juntas cannot insulate themselves from the costs of defeat. Moreover, leaders of juntas do not have the same discretion over the spoils of victory or the same grandiose ambitions that contribute to the allure of war for personalist leaders. Finally, leaders and audiences in juntas are not as likely to overestimate the likelihood of victory as personalist leaders. Personalist strongmen should therefore be more likely to initiate conflict than nonpersonalist juntas, although the difference should be smaller than the differences between bosses and machines, where *both* beliefs and accountability are different. Strongmen should also be less likely to be punished for losing a war than leaders of juntas, because they do not face powerful audiences. Thus, the answer is that strongman regimes should be both more belligerent than juntas, and their leaders less accountable.

[32]

Second, are strongmen more belligerent than bosses? Given that both are personalist regimes in which the leader faces few consequences from a domestic audience, the question is whether the military background of a strongman would favor the initiation of conflict. Because most bosses must have a predilection for violence to survive their ascent to power and then keep their jobs, they will be attracted to violent strategies even if they do not have formal military training. In strongman regimes, the leader's military experience is somewhat redundant given that all personalist regimes select for highly violent and ambitious leaders. On the margins, we would expect military strongmen to be more belligerent than civilian bosses, although the difference is likely smaller than the distance between military strongmen and other regime types. Similarly, we would expect strongmen to lose a slightly higher proportion of the wars they fight. Rates of punishment for defeat should be similarly low in both kinds of regimes. For the above reasons, we might expect that, although the effects of personalism and militarism are additive, there is some redundancy when both attributes are present. I assess this possibility in the quantitative analyses of dispute initiation, outcomes, and punishment. However, because the underlying processes through which strongmen and bosses decide to initiate conflict are so similar, I focus on bosses in the qualitative case studies.

Reverse Causation?

This book treats domestic regime characteristics as causes, rather than consequences, of international conflict. But it is reasonable to ask whether the relationship might run the other way—perhaps it is not that military rule and personalism cause leaders to initiate more conflict and to choose riskier wars, but rather that such regimes are more likely to *emerge* in circumstances in which conflict is more likely. For example, Gibler (2012) argues that centralized, nondemocratic regimes are more likely to emerge and survive in the face of territorial threat. More generally, if a state's security environment affects its domestic political institutions and leaders, this could cause problems of reverse causation (endogeneity) when one evaluates the effect of domestic institutions on international conflict.

Despite this possible concern, existing studies in comparative politics have not considered the international security environment to play an important role in the origins or survival of particular types of authoritarian regimes. For example, in Svolik's (2012) impressive study exploring why absolute or personalist rule emerges in some contexts but not others, war and international conflict are barely mentioned; indeed, where they do come up, they are cast as consequences rather than causes of unconstrained rule.[68] Instead, Svolik and others who have investigated the origins of personalist rule have emphasized purely domestic factors such as the organization of the leader's supporting coalition, the existence of preexisting institutions allowing for elite coordination, and other idiosyncratic factors.[69]

Similarly, scholars who have investigated the conditions under which the military seizes political power rarely invoke the importance of the international security environment. For example, classic texts on the origins of military rule have rarely drawn a connection between external threats and military intervention, and more recently Svolik (2013) finds that having fought an interstate war does not have any effect on the likelihood that the military will intervene to bring a new leader to power.[70]

Despite the lack of a clear theoretical reason to believe that external insecurity is an important determinant of authoritarian regime type, it is worth ensuring that reverse causation is not somehow driving the empirical results. In the chapter on conflict initiation, I discuss a variety of measures I took to ensure that the results were not due to reverse causation or endogeneity. I also describe supplemental analyses, available in the online appendix at https://users.polisci.wisc.edu/jweeks, that indicate that states that have faced security threats in the past are *not* more likely to transition to personalism or military rule. Moreover, the case study chapters explicitly trace the causal effect of domestic political conditions on subsequent decisions and show how *given* a particular external environment, domestic politics affect decision-making.

HYPOTHESES, IMPLICATIONS, AND CASES

The above discussion produced a series of hypotheses about conflict initiation, conflict outcomes, punishment in the aftermath of war, and the decision-making process in individual historical cases. These hypotheses are summarized in table 1.3. To evaluate these hypotheses, I use a combination of cross-national quantitative analyses (chapters 2 and 3) and in-depth case studies of bosses, juntas, and machines (chapters 4, 5, and 6).[71]

One important question is how to choose appropriate cases for deeper historical analysis. Selecting a small number of cases to examine in greater detail naturally involves tradeoffs, and the different chapters take different approaches. For chapters 4 and 5, on personalist bosses and nonpersonalist military juntas, respectively, I select cases that fit the patterns anticipated by the theory by focusing on regimes that initiated significant amounts of conflict. This approach allows me to examine whether the causal mechanisms operate as expected. Moreover, where the empirical predictions of my argument overlap with other theories, I am able to examine whether the causal mechanisms anticipated by

TABLE 1.3 Summary of hypotheses about regime type and international conflict

	Machines	Juntas	Bosses	Strongmen
Initiation	Low	Medium	High	Highest
Probability of defeat	Low	Medium	High	Highest
Probability of punishment after defeat	High	Medium	Low	Low
Process	Consultative, cautious, incorporates civilian and military input (North Vietnam and USSR after Stalin)	Consultative, but focus on military rather than diplomatic or political aspects of decision (Argentina/Falklands War and Japan 1930s/1940s)	Little consultation; violence/military force seen as "business as usual" (Saddam Hussein and Joseph Stalin)	See juntas and bosses.

those theories can account for the behavior I observe. By necessity, I concentrate on cases with a wealth of reliable historical information; for example, it was feasible to study Iraq under Saddam Hussein but not North Korea under the Kims, given the remarkable level of secrecy of the latter regime. Where possible, I choose cases that transitioned from one authoritarian regime type to another so that we can compare foreign policy in the same country under two regime types, and cases for which there is a prominent alternative interpretation for the regime's behavior.

For the cases of boss regimes, this approach led to me to study Saddam Hussein of Iraq and Joseph Stalin of the Soviet Union. In Iraq, the U.S. invasion resulted in an unusual wealth of evidence about the inner workings of the regime. In the Soviet case, we are able to compare foreign policy under Stalin to foreign policy under the "machine" leaders Khrushchev and Brezhnev. In both countries, we can examine whether the general theoretical depiction of how and why policy is made in personalist regimes fits the historical facts in that particular context.

For military juntas, this case selection strategy led me to focus on Argentina under the military dictatorship of the late 1970s and early 1980s and Japan in the 1930s and 1940s as it transitioned from civilian to military rule. The Argentine case is particularly interesting because many scholars have depicted the Falklands/Malvinas invasion as a diversionary war, an explanation that is quite different from mine. I therefore consider diversionary war and related arguments alongside my own. The Japanese case has different merits. Again, this is a case in which the regime's behavior fits the expectations of the argument in that Japan

[35]

initiated a series of armed conflicts. The question is, How did the military backgrounds of key decision-makers influence those decisions? The events in Japan provide a unique opportunity to glean insight into the thinking of both civilian and military leaders about the exact same questions, due to power struggles in the 1930s as the military became more politically prominent, and the wealth of evidence that became available after the end of World War II.

To explore how and why machines are restrained, finally, requires a different approach. Military conflict is rare, and therefore a machine whose foreign policy matched the argument would be one that seldom, if ever, engaged in war. The problem, though, is finding historical information about non-events, particularly in closed regimes. An alternative is to focus on machines that did choose war, and learn whether and how domestic constraints shaped those decisions. But this approach puts the spotlight on circumstances in which hawks prevailed and the leader ultimately decided on war rather than peace. If the domestic constraints faced by leaders of machines induce these leaders to fight mainly popular and uncontroversial wars, domestic debate and consensus-seeking endeavors could appear muted. I nonetheless choose this approach. While focusing primarily on leaders who went to war generates a biased sample of candidate cases, the bias goes against finding evidence of the hypothesized mechanisms. The resulting cases therefore provide a harder test of the argument that machines are more cautious than personalists, are less likely to have hawkish views represented in the domestic audience than juntas, and tend to seek consensus before initiating war. From among the relatively small set of machines that resorted to war, I focus in depth on North Vietnam in its wars against the United States, South Vietnam, and Cambodia, and more briefly revisit the USSR, taking advantage of the opportunity to examine how Soviet decisions about war and peace changed after the death of Stalin due to the greater constraints faced by Khrushchev and Brezhnev.

[2]

Initiating International Conflict

Adolf Hitler, Saddam Hussein, Muammar Gaddafi, and Idi Amin—these names are synonymous not only with domestic repression but also with the provocation of international conflict. In fact, the record of interstate violence committed by such tyrants has fostered the impression that authoritarianism is inexorably linked to war and other international tensions. Policymakers have drawn on this view to recommend democratization and even regime change in the name of international peace.

While some authoritarian regimes fit this stereotype, others have been much less conflict-prone than the headline-grabbing Gaddafis and Husseins of recent history. China after Mao, Tanzania under Nyerere, Kenya under Kenyatta, Mexico under the PRI, and even the former Soviet Union have all been relatively cautious in their decisions to threaten or use military force.[1] Why are some authoritarian regimes less likely to initiate military conflicts than others? The previous chapter argued that the answer lies in the country's combination of institutional constraints and audience preferences. Machines and democracies should be the least likely to initiate international conflict, followed by juntas, bosses, and strongmen. This chapter tests these hypotheses by analyzing patterns of conflict initiation in the second half of the twentieth century.[2]

MEASURING AUTHORITARIAN REGIME TYPE

Assessing these conjectures requires a method for classifying countries according to their proper regime type. Given the theory, this task requires indicators for the extent to which the paramount leader faces a powerful domestic audience, and whether the leader and the audience stem from civilian or military ranks.

While some authors have tried to measure these concepts previously, those attempts have important shortcomings. For example, Lai and Slater (2006) rely on a combination of the Polity executive constraints (*xconst*) variable and the Banks Cross-National Time-Series "regime type" variable, which identifies whether civilians or members of the armed forces control the government.[3] However, the *xconst* variable is problematic for measuring political constraints in authoritarian regimes because it focuses on formal institutional constraints and "regular" limitations on the executive's power, explicitly excluding "irregular limitations such as the threat or actuality of coups and assassinations."[4] It overlooks the possibility that the threat of coups, including both military coups and palace coups at the hands of political elites, is more predictable and credible in some regimes than others.

Other scholars have used Geddes' (2003) typology, which distinguishes among military, single-party, and personalist regimes. An advantage of this classification is that it does not rely purely on formal institutions, which often belie the true rules of the game in authoritarian regimes. However, the Geddes typology does not distinguish between military-led personalist regimes (strongmen such as Idi Amin) and civilian personalist regimes (bosses such as Saddam Hussein or Joseph Stalin). So, as Lai and Slater point out, we cannot assess whether personalist regimes are more conflict-prone because they are personalist, are led by the military, or both. Moreover, Geddes counts some personalist leaders, such as Stalin and Mao, as single-party leaders because of the party institutions that undergird the regime. In contrast, the framework presented here refers to the personal power of the *leader*, suggesting that Stalin and Mao should be considered bosses rather than the overseers of machines.[5]

A different approach allows me to draw on the strengths of the Geddes data while classifying regimes according to both personalism and military background. As part of her research, Geddes gathered information about a large number of domestic political variables for each regime. Three groups of questions reflected the characteristics of three regime types (personalist, single-party, and military); Geddes aggregated the answers from each group of yes/no questions and assigned three regime-type categories based on these subscores. One attractive feature of the raw data is that many of the indicators vary within the regime over time, unlike the tripartite regime typology. For example, the raw data distinguish between the USSR under Stalin, which I code as a "boss," and the post-Stalin Soviet Union, which I code as a "machine." Both of these are coded as single-party regimes in the Geddes typology that other scholars have used, but the raw data indicate that, for example, Stalin chose most of the members of the Politburo and the Politburo acted primarily as a rubber stamp, whereas in the post-Stalin era, neither of these was true.

Because of these advantages, I use the raw Geddes regime-type data to create independent measures of the two dimensions (personalism and military leadership) as well as indicator variables for each of the four regime types: machine, junta, strongman, and boss. To measure the personalist dimension, I create an index incorporating eight of the Geddes variables: (1) Does access to high government office depend on the personal favor of the leader? (2) Do country specialists view the Politburo (or the equivalent) as a rubber stamp for the leader's decisions? (3) Does the leader personally control the security forces? (4) If there is a supporting party, does the leader choose most of the members of the Politburo-equivalent? (5) Was the successor to the first leader, or is the heir apparent, a member of the same family, clan, tribe, or minority ethnic group as the first leader? (6) Has normal military hierarchy been seriously disorganized or overturned, or has the leader created new military forces loyal to him personally? (7) Have dissenting officers or officers from different regions, tribes, religions, or ethnic groups been murdered, imprisoned, or forced into exile? (8) If the leader is from the military, has the officer corps been marginalized from most decision-making? Importantly, these indicators of personalism are coded independently of a leader's subsequent international behavior and are instead based on observable domestic features of a regime.

To measure the military dimension, I use five questions, combining the Geddes data with data from other sources: (1) Is the leader a current or former high-ranking military officer?[6] (2) Do other military officers hold cabinet positions not related to the armed forces? (3) Is the military high command consulted primarily about security (as opposed to political) matters? (4) Are most members of the cabinet or Politburo-equivalent civilians? (5) Does the Banks dataset consider the government to be "military" or "military-civilian"?

I first created indices representing the proportion of "yes" answers.[7] I then created dummy variables for each of the four regime types, using a cutoff of .5 to classify countries as personalist/nonpersonalist and military/civilian and combining the two dimensions to create four regime types.[8] For example, I coded a country-year as a strongman if it scored more than .5 on the personalist index and more than .5 on the military index. Choosing the particular cutoff of .5 did not affect the substantive results, nor did weighting certain important subcomponents of the index more heavily than others or revising the components of the index in reasonable ways. I also show later that the results are similar whether one uses the indices or the categories, and I describe two ways to score democracies on these indices.

Geddes did not code monarchies, theocracies such as Iran, or unconsolidated regimes in her research. These types of regimes could in principle be coded according to my measures, and in the analyses in chapter 3, which focus on a smaller sample, I code missing regimes myself. But, lacking that data for most country-years, I created additional dummy variables to identify "other" nondemocracies (regimes that have Polity scores of 5 or lower but no Geddes regime-type data).

Finally, I treat as a separate category all countries that had recently undergone substantial domestic institutional change.[9] When institutions and ruling coalitions are in flux, it is often difficult to determine what the "rules of the game" are and hence what the appropriate coding of personalism and militarism should be. While in the end it does not matter empirically whether we isolate these regimes, doing so mitigates the possibility that for regimes that recently underwent change, the coding reflects a retrospective rather than contemporary evaluation of who held de facto power. Separating out these regimes also reduces the likelihood of finding that military regimes (which tend to be shorter-lived) are more belligerent *because* they are typically younger than other regime types.

TABLE 2.1 Examples of authoritarian regime type

	Civilian audience or leader	Military audience or leader
	"Machine" 626 country-years	"Junta" 294 country-years
Elite-constrained leaders	China (after Mao) Kenya Malaysia Mexico (until 1997) Poland Senegal Tanzania USSR (after Stalin) (North) Vietnam	Algeria Argentina Brazil Greece Myanmar (after 1988) Nigeria Rwanda South Korea Thailand
	"Boss" 547 country-years	"Strongman" 584 country-years
Personalist leaders	China (Mao) Cuba (Castro) Indonesia (Sukarno) Iraq (Saddam) Libya (Gaddafi) North Korea (Kims) Portugal (Salazar) Romania (Ceauşescu) USSR (Stalin)	Chile (Pinochet) Egypt (Nasser) Indonesia (Suharto) Iraq (Qasim, al-Bakr) Myanmar (until 1988) Pakistan (Ayub Khan) Somalia (Siad Barre) Spain (Franco) Uganda (Idi Amin)

Table 2.1 summarizes the distribution of machines, bosses, juntas, and strongmen for the 1946–99 period and provides examples of each category.[10]

Modeling the Initiation of International Conflict

Next, we require data that capture the initiation of international conflict. Like many previous scholars, I use the Militarized Interstate Disputes (MID) dataset, which identifies all "united historical cases in which the threat, display or use of military force short of war by one member state is explicitly directed towards the government, official representatives, official forces, property or territory of another state."[11] While there are other datasets that measure international disputes, the MID dataset has the advantage of capturing not only intense conflicts that escalate to a fully-fledged crisis or war but also lower-level disputes that do not escalate beyond minor military skirmishes. Casting a wide net is especially important because war and crises are such rare events. Moreover, the MID dataset is the most widely used dataset for measuring international conflict, allowing for greater comparability with previous research.

While the predictions of my argument are monadic in that they focus on how the domestic institutions in one country affect conflict initiation, rather than on how the interactions between different types of polities lead to conflict, I use a dyadic approach to modeling conflict initiation. Some scholars have instead tested monadic arguments using country-years as the unit of analysis.[12] However, a country-year setup makes it difficult, if not impossible, to account for some of the most important correlates of military conflict, such as the balance of military power, alliance relationships, trading relations, and geographic proximity between a country and potential targets of force. All of these are best measured as attributes of a *pair* of states; focusing on dyads therefore allows us to control for these covariates directly, greatly improving our ability to account for potential omitted variables.[13] By including *directed* dyads (for example, one observation for China-USA-1999, and another for USA-China-1999), we can assess which country initiated the conflict, not just whether conflict broke out in the dyad. Given these advantages, I opt for a directed-dyad analysis in which each observation consists of a directed dyad–year.

The outcome of interest is whether Country A in a directed dyad initiated military conflict against Country B during a given year, with one observation per directed dyad–year. Following the bulk of the literature, I code a country as initiating a MID against the other state in the dyad if it is the first to threaten or use military force.

[41]

Because the dependent variable is dichotomous, I estimate the models using logistic regression. To correct for temporal dependence, I follow Carter and Signorino (2010) and include cubic polynomials of the number of years since the last time State A initiated a MID against its opponent. In addition to the cross-sectional analyses, I also carry out the analyses with fixed effects to correct for the possibility of omitted variables that are specific to directed dyads.[14] That alternative modeling approach is described in greater detail below.

Control Variables

Several factors beyond regime type could affect a state's decision to initiate military hostilities against another state. Since some of these factors could be correlated with the type of domestic political regime due to chance, it is important to control for them in the empirical analysis.

Capabilities. Many scholars have argued that more powerful states have wider-ranging interests than minor powers and therefore initiate military force more frequently. Moreover, some countries may simply lack the military capacity to project power across large distances. I therefore include several measures of power, including the raw military capabilities score of each side, the initiator's share of the dyad's total capabilities, and dummy variables marking whether states in the dyad are major powers, with minor power/minor power dyads as the reference category.[15]

Alliances and Geopolitical Interests. Next, I include two measures of alliance similarity, which provide an indication of broader geopolitical interests. First, states that share similar alliances may have fewer competing interests, and therefore be less likely to resort to military conflict, for reasons that have nothing to do with regime type.[16] I therefore include a measure of the similarity of the two states' alliance portfolios (weighted global S-score). Second, states that are more closely allied with the most powerful state in the system may be more satisfied with the status quo, reducing their motivation to fight.[17] Third, states may be deterred from initiating a MID against a state that is closely allied with a superpower. I therefore include a weighted measure of the similarity of each state's alliance portfolio with the system leader.[18]

Geographic Contiguity. Geographically close countries are more likely to have disagreements (such as over the precise location of a border), and it is easier for a country to deploy its military forces against an immediate neighbor. A dummy variable for contiguity marks whether the two states either share a land border or are separated by fewer than 24 miles of water, and another variable measures the logged distance between the capitals of the two countries.[19]

Trade Dependence. Many scholars have argued that trade interdependence can dampen incentives to use military force against a trading partner. For the dyadic analyses, I therefore controlled for trade dependence in the dyad using data by Kristian Gleditsch (2002).[20]

Side B Regime Type. I include a variable that measures whether Side B in the dyad is a democracy. This is not to test hypotheses about target regime type per se but rather to ensure that the results for democratic Side A states are not due to peaceful clusters of democratic neighbors. Although not reported here, I also checked to make sure that the results hold when controlling for the authoritarian regime type of Side B. Importantly, controlling for the regime type of Side B does not affect the significance of the results for the regime type of Side A.

Finally, I lag all of the variables mentioned above, including both the regime type indicators and the control variables. This ensures that annual measures of regime type, trade, military capacity, or alliance status are not a *consequence* of military action that occurred early in a calendar year.

RESULTS

I begin the analysis by estimating models that include the regime-type dummy variables, rather than the raw indices. These results are more straightforward to interpret than the results using the raw indices, though as I show later, the two approaches lead to the same conclusions. All of the following analyses set the base regime-type category for Side A as machine; we would expect junta, boss, and strongman to have positive, significant, and increasingly large coefficients, with strongmen being the most belligerent of all. Machines should not initiate significantly more or less conflict than democracies according to the arguments, and therefore the coefficient on democracy should not be distinguishable from 0.

The results, shown in columns 1 and 2 of table 2.2, support these predictions. Column 1 shows a bare-bones model in which the only control variables are capabilities and distance, two of the strongest and most consistent predictors of military conflict, plus the time polynomials. Column 2 shows the analyses with the full set of predictors of MID initiation. In both models, juntas, bosses, and strongmen are all significantly more likely to initiate MIDs than the base category of machines. Tests of equality between coefficients indicate that juntas, bosses, and strongmen are also all statistically different from democracies.[21] Democracies, in contrast, are not less likely to initiate conflicts than machines.

TABLE 2.2 Directed-dyad logit analysis of dispute initiation

	(1)	(2)	(3)	(4)
			With Fixed Effects	With Fixed Effects
	Pooled	Pooled		
Democracy	0.22	0.28	0.14	0.25
	(0.16)	(0.19)	(0.17)	(0.19)
Junta	0.46**	0.66***	0.50**	0.63***
	(0.20)	(0.21)	(0.22)	(0.23)
Boss	0.67***	0.87***	0.33**	0.54***
	(0.17)	(0.18)	(0.15)	(0.16)
Strongman	0.93***	1.17***	0.45***	0.65***
	(0.16)	(0.18)	(0.17)	(0.18)
Other nondemocracies	0.40**	0.75***	0.30*	0.53***
	(0.15)	(0.17)	(0.16)	(0.17)
New/Unstable regime	0.04	0.28*	0.31**	0.46***
	(0.15)	(0.17)	(0.14)	(0.16)
Side B democracy	0.27**	0.05	−0.02	−0.10
	(0.11)	(0.12)	(0.12)	(0.12)
Military capabilities, Side A	10.42***	5.68***	−0.01	0.44
	(0.86)	(1.50)	(1.43)	(1.75)
Military capabilities, Side B	9.13***	5.75***	1.08	3.51**
	(0.86)	(1.50)	(1.38)	(1.71)
Side A's proportion of dyadic capabilities		0.44***		1.51***
		(0.13)		(0.53)
Lower trade dependence in dyad		−30.55***		0.53
		(11.70)		(8.36)
Major power/major power dyad		1.66***		
		(0.52)		
Minor power/major power dyad		0.75***		
		(0.23)		
Major power/minor power dyad		0.71***		
		(0.21)		
Contiguous countries	1.86***	1.22*		
	(0.54)	(0.67)		
Logged distance between capitals	−0.20***	−0.32***		
	(0.06)	(0.08)		
Alliance portfolio similarity		−0.89***		−0.69***
		(0.14)		(0.22)
Side A alliance similarity with system leader		0.34**		−0.43
		(0.15)		(0.27)

(Continued)

TABLE 2.2 (*Continued*)

	(1)	(2)	(3)	(4)
			With Fixed	With Fixed
	Pooled	Pooled	Effects	Effects
Side B alliance similarity		0.47***		−0.32
with system leader		(0.15)		(0.27)
Time	−30.01***	−31.67***	−6.33***	−6.86***
	(2.02)	(2.06)	(1.51)	(1.55)
Time squared	88.10***	93.67***	−2.44	−0.49
	(9.33)	(9.50)	(8.21)	(8.52)
Time cubed	−73.05***	−78.64***	51.03***	54.02***
	(12.01)	(12.23)	(11.85)	(12.52)
Constant	−3.97***	−2.91***		
	(0.54)	(0.69)		
Observations	947,638	921,732	31,267	28,919
Number of directed dyads			718	701

Robust standard errors in parentheses
*** p<0.01, ** p<0.05, * p<0.1
Note: Machine is the base category

Moreover, there is evidence that strongmen are more belligerent than juntas, and to a lesser extent bosses. The difference between strongmen and juntas is highly significant in both the bare-bones and full models, respectively (using two-tailed tests). The coefficient on strongman is also larger than the coefficient on boss, though the difference is significant only at the .11 and .06 levels, respectively. Later, I explore the interaction between personalism and militarism in more detail by exploiting the raw data.

The other covariates generally perform as expected. Countries are significantly more likely to initiate conflict when they are militarily strong and also when their opponent is strong, as evidenced by the positive coefficients on the military capabilities variables and the indicators for the major power status of each state in the dyad. Countries are also more likely to initiate conflict against targets that are nearby, as indicated by the positive coefficient on contiguity and the negative coefficient on distance between capitals. States are also significantly less likely to initiate conflicts against targets that share their alliance configurations, presumably because they have fewer conflicts of interest. However, they are more likely to initiate conflicts when either they or their targets have a more similar set of alliances with the system leader (in this time period, the United States). Trade interdependence seems to dampen the incidence of military conflict.

I next estimate the analyses with fixed effects to take into account the possibility that omitted variables specific to directed dyads could be affecting the results.[22] This is essentially the same as including a separate intercept for each directed dyad, which means, importantly, that coefficients reflect only *within*-directed-dyad variation in dispute initiation. Moreover, directed dyads in which *no* dispute initiation occurs during the sample period are dropped from the analysis entirely because there is no variation on the dependent variable. The sample therefore consists only of directed dyads in which Side A initiated at least one MID against Side B, dropping all peaceful pairs of states. In this case, including fixed effects has two countervailing effects on the coefficient estimates. On the one hand, it throws out particularly peaceful machines (the base category), leaving only machines that initiated conflicts. On the other hand, peaceful juntas, bosses, and strongmen that never initiated conflicts are thrown out, whereas more conflict-prone ones are retained in the sample. This means not only that the sample is nonrepresentative and potentially biased but also that the sample is much smaller (31,267 instead of 947,638 observations, indicating that nearly 97% of the observations were dropped). For these reasons, some argue against fixed-effects analyses, and the coefficients should be interpreted with caution.[23]

Despite these potential issues, the results of the fixed-effects analysis support the hypothesis that juntas, bosses, and strongmen are more likely to initiate conflicts than machines and, for the most part, democracies. Machines, again, are no more belligerent than democracies. The one unexpected result in the fixed-effects models is that the coefficient on junta is larger, in a relative sense, than it was in the cross-sectional analysis—around the same size as the coefficient on strongman. Again, this could be because many peaceful dyads were dropped from the analysis entirely, leaving only the most conflict-prone juntas in the sample. Another reason, as described above, is that the fixed-effects analysis identifies coefficients based only on within-directed-dyad variation in the predictor variables; countries only contribute to the regime-type parameter estimates when they change their regime type. The results therefore depend on which countries happened to switch regime type during the sample period. This means that the results indicate that among the countries that switched regime type in the sample period and initiated at least one MID, juntas are about as violent as strongmen. Despite these caveats, the positive and significant coefficients on the regime-type variables in the fixed-effects analysis increase our confidence that the effect of regime type is not due primarily to omitted variables that happen to be correlated with regime type.

What are the substantive effects of these differences in regime type? I use CLARIFY to estimate the predicted probability of conflict initiation in a hypothetical scenario.[24] Figure 2.1 shows the predicted probability that a state initiates a MID when all of the covariates are set to the observed values for an interesting directed dyad-year: Iraq vs. Kuwait in 1990 (based off of column 2 of table 2.2). Note that because the figure plots predicted probabilities based on *all* of the variables in the model, there is considerably more uncertainty around the point predictions than there is around the estimates of coefficients shown in table 2.2. Nonetheless, the figure indicates that, even when factoring in all of the covariates, juntas are nearly twice as likely to initiate disputes as machines, and bosses and strongmen are even more belligerent in comparison. In contrast, the rates of dispute initiation of democracies and machines are not distinguishable from each other.

The previous analyses distilled the raw personalism and militarism scores into dummy variables for ease of interpretation. A different approach is to directly analyze the raw scores on the personalist and military indices, which range between 0 and 1. The advantage here is that it does not force one to define a particular cutoff between "personalist" and "nonpersonalist" or "military" and "civilian." I enter the indices in two ways. First, in columns 1 (cross-sectional) and 2 (with fixed effects) of table 2.3, the sample includes only countries where I have enough data to construct the indices for personalism and militarism. This eliminates democracies, for which we do not have data on personalism and only

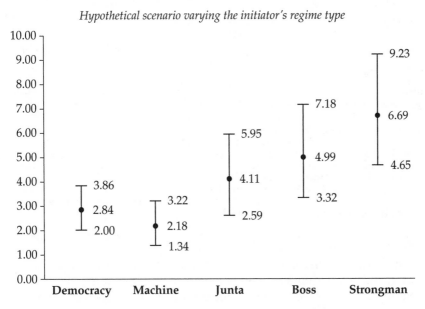

Hypothetical scenario varying the initiator's regime type

FIGURE 2.1 Predicted percent of the time that Side A will initiate conflict

TABLE 2.3 Directed-dyad logit analysis of dispute initiation, using the raw indices

	(1)	(2)	(3)	(4)
	Code democracies as "missing" on the personalism and militarism indices		Code democracies as "0" on the personalism index and "0" or "0.2" on the militarism index	
	Pooled	FE	Pooled	FE
Personalism index	1.08***	1.12***	0.65***	0.60**
	(0.23)	(0.33)	(0.18)	(0.24)
Militarism index	1.26***	1.48***	0.78***	0.76***
	(0.28)	(0.53)	(0.17)	(0.27)
Personalism*militarism	−0.81***	−1.29**	−0.26	−0.73
	(0.31)	(0.61)	(0.28)	(0.47)
Military capabilities Side A	12.72**	1.55	4.89***	−1.10
	(5.35)	(10.68)	(1.51)	(2.19)
Military capabilities Side B	3.74**	9.17***	4.35***	6.20***
	(1.77)	(2.91)	(1.67)	(2.37)
Lower trade dependence in dyad	16.06***	27.72	−28.83**	8.51
	(3.58)	(17.16)	(13.68)	(10.57)
Alliance portfolio similarity	−0.04	0.00	−0.98***	−0.64**
	(0.31)	(0.51)	(0.16)	(0.30)
Additional controls				
Constant	−4.84***		−2.64***	
	(0.72)		(0.61)	
Observations	268,458	8,178	557,458	16,047
Number of directed dyads		265		449

Robust standard errors in parentheses
*** $p < 0.01$, ** $p < 0.05$, * $p < 0.1$
Notes: In addition to the variables listed in the table, as in table 2.2 all models include temporal controls (years since last conflict initiation and cubic polynomials of that variable), initiator share of dyadic military capabilities, alliance portfolio similarity, each states similarity of alliance portfolio with the most powerful state in the system, and Side B democracy. I omit them here for the sake of brevity. Models 1 and 3 also include contiguity, logged distance between capitals, and the major power status of the dyad. These latter variables are not included in the fixed-effects models shown in columns 2 and 4 because they do not vary significantly over time.

limited data on militarism, and also the autocracies that Geddes did not code.[25] The analyses in the first two columns therefore assess the effect of personalism and militarism among autocracies. Columns 3 and 4 show the results when we code all democracies as "0" on personalism and code democracies as "0" on all components of the military indicator other than the leader's military background, which is known for democratic leaders through the Cheibub, Gandhi, and Vreeland (2010) data. For all of the models, I also include an interaction term between militarism and personalism. This allows us to assess whether the two factors are additive or, as hypothesized, partially redundant.

The results reveal the importance of both militarism and personalism. To interpret the interaction effects, we must consider both the constitutive terms and the interaction term.[26] To aid interpretation, figure 2.2 shows how the marginal effect of a unit change in militarism changes as the level of personalism increases and vice versa.[27] The effect of a unit change in militarism is positive and significant over the entire range of the personalism index. Similarly, the effect of a unit change in personalism on conflict initiation is positive and significant, except when militarism is at its very highest values. Thus, personalism and militarism have significant effects no matter what the value of the other dimension.

The graph also indicates that the effects of personalism and militarism are somewhat redundant: The effect of personalism decreases as militarism increases and vice versa. If the two dimensions were perfectly additive, meaning that the effect of one dimension (personalism or militarism) does not depend on the value of the other dimension, then the lines would be flat. If the two dimensions had a positive interactive effect, meaning for example that the effect of personalism increases as the value of militarism increases, then the slope would be positive. In contrast, the negative slopes of the lines suggest some redundancy in personalism and militarism: The effect of personalism appears to be slightly lower at high levels of militarism and vice versa.

Checking Robustness

I also carried out an extensive additional set of robustness checks to ensure that the findings are not driven by particular modeling choices or the inclusion of particular covariates.[28] I began by including additional control variables in the analysis to address potential omitted variable bias. First, I included Side B regime type in the model (that is, whether the potential target in the dyad was a democracy, machine, junta, boss, strongman, or other regime) to ensure that certain regime types were not disproportionately likely to have more conflict-prone neighbors. I also estimated models that control for Polity score in order to ensure that machines are not simply the "most democratic" or participatory of the authoritarians. I next controlled for whether either country in the dyad was undergoing a civil war; Gleditsch, Salehyan, and Schultz (2008) show

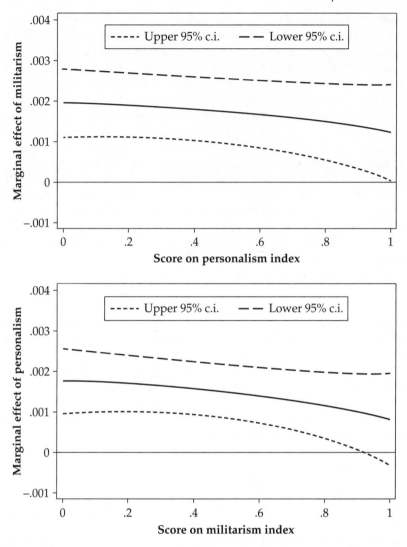

FIGURE 2.2 The interaction between personalism and militarism

that states undergoing civil war are significantly more likely to become involved in international conflict. None of these additional controls made any difference to the results in either the cross-sectional or fixed effects analyses.

Another approach is to drop countries from the sample to ensure that the results hold among important subsets of the population. For example,

I dropped the Warsaw Pact countries (other than the USSR) since these countries might not have foreign policies that were truly independent. I also restricted the sample to dyads that were not allied, to make sure that alliance patterns were not driving the results in some way that was not controlled for in the earlier analyses. Next, I dropped individual countries, such as the USSR, China, Iraq, and the United States, from the sample, both individually and in various combinations, in order to make sure that outliers were not driving any of the results. Again, none of these changes altered the central regime-type findings in the cross-sectional analyses. Although the more restrictive fixed effects analyses are slightly less robust, they also hold given most changes.

Alternative Explanations

Finally, the findings do not support existing alternative arguments about variation in the conflict propensity of dictatorships. First, the evidence does not appear to bear out the expectations of Lai and Slater's (2006) infrastructural-power theory of conflict. According to their arguments, bosses should be no more conflict-prone than machines, because what matters is not the level of personalism of the regime but rather whether the regime has a party infrastructure that provides stability and allows the leader to coopt dissent. This argument is not supported by an analysis of the improved measures of autocratic institutions that I present here, as bosses are consistently more conflict-prone than machines.[29]

Second, the evidence appears inconsistent with selectorate theory. Previous research assessing the ability of selectorate theory to explain conflict among autocracies, such as Peceny and Butler (2004), was forced to rely on less accurate measures of autocratic institutions, for example classifying Mao and Stalin as single-party leaders rather than personalist ones. That earlier research also made it difficult to gain a picture of overall patterns of dispute initiation by the initiator's regime type. Although selectorate theory's predictions are usually dyadic (that is, they take into account the interaction between the regime types of the initiator and target), we would still expect that, averaging across all of the types of dyads, small-coalition regimes should initiate more conflict than large-coalition regimes.[30] Instead, we find that machines, which have small winning coalitions (w) both in absolute size and relative to the selectorate (s)—i.e. a small w/s ratio—are no more belligerent than democracies, which have much larger coalitions and w/s scores.[31] Moreover, small-coalition bosses do not initiate significantly more conflicts than juntas, which should also have a larger w/s.[32] A related question is whether the fear of severe punishment could explain the findings. This question is taken up in more detail in the next chapter.[33]

Finally, it is important to ask whether the findings could be a product of reverse causation or endogeneity. Perhaps it is not that military rule and personalism *cause* leaders to initiate more conflict, but rather that such regimes tend to *emerge* in circumstances in which conflict is more likely for other, unrelated reasons.

As we saw in chapter 1, despite the plausibility of this idea, it is not one that scholars of comparative politics have deemed important, at least in existing studies of the origins of different types of authoritarianism. Nonetheless, the previous analyses attempted to account for the possibility of reverse causation in several ways. Recall that all of the predictor variables are lagged by one year. Moreover, I showed that the results persist even when controlling for a whole host of variables thought to increase the likelihood of international tensions—geography, military power, trade relationships, civil war, and others. I found that even when controlling for these observable indicators of international tension, regime type exerts a significant effect. In addition, I showed the results of the analysis when I include fixed effects. This allows us to account not only for measurable factors but also for *unmeasurable* attributes of a dyad, such as its "innate" level of international tension. Again, there was strong evidence that authoritarian regimes exhibit substantial variation in their conflict behavior, even when only estimating variation *within* directed dyads.

Of course, it is still possible that there are unmeasured changes in the security environment even within directed dyads that none of these approaches picks up. Therefore, in a supplemental appendix, I carry out a more extensive analysis in which I demonstrate that preexisting levels of international conflict do not increase the likelihood that a personalist regime or military junta will seize power.[34] I find, for example, that the number of MIDs a country has experienced in recent years has no significant correlation with the likelihood of transition to a personalist dictatorship or a military junta. For example, countries that are involved in more military conflict—whether as initiators or targets—are neither more nor less likely to transition to a "conflict-prone" type of regime. This lack of correlation is evident whether or not we control for other predictors of regime transition such as GDP, civil war, and population size and holds given a variety of ways of measuring both transition and involvement in past conflict.

Together, these findings suggest that international conflict is a consequence of regime type and not vice versa. While a deep treatment of the causes of authoritarian regime type is beyond the scope of this book, the

available evidence suggests that regime type leads to differences in conflict behavior and not the other way around.

The initiation of international conflict, however, is only part of the
story. What about the outcomes of these disputes? And how do leaders
of different regime types fare in the aftermath of conflicts? The following
chapter takes up those questions.

[3]

Winners, Losers, and Survival

Why are some regimes so much more successful in war than others? The previous chapters established that domestic political pressures cause some authoritarian leaders to be highly selective about resorting to military force, while other leaders are either freer to indulge in riskier behavior or are, by reason of military background, more likely to see force as preferable to diplomacy. In this chapter I explore whether the same arguments explain success and failure on the battlefield.

SELECTING WARS

To review, civilian-led "machines" in which the leader is constrained by a powerful domestic audience are, like democracies, selective in their use of military force. While the political process in these regimes is restricted to a rather narrow segment of elites, the leader's fear of punishment at the hands of those regime insiders induces a level of caution and selectivity that defies the stereotype of the reckless, belligerent dictator. In these regimes, the domestic audience consists of bureaucrats and technocrats who have little to gain personally from war and whose civilian backgrounds encourage them to consider diplomacy a viable tool of foreign policy. The audience's skepticism about using military force urges leaders to proceed cautiously in matters of war. Those leaders are particularly likely to avoid conflicts that could result in defeat because this could lead to punishment.

In juntas, leaders are also accountable to a domestic audience for failure in war, but war outcomes are nonetheless slightly more mixed. The preceding chapter explained that, as in machines, leaders of juntas have incentives to avoid becoming involved in losing wars. Defeat may cause the audience to infer that the leader is incompetent or overly risk-acceptant, increasing the likelihood of ouster. On the other hand, the dominant decision-makers in juntas—military officers—are more likely than civilians to feel that it is necessary to take on risky wars, due to their failure to recognize viable peaceful alternatives. As demonstrated by Argentina's invasion of the Falkland Islands in 1982, El Salvador's aggression against Honduras in 1969, and Japan's reckless adventures in the 1930s and 1940s, military officers are more likely than civilians to see war as inevitable and to discount possible diplomatic solutions to a conflict. The competing pressures of a bias in favor of military over diplomatic options and yet high leader vulnerability in the event of defeat imply that leaders of military juntas should take on greater risks of defeat than leaders of democracies or machines, but have greater incentives to avoid defeat than leaders of personalist regimes, in which there is little or no accountability. If their gambles do not pay off, leaders of juntas face a level of punishment that should fall between that in machines and democracies and that in personalist boss and strongman regimes because the audience imposing punishment shares the general belief that war is often necessary.

Finally, for personalist boss and strongman regimes in which the leader does not face a powerful domestic audience, defeat is a common occurrence. These leaders are more likely to choose high-risk wars for several reasons. First, this type of regime selects for leaders who harbor expansive domestic and international ambitions, and these leaders are more likely than other kinds of leaders to desire to expand their borders or dominate their neighbors in order to enhance their personal glory. This is, of course, in addition to motives typical of other regime types, such as wishing to increase national security or furthering some ideological goal. Second, because these leaders are significantly more insulated from the domestic consequences of costly wars and defeat than their nonpersonalist counterparts, they can take gambles on wars with substantially less concern for the domestic aftermath. In other words, these leaders place a high value on the possibility of winning but pay few of the costs of defeat. Accordingly, Saddam Hussein decided to invade Kuwait without even consulting his own generals, Muammar Gaddafi engaged in a series of reckless military adventures in North Africa with little serious planning, and Mao Zedong and Joseph Stalin, while lucky enough to escape serious defeat, both became involved in several conflicts that a less ambitious and more constrained leader might have eschewed. This lack of selectivity should be even more pronounced in strongman regimes led by a military officer, where the leader's military background could further lead him to perceive high threat and to discount diplomatic alternatives.

Finally, personalist leaders are likely to harbor positive illusions about their own (and by extension, their country's) prowess, which causes them to overestimate the likelihood of victory. The dictator's entourage in turn has few incentives to dispel such notions.

These arguments suggest that democracies and machines, which according to the theory choose their wars the most carefully, should lose the smallest proportion of their wars. When these leaders do miscalculate and lose wars, they should also face high rates of domestic punishment. Juntas are slightly more likely to become involved in losing wars due to their fear of the status quo and disdain for diplomatic solutions. But their leaders nonetheless face moderately high rates of punishment for defeat because the audience may infer that the leader has undesirable qualities, and has the power to act on that inference. In contrast, bosses and strongmen choose wars the least carefully, losing the highest proportion, with strongmen being particularly likely to select low-odds wars. Both of these types of leaders, moreover, are better able to escape domestic punishment than their more constrained counterparts.

These views are counter to two common propositions: that regime type has little relationship with war outcomes and postwar punishment,[1] and that democracies have unique advantages when it comes to choosing and fighting wars, due in part to their greater domestic accountability.[2] In this chapter, I show that regime type does affect patterns of victory and defeat in war, and that the differences among nondemocracies are even more consequential than those between democracies and dictatorships.

Why Focus on Selection Rather than War-Fighting?

Once a state has chosen to enter a war, a new stage begins: fighting. This has led some scholars to focus on a second, complementary explanation for variation in war outcomes—regimes could differ in their ability to generate and *deploy* military power effectively, no matter what their incentives to win. Reiter and Stam (2002) call this the "war-fighting" explanation and, like other scholars, have focused on the purported advantages of democratic institutions in producing victory.

There are a variety of pathways through which domestic regime type could affect a state's ability to fight successfully. One is that some regimes can mobilize resources for war more effectively than others, for example by harnessing the power of free enterprise.[3] Another is that some regimes can create more effective alliance relationships, therefore multiplying their military power.[4] A third possibility is that some regimes produce better soldiers and better fighting practices; countries with democratic culture and institutions could cultivate soldiers who demonstrate greater initiative and leadership on the battlefield.[5] Focusing more specifically on autocracies, some have argued that personalist regimes systematically undermine their own military effectiveness in order to prevent future coups. Authors such as Risa Brooks (1998) and James Quinlivan (1999) have documented the many ways in which "coup-proofing" a regime, or insulating the leader's power by tinkering with military institutions, can undermine the effectiveness of those institutions.[6] Saddam Hussein, for example, organized the military hierarchy specifically in order to prevent coups, resulting in drastically reduced military effectiveness.[7]

These are all possible reasons why countries, if war were forced on them in a vacuum, might fight more effectively or more poorly. However, war is almost never thrust upon states—it is the product of two countries choosing the gamble of fighting over the relative certainty of bargaining. If leaders choose wars on the basis of their likely consequences, then they will already have taken into account these anticipated advantages or deficiencies in war-fighting at the bargaining stage.[8]

This is particularly true when leaders *initiate* or *join* wars of their own volition. At the core of my argument is the assumption that leaders wish to protect their authority and prolong their survival in office. For this reason they strive to avoid involvement in wars that will imperil their grip on power. This implies that when leaders initiate wars despite their army's poor condition, it is either because they can afford to or because they miscalculated during the selection stage. As I argued earlier, regime type can affect both the perceived costs and benefits of fighting a war, and perceptions of the likelihood of winning. The most interesting influence on war outcomes, therefore, takes place when states *choose* wars, for example when countries with objectively weaker military capabilities nonetheless choose to fight wars against stronger or more motivated adversaries or in the face of international opprobrium. Understanding how states choose wars is key to explaining patterns in outcomes.

How does the argument's logic apply to *targets* of wars? Despite the term *target*, targets frequently do choose whether or not to become involved in a war—for example, Saddam Hussein chose not to allow more thorough weapons inspections in 2003, perhaps because in his view the worst-case scenario was another limited war that he could survive politically. Moreover, even when they are targeted, leaders choose the level of effort to commit to a conflict based on how the outcome of the war will affect them politically, thus further "selecting" into the war outcome.[9] As with initiators, the interesting question is why the potential target of a war chose to stand firm and incur the risk of fighting rather than deescalate tensions and reach a peaceful bargain. Again, leaders' decisions *before* the war broke out are key.

On the other hand, targets do potentially exercise less autonomy over the decision to fight; while the selection stage should still influence the war outcomes on average, the link could be somewhat more tenuous. To ensure that the patterns are driven by selection into wars rather than factors that come into play after a war has been forced on a country, I show that similar patterns hold when targets are excluded from the analysis entirely.

WAR OUTCOMES IN THE PAST CENTURY

The first question is whether domestic regime type affects how selective leaders are about choosing their involvement in conflict. To that end, I evaluate the relationship between regime type and war outcomes for all major participants of interstate wars initiated between 1921 and 2007 and, later, check whether similar patterns emerge in lower-level Militarized Interstate Disputes (MIDs).[10]

Given the rarity of full-blown war, generating the correct list of war participants is important. I begin with the most recent update to the Correlates of War Interstate War dataset, which contains 192 cases of war participation in this time period.[11] I then limit that list to major combatants in wars—states that contributed at least 10 percent of the maximum troop strength deployed by all countries fighting on its side during the conflict.[12] We can be reasonably certain that if domestic politics matter, these are the cases in which audiences—if they exist—are the most likely to hold leaders responsible for their country's involvement in the war. I also differentiate between states that initiated or joined a conflict and countries that were directly targeted by another state and therefore had less autonomy over their decision to enter the war. Table 3.5, shown at the end of the chapter, lists the resulting 120 major participants in interstate wars between 1921 and 2007.

To measure authoritarian regime type, I collected information about the regime type of every authoritarian war participant. For the tests in the previous chapter, I was able to rely to a large extent on data collected by other scholars, which I used to generate a new measure of authoritarian regime type that matches the dimensions highlighted by my argument. However, the tests in this chapter require me to collect much of the data from scratch, since many of the wars took place before 1945 or among countries that had not been coded by Geddes (such as monarchies). Working with a team of research assistants to ensure inter-coder reliability, I therefore coded the regime type of each war participant to assess whether the leader was effectively constrained by a domestic audience.[13] If the leader was constrained by a domestic audience, I assessed whether that audience was composed primarily of civilians (machines) or stemmed from the military ranks (juntas). Among unconstrained regimes, I coded leaders as civilian bosses if they did not have an extensive professional military career (typically, at the level of general or equivalent) prior to taking power. If the leader had an extensive career in military service, I coded the regime as a strongman regime. As before, however, the differences between bosses and strongmen are predicted to be less important than the differences among machines, juntas, and unconstrained (personalist) regimes. The precise coding rules and procedures, which are adapted from those that produced the dataset used in chapter 2, are described in detail in the appendix.

One possible concern is that the coding of regime type could be influenced by information that occurred during or after the war, such as whether the leader was punished. In each case, I was extremely careful to consider only evidence of the regime's rules prior to the start of the war, such as whether the leader had established a clear pattern of dominance over high appointments or had purged individuals who opposed him. Because it is not often immediately clear what the "rules of the game" are in a new regime—that is, whether the leader has truly consolidated power—I code all regimes as "new/unstable" if they underwent significant institutional change up to two years before the initiation of the war. In these new regimes, it is too difficult to establish a clear record of the leader's power vis-à-vis his audience to reach a reliable coding of the constraints on the leader. Further details on all of these coding procedures are provided in the appendix.

Finally, we require information about the outcome of the war. I use Croco's (2011) coding of war outcomes, which takes into account the state's own specific, stated objectives for the war.[14] This approach is most appropriate for the question at hand because domestic audiences will judge their leaders' success according to what the leaders stated they wished to achieve both militarily and politically, rather than according to only military performance or some external criterion.[15] Outcomes are considered victories if a significant portion of the war aims were achieved, draws if the objectives were not achieved and the status quo did not worsen, and losses if the status quo deteriorated.[16] This implies that the outcomes are not always zero-sum, with a victory for one side automatically implying defeat for the opponent. For example, when Taiwan repelled Chinese attacks in 1958, this is considered a victory for Taiwan because its goal was to defend the status quo. It is considered a draw for China because even though China failed to dislodge Taiwan from Quemoy and Matsu, the status quo did not deteriorate appreciably. Based on the military outcome, however, the Correlates of War (COW) dataset considers this war as a stalemate for both sides despite Taiwan's success at holding out against Chinese attacks. Similarly, Croco considers the Sino-Vietnamese Punitive War of 1979, in which China attacked Vietnam, a draw for China: although the status quo did not deteriorate, China did not succeed in convincing Vietnam to withdraw from Cambodia. The outcome is coded as a victory for the target, Vietnam, because it withstood Chinese attacks and was not coerced into altering its Cambodia policy. Of course, for other questions—such as how states perform in purely military terms—the traditional COW scheme may be more appropriate. But for the question at hand, it is essential to take into account the objectives of the war, because this better reflects how audiences will judge success.

Of the 120 war participants in the sample, 47 of the war participants won, 20 drew, and 53 lost. The war participants, their role as initiator, joiner, or target, my regime type codings, and the war outcome are listed in table 3.5.

To begin the analysis, figure 3.1 shows the relationship between "regime type" as scholars typically use the concept—whether or not the initiator was a democracy with a Polity score of 6 or higher—and defeat in war.[17] Consistent with previous research, nondemocracies appear substantially more likely to lose their wars than democracies. Between 1921 and 2007, countries that were not fully fledged stable democracies lost 49 percent of their 91 wars, whereas democracies lost only 28 percent of their 29 wars. Ninety-five percent confidence intervals appear around the mean number of losses, and the difference in rate of defeat between

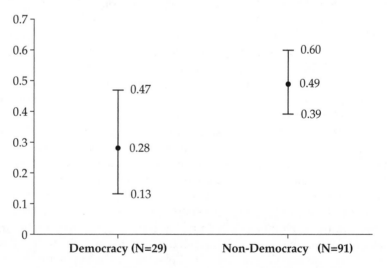

FIGURE 3.1 Proportion of defeats, democracies vs. non-democracies, 1921–2007

democracies and nondemocracies was significant at the .04 level using a chi-square test. Among the subset of countries that initiated or joined a war, the differences were equally stark: nondemocracies lost 36 percent (16 of 44 war initiations), whereas stable democracies lost none (0 of 15 war initiations), a difference that was significant at the .01 level.

A deeper look, however, reveals that this pattern is driven by a distinct subset of authoritarian regimes. Figure 3.2 distinguishes war outcomes not simply between democracies and nondemocracies but also among different types of dictatorships. I first focus on all war participants and then examine the subset of initiators and joiners to make sure that the results are the same for the countries that had the most autonomy over the decision to fight.

Figure 3.2 indicates that the blunt distinction between democracies and nondemocracies masked substantial variation in war outcomes among authoritarian regimes. Elite-constrained civilian machines lost 25 percent of their 20 wars, similar to democracies' 28 percent out of 29 wars. Juntas lost 38 percent of their 8 wars, a proportion that is higher than that of democracies and machines, though not significantly so in a statistical sense, perhaps due to the small number of observations. Personalist civilian bosses in contrast lost 56 percent of their 25 wars, and strongmen lost an abysmal 73 percent of 15 wars. In sum, it is unconstrained personalists who drove the finding of a democratic advantage. Elite-constrained civilian machines fared nearly as well as democracies when they initiated wars. Juntas did slightly worse than machines.

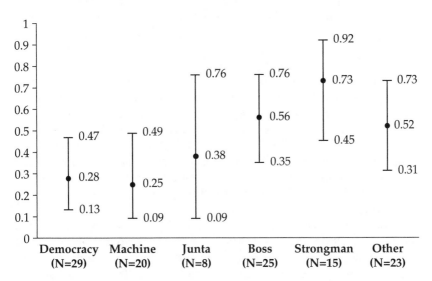

FIGURE 3.2 Proportion of defeats by regime type, 1921–2007

[61]

What historical cases underlie these patterns? Among machines, the Soviet Union counts for two observations; the first when Stalin—who had not yet carried out the purges that gave him total domination over his domestic rivals—started the short and victorious Sino-Soviet War against a weak and fractured China in 1929. (After Stalin carried out the purges, he is coded as a boss.) In 1956, Stalin's successor Khrushchev presided over the successful invasion of Hungary, another victory for the Soviets. Other victorious machines include Paraguay in the Chaco War, Tanzania in its 1979 war against Idi Amin's Uganda, and North Vietnam in a series of wars against the United States, Cambodia, and China in which, at a minimum, it successfully defended the status quo. Not all machines were victorious, of course: for example, Syria lost the 1948 Arab-Israeli War during a brief period in which it is coded as a machine; Taliban-led Afghanistan lost in 2003 against the United States; and China under Deng drew in its two wars against Vietnam. Nonetheless, the low rate of defeat among machines is driven by a geographically and temporally diverse set of countries.

A skeptic might argue that a universe of twenty cases of war involvement for machines is not large enough to establish a convincing pattern. But as we saw in chapter 2, that leaders of machines have incentives to be highly selective about their wars implies that machines would fight a relatively small number of conflicts, a pattern demonstrated in the analysis of conflict initiation. Machines, according to the argument, initiate wars only when their objective chances of victory are high. The small number of war initiations by machines is therefore consistent with the idea that some types of autocracies use force more selectively, and hence more sparingly, than others.

Among juntas, the number of observations is even smaller—only eight wars. This small number is due in part to juntas' incentives to win their wars, but also because juntas are a relatively rare type of government. Among the juntas coded as achieving at least some of their war objectives are Ethiopia in the 1977 Ogaden War, El Salvador in the 1969 Football War, and Japan in the 1937 Third Sino-Japanese War. Japan also racked up two draws (both against the USSR, in 1938 and 1939) and a major defeat in World War II, to be discussed in detail in chapter 5.[18] Other defeated juntas are Argentina in the 1982 Falklands War, in which diplomatic alternatives were clearly discounted, and Honduras in the Football War.

Bosses and strongmen, finally, were much less selective about the wars they fought. Of the 25 wars that bosses fought, they won only nine, and of these nine, two-thirds were due to Stalin or Mao. Among the defeated boss regimes were Ethiopia under Haile Selassie, Iraq under Saddam

Hussein, Libya under Gaddafi, and many more. Strongmen, who did even more poorly on average, featured defeated leaders including Chiang Kai-shek of China and later Taiwan, Gamal Abdel Nasser of Egypt, Hafez al-Assad of Syria, and others.

Finally, while the theoretical arguments do not pertain directly to the diverse set of countries that are coded as new or unstable regimes, it is interesting to note that these regimes tended not to fare particularly well.

Confounding Factors?

One possible explanation for the results uncovered here is that machines are, due to chance, different from other autocracies in ways that affect their success in war. Perhaps machines are typically stronger or richer than their military-led or personalist counterparts, and it is this that explains their relative success in war. We must confront the possibility that machines are more likely to win the wars they initiate not because their leadership is more selective but because of other confounding factors.

Scholars often address such questions by including control variables in a multivariate framework. For the research question at hand, however, we must be careful about what types of variables to include, because some common control variables are likely "post-treatment" to regime type, and including them in the analysis could bias the results. My argument suggests that constrained leaders estimate the relative costs and benefits of fighting before initiating a war, taking into account the relative balance of capabilities (including the capabilities of key allies), the favorability of the terrain, and other observable factors related to the likelihood of victory. If that is the case, then we should *not* control for those factors in estimating the effects of regime type on war outcomes. Put another way, leaders select into conflicts based on publicly and privately observed information about factors that will affect the war outcome. For example, the United States invaded Iraq and Afghanistan because it believed it could defeat these countries militarily, but it never attacked the Soviet Union directly because it knew that a fight could be devastating. Factors such as relative military capabilities clearly played a direct role in the war selection process; this balance of capabilities is part of the "outcome" to be analyzed. Unconstrained leaders, the argument implies, are more likely to select into wars against powerful targets or under unfavorable strategic circumstances precisely because they have little to lose for doing so. Thus, for this particular research question, the characteristics of the target states, terrain, relative capabilities, and so on are part of what is to be explained and are not to be treated as independent predictor variables. Including them in the analysis could induce post-treatment bias, since we would be controlling for a *consequence* of regime type.[19]

Nonetheless, for interested readers, I show an analysis that controls for absolute military capabilities, the country's degree of alliance similarity with the most powerful state in the international system, and the number of bordering countries, which proxies for the security threats that a country faces. Such an analysis is problematic for the reasons described above. But if the findings hold, it forestalls the critique that the findings are driven by omitted factors that are correlated with regime type by chance. Table 3.1 presents the results of an ordered logistic regression of war outcome on regime type and covariates such as military capabilities, alliance with the system leader, and the number of neighboring states a country has. The dependent variable, *outcome*, is coded lose = −1, draw = 0, and win = 1. Thus, positive coefficients indicate a higher likelihood of favorable war outcomes, whereas negative coefficients indicate a higher probability of adverse outcomes.[20] The first column shows the results without any control variables. The remaining columns include these control variables, though readers are reminded of the caveats about post-treatment bias.[21] Standard errors are clustered by war, since war outcomes are not independent across participants of the same war.

Including these control variables does not, in fact, change the finding that democracies and machines lose wars at similar (low) rates, while personalist bosses and strongmen lose at significantly higher rates than machines. Juntas, as before, place somewhere in between. In these analyses, machines are the base category. The coefficients on bosses and strongmen are negative and significant at the .05 level or higher. The coefficient on junta is negative but not significant at conventional levels. Furthermore, Wald tests indicate that bosses and strongmen are different from democracies.[22]

Finally, we might check whether other domestic factors are driving the differences between authoritarian regime types. For example, perhaps it is not that machines feature leaders who are constrained by an elite civilian audience; maybe it is that they are more "democratic" than other regime types in the sense that they allow greater public participation in politics and therefore greater scrutiny of policy options. If so, a healthier democratic marketplace of ideas could account for machines' greater selectivity.

To address this possibility, table 3.1 includes the results of several ordered logit analyses of war outcomes for nondemocratic war participants while controlling for mass political participation. I use two measures of participation: overall Polity scores and the Polity dataset's *Competitiveness of Participation* or *parcomp* variable. This latter measure captures "the extent to which alternative preferences for policy and leadership can be

TABLE 3.1 Regime type and war outcomes, 1921–2007

	Model 1	Model 2	Model 3	Model 4
Democracy	−0.18	−0.34		
	(0.60)	(0.62)		
Junta	−0.77	−0.51	−0.91	−1.06
	(0.63)	(0.72)	(0.90)	(0.90)
Boss	−1.23**	−1.45**	−1.94***	−1.95***
	(0.60)	(0.58)	(0.64)	(0.69)
Strongman	−2.26***	−2.19***	−2.52***	−2.53***
	(0.69)	(0.72)	(0.79)	(0.75)
Other	−1.30**	−1.24**	−1.30*	−1.11*
	(0.58)	(0.62)	(0.68)	(0.64)
Material capabilities		1.07	7.92	8.03*
		(3.72)	(5.11)	(4.71)
Alliance similarity with system leader		0.43	2.11**	2.38**
		(0.68)	(0.94)	(0.94)
Number of bordering countries		0.08	0.05	0.04
		(0.06)	(0.07)	(0.07)
Polity score			−0.09	
			(0.07)	
Competitiveness of participation				−0.35
				(0.28)
Cut point 1	−1.15***	−0.49	−0.15	−1.28
	(0.44)	(0.63)	(0.67)	(0.88)
Cut point 2	−0.39	0.30	0.70	−0.41
	(0.40)	(0.62)	(0.67)	(0.85)
Observations	120	120	85	85

Robust standard errors in parentheses (clustered by war)
*** $p < 0.01$, ** $p < 0.05$, * $p < 0.1$
Notes: Results are from an ordered logit model. The base category is machines. Standard errors are clustered by war. The category Other includes all regimes that are not stable democracies or stable autocracies or for whom it was simply not possible to reach a reliable determination of regime type due to data availability (e.g., Saudi Arabia and Yemen in 1934). Table 3.5 lists each of the regime codings, and the appendix describes in greater detail how the codings were reached.

pursued in the political arena."[23] Polities are scored from 1 to 5. Countries with a score of 1 are considered "Repressed"; countries with a score of 2 are considered "Suppressed"; up to a score of 5, "Competitive." Nearly 70 percent of the machine initiators in the sample have the worst competitiveness score, "Repressed," although three—Japan in 1931, Paraguay in 1932, and Ethiopia in 1998—are considered "Factional" (with a competiveness score of 3). The differences among authoritarian regime types are not statistically significant, with the exception that the juntas in this sample appear to have higher *parcomp* scores (greater competitiveness) than other regimes. This seems to be due to several observations involving Japan, which was led by the military in practice but retained a nominal parliamentary system in which participation is (probably erroneously) coded as "Factional." I restrict the comparisons to nondemocratic states only, since otherwise there would be collinearity between the participation variables and the dummy for democratic regime type (the base category for the analyses that include democracies).

Table 3.1 indicates that neither measure of democratic participation explains the variation among authoritarian regime types. Even when I control for competitiveness of participation, bosses and strongmen are significantly more likely to face defeat than machines, with juntas more likely to lose but not significantly so.

In sum, the findings corroborate the hypothesis that only some types of autocratic states lack the domestic incentives to be selective in war. Like democracies, elite-constrained civilian dictatorships are careful to avoid losses. Bosses and strongmen, however, choose their wars less wisely, with juntas falling in between the two extremes. The findings also potentially reconcile previous disagreements about the role of democracy in war outcomes (e.g. Reiter and Stam 2002 and Downes 2009). Democracies *are* relatively successful in war—just not more successful than *all* kinds of non-democracies.

Initiators and Targets

The analysis above pooled initiators and targets together, since in most cases even targets have opportunities to avoid war, whether or not they officially initiate hostilities. It is, however, worthwhile to consider whether the same patterns hold for the subset of countries that unequivocally selected into war by taking the first shot or joining the war freely.[24] If these initiators and joiners exhibit distinct patterns of war outcomes by regime type, we can be especially confident that the differences we observe here are due to how leaders choose wars in the first place, not how they fight wars that are thrust upon them.

Figure 3.3 shows the results when we restrict the sample to states that either initiated a war or joined it without being attacked directly first. As before, democracies and machines are particularly unlikely to lose the wars they initiate or join. Juntas trail machines, though the difference between the two is again not statistically significant. Personalist bosses and strongmen, in contrast, are significantly more likely to lose the wars they choose. Their rate of defeat is significantly higher than that of

[66]

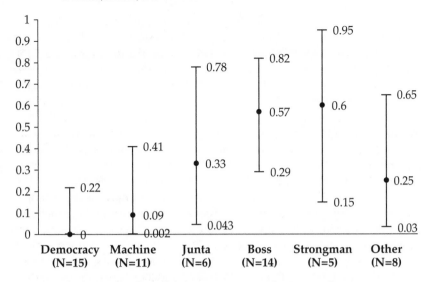

FIGURE 3.3 The probability of defeat, initiators and joiners only

democracies and machines despite the small number of observations. The replication files available online show that these patterns hold when carrying out the same ordered logit analyses estimated earlier, but restricting the sample to only initiators and joiners.

Outcomes of Militarized Interstate Disputes, 1946–2000

Above, I analyzed rates of defeat in the most serious types of international conflicts: war. However, the selection logic should also operate at lower levels of conflict, such as militarized disputes short of war. Moreover, carrying out similar analyses on a larger sample drawn from an entirely different dataset increases our confidence that the results for war outcomes are not spurious. I therefore return to militarized interstate disputes (MIDs), whose initiation I analyzed in the previous chapter.[25]

While all MIDs involve the threat or use of force, many MIDs consist of minor events such as seizures of stray fishing vessels, accidental border crossings, and threats that never escalate to the actual use of force. For this reason, *targets* of MIDs probably do not consistently "select into" MIDs in the same way that they select into wars. I therefore limit the sample to states that either initiated or joined a MID on the initiating side and evaluate how regime type influences the outcomes of the MIDs in which these states choose to become involved.[26]

[67]

The MID *outcome* variable differentiates among victory, yields, and other outcomes such as the release of naval vessels. I recode these outcomes as "win" if the dispute ends in victory for the initiator or yield for the target; "draw" if the dispute ends in compromise, stalemate, release, or is "unclear; "lose" if the initiator yields or the target is victorious; and missing otherwise.[27] Unlike wars, the vast majority of MIDs end in a stalemate or draw: In this sample, around 7 percent of MID initiations result in clear-cut victory, and around 4 percent of MIDs result in clear-cut defeat. For data on regime type, I use the same data I used to study the initiation of MIDs in chapter 2.

Table 3.2 reports average rates of victory, draw, and loss for MIDs between 1946 and 2000, by regime type. Democracies enjoy the highest proportion of wins (.15) and they lose disputes at low rates (.03). Machines win disputes at a slightly lower rate than democracies (.08), though they lose disputes at the same low rate (.02). Bosses and strongmen almost never win disputes (.01 and .01, respectively), and on average they lose disputes at higher rates than machines (.03 and .06). Juntas, as in the case of wars, fall between these extremes.

To gain a clearer picture of the significance of regime type, I next carry out a multinomial logit analysis of dispute outcomes (unlike the analysis of war outcomes, a test of the proportional odds assumption indicates that an ordered logit is not appropriate here). Before proceeding, it is important to note that as with the analysis of war participants above, including control variables could actually distort the effects of regime

TABLE 3.2 MID outcomes

	Lose	Draw	Win
Democracy	0.03	0.82	0.15
	15	*351*	*64*
Machine	0.02	0.90	0.08
	4	*159*	*14*
Junta	0.04	0.92	0.04
	2	*47*	*2*
Boss	0.03	0.96	0.01
	7	*193*	*1*
Strongman	0.06	0.93	0.01
	12	*178*	*2*
Other	0.04	0.92	0.04
	26	*596*	*25*
Total	0.04	0.90	0.06
	66	*1524*	*108*

type. If regime type affects whether leaders are willing to initiate MIDs against powerful opponents, for example, then including those variables in the analysis could induce post-treatment bias. The attributes of the conflict dyad are not exogenous control variables; they are part of what we are trying to explain.

With these issues in mind, the first column of table 3.3 shows the results of a multinomial logit analysis without any control variables. Standard errors are clustered by dispute, since outcomes are not independent for participants within the same dispute. The base category is machines, allowing for a simple comparison both between machines and democracies and between machines and other regime types. The base outcome is draws.

TABLE 3.3 Multinomial logit analysis of MID outcomes

	Model 1		Model 2	
	Lose	Win	Lose	Win
Democracy	0.53	0.73	0.20	−0.03
	(0.70)	(0.61)	(0.75)	(0.64)
Junta	0.53	−0.73	0.30	−1.32
	(0.88)	(0.84)	(0.91)	(0.91)
Boss	0.37	−2.83***	0.18	−3.61***
	(0.64)	(1.09)	(0.63)	(1.12)
Strongman	0.99	−2.06**	0.81	−2.80***
	(0.60)	(0.83)	(0.61)	(0.91)
Other	0.55	−0.74	0.24	−1.26**
	(0.58)	(0.48)	(0.59)	(0.57)
Capabilities			−3.34	−6.72**
			(3.50)	(2.70)
Trade openness (logged)			0.12	0.46***
			(0.19)	(0.17)
Number of bordering countries			0.02	0.02
			(0.04)	(0.03)
Civil war in progress			−1.63*	−0.28
			(0.95)	(0.50)
Number of allies			0.02	0.03**
			(0.01)	(0.01)
Constant	−3.68***	−2.43***	−4.10***	−3.47***
	(0.51)	(0.44)	(0.96)	(0.84)
Observations	1,698	1,698	1,629	1,629

Robust standard errors in parentheses
*** $p < 0.01$, ** $p < 0.05$, * $p < 0.1$

The table indicates that that there are significant differences in outcomes by regime type. When it comes to defeat, the authoritarian regime coefficients are in the anticipated direction but not statistically significant, though this may be due to the very low incidence of defeat in the sample as a whole. However, there are significant differences in the likelihood of victory by regime type. As hypothesized, no meaningful differences exist between democracies and machines, while the negative and significant coefficients on bosses and strongmen indicate that they are significantly less likely to win disputes than machines. The difference between juntas and machines is in the anticipated direction, but not statistically significant. When it comes to comparisons between the authoritarian regime types and democracies, Wald tests indicate that juntas, bosses, and strongmen are different from democracies at the $p < 0.083$, $p < 0.001$, and $p < 0.001$ levels, respectively.

The succeeding columns of table 3.3 show the results when including control variables such as the initiator's military capabilities, trade openness, the number of borders a country has, the presence of a civil war, and the country's number of formal allies. As before, we see that democracies do not have different MID outcomes than machines, while bosses and strongmen are significantly less likely to have favorable outcomes (and Wald tests indicate that bosses and strongmen are, again, significantly less likely to win than democracies).[28]

As before, I also consider the possibility that the authoritarian regime type categories simply reflect heterogeneity in the level of democracy among authoritarian regimes. Perhaps it is not that civilian leadership and elite constraints are producing the patterns of MID outcomes by regime type but rather the repression of public political participation. However, controlling for *parcomp* or Polity scores among nondemocratic regimes does not alter the results.[29] In sum, the evidence indicates that machines fare as well as democracies in both wars and lower-level militarized disputes. Juntas follow, and bosses and strongmen trail far behind.

THE CONSEQUENCES OF DEFEAT

What happens to leaders in the aftermath of defeat? The argument in this book suggests that constrained leaders believe they will face domestic punishment for wars that end in defeat. In contrast, when the leader does not face a powerful domestic audience, as in personalist boss or strongman regimes, leaders do not expect that they will be punished for defeat because there are few actors in the regime with the ability to jettison the leader. The hypothesis developed earlier was that leaders of democracies and machines should be the most likely to face punishment for defeat in war, followed by juntas and then bosses and strongmen.

Of course, a potential complication is that if leaders know that certain actions are likely to invite punishment, they will avoid those very actions. This creates two possible issues for the data analysis. The first is that we are unlikely to observe large numbers of leaders of democracies, machines, or juntas becoming involved in conflicts that they go on to lose. Indeed, earlier we established precisely that pattern: Only very few constrained leaders lost the wars they fought. A second potential problem is that if leaders do act strategically in order to avoid punishment, then the rates of punishment we observe in practice will be lower than the "theoretical" likelihood of punishment leaders would face if they were not acting in anticipation of punishment.[30] For example, the leaders who do fight losing wars may have chosen those wars because they had reason to believe that punishment was unlikely for that particular conflict. Alternatively those leaders may have unusual concerns and thus may be unrepresentative in some important way. Therefore, an analysis of rates of punishment would be biased against finding evidence of punishment. Despite these complications, we should still observe a fairly large number of unconstrained (boss and strongman) leaders losing wars and yet surviving in office at higher rates than leaders of other regime types, even if strategic selection may mute the differences among regimes.

Two additional questions arise. The first is whether we should examine the absolute likelihood of ouster or the probability of ouster after defeat *relative to* the likelihood of ouster during peacetime. Both likely play an important role in the leader's calculation. For simplicity, here I focus on absolute rates of punishment, though elsewhere I carry out a more sophisticated analysis that compares the rate of ouster in the aftermath of each war outcome to the rate of losing office during peacetime, reaching similar conclusions.[31]

A second question is whether to look only at the likelihood of ouster or also at the severity of the punishment. Hein Goemans (Goemans 2000, Chiozza and Goemans 2011, and Debs and Goemans 2010) in particular has argued that leaders are especially motivated to avoid severe punishment such as house arrest, exile, or death. Leaders, this research argues, are more likely to gamble on military conflict the more likely they are to lose office through "irregular" violent means. Thus, perhaps the patterns evident here could be due to leaders' desire to avoid *severe* punishment and not their desire to avoid punishment in general. While I focus primarily on the overall likelihood of punishment, I later discuss the possibility that the patterns are driven by leaders' fear of irregular removal. Moreover, in the case study chapters I discuss evidence that the greater conflict initiation of juntas and personalists does not appear to be due to an imminent fear of violent punishment.

To assess my hypotheses about variation in the rate of punishment by regime type, I return to the sample of war participants used at the beginning of this chapter: all major combatants in wars beginning between 1921 and 2007. In order to capture whether the leader was ousted following the conclusion of each war, I define a dichotomous variable that measures whether the leader remained in power two years after the conclusion of the war, based on the Archigos database on political leaders.[32] I chose the two-year cutoff to reflect the fact that it may take some time after the end of the war for the leader to be removed from office in practice, though the particular choice of cutoff (one year or three years, for instance) does not affect the substantive results. Leaders who were removed before the war ended also receive a "1" on this variable. I treat cases of natural death, retirement due to ill health, and suicide as censored, since we do not have the opportunity to observe whether the leader was punished.[33]

Table 3.4 displays the proportion of leaders who lost office within two years of the end of the war, according to war outcome (defeat vs. draw or victory) and regime type.[34] The table indicates that machines are surprisingly similar to democratic leaders and sharply different from other types of authoritarian leaders in terms of the likelihood of losing office after defeat in an interstate war. Of the 7 democratic leaders who lost wars, 86 percent lost office within two years, compared to only 53 percent of the 17 democrats who won or drew wars.[35] (Keep in mind that for democratic leaders the rates of losing office can be affected by term limits.) Of the four leaders of machines who embroiled their country in a war that ended in defeat, all lost office, compared to only 15 percent of the 13 cases when war ended in a draw or victory.

I hypothesized that juntas would experience rates of punishment after defeat that fall between machines and personalists. The three leaders of junta regimes who lost wars all lost office within two years, compared to three of the five junta leaders who drew or were victorious. Here, the limitations of a small sample make it difficult to say whether these rates of punishment for defeat would be the same as or lower than the rates for machines if we had more data. For the time being, we can say that in the few cases in which leaders of democracies, machines, and juntas became involved in a losing war, they also lost office.

In sharp contrast, leaders of boss and strongman regimes demonstrate surprising resilience even in the face of defeat. Of the 13 bosses who steered their country to a loss, less than 40 percent lost office as a consequence. While this is much higher than the rate of ouster for leaders who won or drew wars (0 of 11), it is still much lower than the 75–100 percent rates of ouster for defeated democrats, machines, and juntas. Despite the small sample size, these differences are large enough that a chi-square test indicates that the rate of ouster after defeat for bosses is significantly different from that of democracies, machines, and juntas at the $p < 0.043$, $p < 0.031$, and $p < 0.055$ levels, respectively. Moreover, it is noteworthy that of the five bosses who were ousted in the aftermath of defeat, three were driven out by foreign forces: Haile Selassie of Ethiopia in 1936, who was later reinstated; Pol Pot of Cambodia; and Saddam Hussein of Iraq. In other words, the rate of *domestic* punishment is even lower than the estimates shown in the table.

The treatment of strongmen in the aftermath of defeat is even more lenient. Of the 10 strongman leaders who guided their countries to defeat, only two (20%) lost office within two years. And both of these leaders—Chiang Kai-shek in 1937, who continued to lead the Kuomintang, and Idi Amin of Uganda in 1979—were driven out by foreigners rather than being removed by a domestic audience. Chi square tests indicate that the rate of post-defeat punishment for strongmen is significantly different from the rates for democracies, juntas, and machines.

TABLE 3.4 Proportion of leaders ousted within two years, by war outcome

	Lose	Win or draw	Total
Democracy	0.86	0.53	0.63
	7	17	24
Machine	1.00	0.15	0.35
	4	13	17
Junta	1.00	0.60	0.75
	3	5	8
Boss	0.38	0.00	0.21
	13	11	24
Strongman	0.20	0.00	0.15
	10	3	13
Other	0.50	0.11	0.33
	12	9	21
Total	0.53	0.28	0.39
	49	58	107

The patterns look very similar when the sample is restricted to initiators and targets.[36]

As mentioned earlier, a different way to put leaders' postwar fates into context would be to compare rates of post-defeat punishment to the rate of ouster of similar leaders during peacetime. When making a decision to go to war in the first place, leaders may take into account not only the absolute probability of losing office but also the relative probability of losing office after going to war compared to the probability of retaining power if they avoid international bloodshed. Elsewhere I carry out a more complicated analysis in which I compare the rate of ouster in the aftermath of defeat to the probability of ouster during peacetime, while controlling for a whole host of covariates.[37] The results are the same: Democrats and constrained authoritarians (leaders of machines and juntas) who lead their countries to defeat are ousted at much higher rates compared to their peacetime rates of survival. Unconstrained bosses and strongmen who are defeated lose office at rates that are low both in an absolute sense and low compared to their peacetime rates of losing office.

Finally, it is worth considering the alternative hypothesis that the leaders of boss, strongman, and junta regimes are motivated to gamble on war out of fear of losing office and then facing severe punishment such as death, imprisonment, or exile. Chiozza and Goemans 2011 argues that leaders who anticipate irregular removal from office have increased incentives to fight. The very act of sending troops to another country, they argue, allows leaders to marginalize potential coup plotters, regardless of whether the war ultimately results in victory (19-25). Moreover, winning a war could prevent the risk of irregular removal by increasing the leader's legitimacy, prestige, and resources (25). Finally, defeat could carry "a significant risk of forcible removal from office" (28). Therefore, when leaders already face a relatively high risk of forcible removal from office, their punishment is effectively truncated, meaning they have much to gain from gambling on the possibility of victory or a draw.

According to this logic, an alternative explanation for the findings I presented earlier—that juntas, bosses, and strongmen initiate conflict at much higher rates than democracies or machines—might be that leaders of juntas, boss, and strongman regimes are actually so fearful of the possibility of forcible removal from office that they "gamble for survival." In other words, they initiate conflicts that they have a high probability of losing because they will be punished severely either way. While a thorough examination of the Chiozza and Goemans hypothesis is beyond the scope of this book, it is interesting to note that leaders of the most belligerent regimes—boss and strongman regimes—

[74]

experienced severe punishment after defeat at very low rates. For example, among strongmen, the most belligerent leaders, only Idi Amin faced severe punishment after a defeat (a peaceful exile in Saudi Arabia after the Ugandan/Tanzanian war). Given that punishment in the aftermath of defeat likely represents an upper bound on the leader's prewar probability of punishment, this suggests that fear of severe punishment is not the primary factor driving the belligerence of this most conflict-prone of regime types.

Conclusion

This chapter revisited the finding that democratic polities, in which ordinary citizens have civil and political liberties and freely elect their leaders, enjoy unique advantages in terms of avoiding defeat in war. Civilian elite-constrained autocrats—machines—are as likely to avoid defeat as democratic leaders, regardless of the overall level of democracy in their country. Moreover, these same autocrats are punished at high rates for losing wars. They therefore have every incentive to be selective and cautious in their foreign policy decisions.

Elite-constrained regimes led by military officers—juntas—lose wars at slightly higher rates than machines. They can still anticipate relatively high rates of punishment for defeat, though, because their audiences will judge them for defeat and have the means to mete out punishment. As I argued in chapter 1 and show in more depth in chapter 5, leaders and audiences in juntas are biased in favor of using military force over other means because they fear the consequences of inaction and view few alternatives as viable. This results in a moderate level of defeat and a moderate rate of punishment.

In contrast, domestically unfettered leaders—bosses and strongmen—are, as the conventional wisdom anticipates, less cautious about initiating military conflicts. These leaders have fewer incentives to scrutinize their decisions to go to war, and they may suffer from overoptimism. Their rates of defeat in wars and MIDs are therefore substantially higher than those of other states. At the same time, they typically survive even defeat in war.

Thus, the patterns of defeat and postwar ouster uncovered here are consistent with the theoretical arguments laid out in chapter 1. But while evidence of these associations helps us rule in or rule out certain explanations, it does not prove that the relationships are due to the hypothesized mechanisms. The next three chapters turn to historical case studies to shed further light on the processes linking regime type to patterns of war and peace.

TABLE 3.5 War participants, war outcomes, and leader fates

COW War #	War name	Country	Leader	War began	Regime type	Role	War outcome	Out in 2?
118	Manchurian	USSR	Stalin	1929	Machine	Initiator	Win	0
118	Manchurian	China	Chiang Kai-shek	1929	Other	Target	Lose	0
121	Second Sino-Japanese	China	Chiang Kai-shek	1931	Strongman	Target	Lose	0
121	Second Sino-Japanese	Japan	Inukai	1931	Machine	Initiator	Win	1
124	Chaco	Paraguay	Guggiari	1932	Machine	Initiator	Win	1
124	Chaco	Bolivia	Salamanca	1932	Other	Target	Lose	1
125	Saudi-Yemeni	Yemen A. R.	Yahya	1934	Other	Target	Lose	0
125	Saudi-Yemeni	Saudi Arabia	Aziz	1934	Other	Initiator	Win	0
127	Conquest of Ethiopia	Italy	Mussolini	1935	Boss	Initiator	Win	0
127	Conquest of Ethiopia	Ethiopia	Selassie	1935	Boss	Target	Lose	1
130	Third Sino-Japanese	China	Chiang Kai-shek	1937	Strongman	Target	Lose	1
130	Third Sino-Japanese	Japan	Konoe	1937	Junta	Initiator	Win	1
133	Changkufeng	Japan	Konoe	1938	Junta	Initiator	Draw	1
133	Changkufeng	USSR	Stalin	1938	Boss	Target	Win	0
136	Nomonhan	USSR	Stalin	1939	Boss	Target	Win	0
136	Nomonhan	Mongolia	Choibalsan	1939	Other	Target	Win	0
136	Nomonhan	Japan	Hiranuma	1939	Junta	Initiator	Draw	1
139	World War II	Germany	Hitler	1939	Boss	Initiator	Lose	.
139	World War II	France	Daladier	1939	Democracy	Target	Lose	1
139	World War II	Poland	Śmigły-Rydz	1939	Other	Target	Lose	1
139	World War II	UK	Chamberlain	1939	Democracy	Target	Win	1
139	World War II	Italy	Mussolini	1940	Boss	Joiner	Lose	1

139	World War II	Netherlands	De Geer	1940	Democracy	Target	Lose	1
139	World War II	Greece	Metaxas	1940	Strongman	Target	Lose	.
139	World War II	Belgium	Pierlot	1940	Democracy	Target	Lose	1
139	World War II	USA	Roosevelt, F.	1941	Democracy	Target	Win	.
139	World War II	Yugoslavia	Peter II	1941	Other	Target	Lose	1
139	World War II	USSR	Stalin	1941	Boss	Target	Win	0
139	World War II	Japan	Tojo	1941	Junta	Joiner	Lose	1
142	Russo-Finnish	USSR	Stalin	1939	Boss	Initiator	Win	0
142	Russo-Finnish	Finland	Kallio	1939	Machine	Target	Lose	.
147	First Kashmir	India	Nehru	1947	Other	Initiator	Lose	0
147	First Kashmir	Pakistan	Jinnah	1947	Other	Target	Win	.
148	Arab-Israeli	Egypt	Farouk	1948	Boss	Initiator	Lose	0
148	Arab-Israeli	Israel	Ben-Gurion	1948	Other	Target	Win	0
148	Arab-Israeli	Iraq	Abdul-Ilah	1948	Boss	Initiator	Lose	0
148	Arab-Israeli	Syria	Kuwatli	1948	Machine	Initiator	Lose	1
148	Arab-Israeli	Jordan	Abdullah 1	1948	Other	Initiator	Lose	0
151	Korean	South Korea	Rhee	1950	Other	Target	Draw	0
151	Korean	North Korea	Kim Il-sung	1950	Other	Initiator	Draw	0
151	Korean	China	Mao Zedong	1950	Other	Joiner	Draw	0
151	Korean	USA	Truman	1950	Democracy	Joiner	Draw	1
153	Off-Shore Islands	China	Mao Zedong	1954	Boss	Initiator	Win	0
153	Off-Shore Islands	Taiwan	Chiang Kai-shek	1954	Strongman	Target	Lose	0
155	Sinai War	UK	Eden	1956	Democracy	Initiator	Draw	.
155	Sinai War	France	Mollet	1956	Democracy	Initiator	Draw	1
155	Sinai War	Egypt	Nasser	1956	Strongman	Target	Lose	0

(Continued)

TABLE 3.5 (*Continued*)

COW War #	War name	Country	Leader	War began	Regime type	Role	War outcome	Out in 2?
155	Sinai War	Israel	Ben-Gurion	1956	Democracy	Initiator	Win	0
156	Soviet Invasion of Hungary	USSR	Khrushchev	1956	Machine	Initiator	Win	0
156	Soviet Invasion of Hungary	Hungary	Gerő	1956	Machine	Target	Lose	1
159	Taiwan Straits	Taiwan (ROC)	Chiang Kai-shek	1958	Strongman	Target	Win	0
159	Taiwan Straits	China (PRC)	Mao Zedong	1958	Boss	Initiator	Draw	0
160	Assam	China (PRC)	Mao Zedong	1962	Boss	Initiator	Win	0
160	Assam	India	Nehru	1962	Democracy	Target	Lose	.
163	Vietnam War, Phase 2	USA	Johnson	1965	Democracy	Target	Lose	1
163	Vietnam War, Phase 2	Vietnam	Ho Chi Minh	1965	Machine	Initiator	Win	.
163	Vietnam War, Phase 2	South Vietnam	Khahn	1965	Other	Target	Lose	1
166	Second Kashmir	India	Shastri	1965	Democracy	Initiator	Draw	.
166	Second Kashmir	Pakistan	Ayub Khan	1965	Strongman	Target	Draw	0
169	Six-Day War	Jordan	Hussein Ibn Talal El-Hashim	1967	Boss	Target	Lose	0
169	Six-Day War	Syria	Jadid	1967	Strongman	Target	Lose	0
169	Six-Day War	Egypt	Nasser	1967	Strongman	Target	Lose	0
169	Six-Day War	Israel	Eshkol	1967	Democracy	Initiator	Win	.
170	Second Laotian, Phase 2	Laos	Souvanna Phouma	1968	Other	Target	Lose	0
170	Second Laotian, Phase 2	USA	Johnson	1968	Democracy	Target	Lose	1
170	Second Laotian, Phase 2	Vietnam	Ho Chi Minh	1968	Machine	Initiator	Win	.
172	War of Attrition	Israel	Allon	1969	Democracy	Target	Win	1
172	War of Attrition	Egypt	Nasser	1969	Strongman	Initiator	Draw	.
175	Football War	Honduras	López Arellano	1969	Junta	Target	Lose	1

[78]

175	Football War	El Salvador	Sánchez Hernández	1969	Junta	Initiator	Win	0
176	Communist Coalition	USA	Nixon	1970	Democracy	Target	Lose	0
176	Communist Coalition	Vietnam	Le Duan	1970	Machine	Initiator	Win	0
176	Communist Coalition	South Vietnam	Van Thieu	1970	Other	Target	Lose	0
176	Communist Coalition	Cambodia	Lon Nol	1970	Boss	Target	Lose	0
178	Bangladesh	India	Gandhi, I.	1971	Democracy	Initiator	Win	0
178	Bangladesh	Pakistan	Yahya Khan	1971	Other	Target	Lose	1
181	Yom Kippur War	Syria	Al-Assad H.	1973	Strongman	Initiator	Lose	0
181	Yom Kippur War	Egypt	Sadat	1973	Strongman	Initiator	Lose	0
181	Yom Kippur War	Israel	Meir	1973	Democracy	Target	Win	1
184	Turco-Cypriot	Cyprus	Sampson	1974	Democracy	Target	Lose	1
184	Turco-Cypriot	Turkey	Ecevit	1974	Other	Initiator	Win	1
186	War over Angola	Dem. Rep. Congo	Mobutu	1975	Boss	Initiator	Draw	0
186	War over Angola	South Africa	Vorster	1975	Machine	Initiator	Draw	0
186	War over Angola	Cuba	Castro	1975	Boss	Target	Win	0
187	Ogaden	Ethiopia	Mengistu Mariam	1977	Junta	Target	Win	0
187	Ogaden	Cuba	Castro	1977	Boss	Target	Win	0
187	Ogaden	Somalia	Siad Barre	1977	Strongman	Initiator	Draw	0
189	Vietnamese-Cambodian	Vietnam	Le Duan	1977	Machine	Target	Win	0
189	Vietnamese-Cambodian	Cambodia	Pol Pot	1977	Boss	Initiator	Lose	1
190	Ugandian-Tanzanian	Uganda	Amin	1978	Strongman	Initiator	Lose	1
190	Ugandian-Tanzanian	Tanzania	Nyerere	1978	Machine	Target	Win	0
190	Ugandian-Tanzanian	Libya	Gaddafi	1979	Boss	Joiner	Lose	0
193	Sino-Vietnamese Punitive	Vietnam	Le Duan	1979	Machine	Target	Win	0

(Continued)

Table 3.5 (Continued)

COW War #	War name	Country	Leader	War began	Regime type	Role	War outcome	Out in 2?
193	Sino-Vietnamese Punitive	China	Deng Xiaoping	1979	Machine	Initiator	Draw	0
199	Iran-Iraq	Iraq	Saddam Hussein	1980	Other	Initiator	Draw	0
199	Iran-Iraq	Iran	Ayatollah Khomeini	1980	Other	Target	Draw	.
202	Falkland Islands	Argentina	Galtieri	1982	Junta	Initiator	Lose	1
202	Falkland Islands	UK	Thatcher	1982	Democracy	Target	Win	0
205	War over Lebanon	Syria	Al-Assad H.	1982	Strongman	Target	Lose	0
205	War over Lebanon	Israel	Begin	1982	Democracy	Initiator	Win	1
207	War over Aouzou Strip	Libya	Gaddafi	1986	Boss	Target	Lose	0
207	War over Aouzou Strip	Chad	Habré	1986	Other	Initiator	Win	0
208	Sino-Vietnamese Border	China	Deng Xiaoping	1987	Machine	Initiator	Draw	0
208	Sino-Vietnamese Border	Vietnam	Nguyen Van Linh	1987	Machine	Target	Win	0
211	Gulf War	Kuwait	Jaber Al-Sabah	1990	Machine	Target	Lose	1
211	Gulf War	Iraq	Saddam Hussein	1990	Boss	Initiator	Lose	0
211	Gulf War	USA	George H. W. Bush	1991	Democracy	Joiner	Win	1
216	Azeri-Armenian	Azerbaijan	Abulfaz Elchibey	1993	Other	Target	Lose	1
216	Azeri-Armenian	Armenia	Ter-Petrosyan	1993	Democracy	Initiator	Win	0
219	Badme Border	Eritrea	Isaias Afewerki	1998	Boss	Initiator	Lose	0
219	Badme Border	Ethiopia	Meles Zenawi	1998	Machine	Target	Win	0
221	War for Kosovo	USA	Clinton	1999	Democracy	Initiator	Win	1
221	War for Kosovo	Yugoslavia	Milošević	1999	Boss	Target	Lose	1
221	War for Kosovo	UK	Blair	1999	Democracy	Initiator	Win	0

223	Kargil War	India	Vajpayee	1999	Democracy	Target	Win	0
223	Kargil War	Pakistan	Sharif	1999	Democracy	Initiator	Draw	1
225	Inv. of Afghanistan	USA	George W. Bush	2001	Democracy	Initiator	Win	0
225	Inv. of Afghanistan	Afghanistan	Mullah Omar	2001	Machine	Target	Lose	1
227	Invasion of Iraq	USA	George W. Bush	2003	Democracy	Initiator	Win	1
227	Invasion of Iraq	Iraq	Saddam Hussein	2003	Boss	Target	Lose	1

[4]

Personalist Dictators: Shooting from the Hip

The previous chapters showed that dictatorships vary in the rates at which they initiate conflict, the likelihood that they will be defeated in the conflicts in which they do become involved, and the probability that the leader will be ousted in the wake of defeat. On each of these dimensions, personalist boss and strongman regimes are the most extreme: They initiate the most international conflict, they are the least likely to win, and yet their leaders typically survive even defeat in fully-fledged war.

This book attributes those patterns to a combination of a lack of institutional incentives and the preferences of the leaders who preside over those regimes. First, the personal characteristics of the kinds of individuals who become personalist leaders cause them to have more ambitious foreign policy goals, and hence more revisionist preferences, than leaders of other kinds of regimes. Second, personalist leaders perceive lower costs of fighting than leaders of democracies or machines because they have few normative aversions to force, view force as effective, and do not internalize the costs of fighting to the same extent as typical regime insiders or more accountable leaders. Third, rulers of personalist regimes perceive lower costs of defeat than other leaders, again because their regimes lack institutions facilitating *ex post* punishment. Finally, because fearful subordinates are unwilling to correct the leader's personal biases, personalist leaders often overestimate the likelihood of victory.

While previous chapters showed evidence consistent with these propositions, the cross-national analyses provided little evidence of the more detailed causal factors at play. To further assess the plausibility of these characterizations of personalist leaders and whether they can provide a causal explanation for the cross-national patterns uncovered earlier, this chapter investigates the foreign policy decisions of two infamous bosses:

Saddam Hussein of Iraq and Joseph Stalin of the Soviet Union. I focus on civilian personalist bosses rather than strongmen because this allows us to isolate the effect of personalism from the effect of military rule.

The first part of this chapter deals with Saddam Hussein. Saddam's regime is a clear-cut case of personalist dictatorship, and a relative wealth of evidence is available about the inner workings of the regime due to documents and interviews retrieved after the U.S.-led invasion of Iraq. I first establish that Saddam's regime was indeed a "boss" regime: No institutions or domestic actors existed to constrain him or credibly threaten punishment in the aftermath of defeat, and Saddam and most of his inner circle did not have formal military training. Second, I show that Saddam had personal characteristics and preferences that differed from those usually found in leaders of democracies or machines. This is important because the lack of constraints in his regime meant that his *own* preferences, ambitions, and perceptions directed policy. I therefore discuss Saddam's rise to power and how his ruthlessness, ambition, and penchant for violence made him quite different from typical leaders of democracies or machines. Third, I show how this combination of personal preferences and a lack of constraints helps explain why Saddam invaded Kuwait in 1990, stood firm against U.S. threats, and yet escaped punishment when Iraq's army was crushed by coalition forces.

After analyzing the Iraqi case, I turn to another personalist boss regime: the Soviet Union under Stalin. Studying this regime allows me to compare foreign policy decision-making under Stalin to decision-making once the regime's institutions became less personalistic under Stalin's successors. Moreover, this is a "harder" test of the argument than the Iraqi case in that Stalin was widely viewed as particularly *successful* in his uses of force compared to other bosses. In addition, scholars have often explained Stalin's foreign policy decisions in "realist" terms, seeing his decisions to use force as consequences of the pressures of the international system. However, here I argue that even in this relatively hard case, there is evidence that a different leader faced with the same international circumstances would have used force more sparingly. I first briefly summarize what is known about Stalin's personal history, particularly early evidence of a predilection for political violence and signs of unusual ambition. I then comment on the structure of the regime and how the lack of constraints, combined with the leader's personal qualities, increased the regime's propensity to initiate international conflict. This provides a baseline for a comparison with Soviet policy under Stalin's immediate successors, Khrushchev and Brezhnev, in chapter 6.

To a large extent, these two case studies are consistent with what we think we know about dictatorships and war, particularly the idea that a lack of domestic political constraints fosters conflict. On the other hand, the case studies show evidence of the details of the theoretical argument advanced in this book, demonstrating that the leaders' personal characteristics and worldviews, when combined with a lack of constraints, led them down seemingly irrational paths. Importantly, these two cases also pave the way for the later analyses of juntas and machines, which, as we shall see, operate in decidedly different ways.

SADDAM HUSSEIN AND THE 1990 INVASION OF KUWAIT

The Regime

Saddam Hussein's Iraq clearly fits the characterization of a "boss" regime—a personalist regime in which no institutions exist that allow domestic actors to constrain the leader and in which the key decision-makers are civilians rather than professional military men. Saddam's dictatorship represents a clear example of personalist authoritarianism and its consequences for foreign policy.

Saddam Hussein came to power in July of 1979, having worked his way through the ranks of the Ba'ath Party, which had ruled Iraq since 1968. Analysts agree that from the year he took power until the United States toppled him in April 2003, Saddam's Iraq was one of the most autocratic countries in the world. It lacked freedom of the press, competitive elections, or any other institutionalized methods through which ordinary citizens were able to influence their country's political direction or leadership.

But as previous chapters have argued, nondemocratic regimes vary greatly in the extent to which leaders are constrained by their fellow elites. Saddam's Iraq featured some of the trappings of elite power-sharing—a cabinet, an executive body called the Revolutionary Command Council (RCC), and a 250-member national assembly nominally elected by Iraqi men. But in reality Iraq was a highly personalized regime dominated by one man, Saddam Hussein. Saddam controlled every important position in the regime, both in name and in deed. He held the offices of prime minister, commander-in-chief of the armed forces, chairman of the RCC, and secretary-general of the Ba'ath Party Regional Command.[1] Just as important, he controlled political appointments, allowing him to confer top positions on close allies and family members whose fates were closely aligned with his own.[2]

Saddam also built an extensive internal security apparatus, with overlapping internal intelligence agencies reporting directly to him about the activities of citizens, regime insiders, and the other intelligence agencies themselves.[3] These agencies gave Saddam the power to monitor potential enemies and command their immediate arrest. Ministers and high government officials knew their position was always precarious.

Using the intelligence services and the Ba'ath Party apparatus, Saddam not only monitored civilian officials but also tampered with the military extensively to insulate himself from the possibility of a military coup. He believed that holding on to power required keeping close tabs on military officers and purging anyone who displayed any hint of disloyalty.[4] Although he lacked military training, Saddam had himself appointed a general and promoted his sons to high military positions.[5] Several new studies, based on documents and interviews acquired by the U.S. military after Saddam's fall in 2003, reveal various ways in which he engineered the regime's stability against coups. Saddam carefully screened applicants to military academies; created a proliferation of parallel hierarchies and competing security forces, such as the Republican Guard and the Special Republican Guard; frequently rotated top commanders so that they could not build their own loyal power bases; based promotions on loyalty rather than merit; used the Ba'ath Party and the intelligence services to monitor officers (even going so far as to require extensive background checks of potential brides before officers married); and lavishly rewarded those who remained loyal.[6]

Saddam's emphasis on loyalty had important consequences. For one, it encouraged him to dismiss anyone who appeared too ambitious or too "clever," because intelligence and political acumen could pose a threat.[7] Moreover, since criticism is a potential indicator of disloyalty, Iraqi political elites and military officers had incentives to tell the commander-in-chief what he wanted to hear rather than question Saddam's judgment, no matter how poor.[8] It was better to stand back and hope that Saddam's plans turned out all right than to step forward and incur his wrath. Military officers who in other regimes would have given candid professional advice instead "understood that their role was to ensure Saddam's dictates were followed to the letter, often no matter how infeasible or irrelevant to the military problem."[9] Perhaps for these reasons, Ali Hassan al-Majid—Saddam's cousin, defense minister, and chief of intelligence—told U.S. interrogators in 2003 that he could not recall any instances of anyone bringing bad news to Saddam.[10]

In sum, Saddam represented the quintessential boss, "unconstrained by any group or institution."[11] Those in any realistic position to work together to remove Saddam from power—government and military officials—had virtually no incentives to do so because their own political survival depended on Saddam's continued reign. Moreover, the extensive internal security apparatus meant that any hint of disloyalty would have been detected quickly, with dire consequences for the unlucky culprit. The personal preferences, whims, and instincts of the man in charge

[85]

were therefore unusually important to understanding the regime's foreign policy decisions.

Saddam the Leader

On their own, a lack of constraints and a low likelihood of being punished for risky foreign policy decisions could explain some of the belligerence and incautious behavior of personalist bosses. However, this book also suggests that the kinds of individuals who come to power in personalist regimes—or, as is often the case, deliberately create this type of political regime—share certain traits and worldviews that make them unusually disposed to using violence abroad. These leaders tend to be ambitious to an extent unusual even among other political leaders and also tend to believe that violence is an effective tool for solving conflicts of interest. In other words, personalist bosses not only pay fewer costs for using violence internationally but are also unusually motivated to resort to force.

Saddam's longstanding personal characteristics certainly fit this description. Saddam was not just an ordinary person who took on risk due to the absence of political constraints. Instead, from very early in his life, he evinced a high degree of ambition as well as an attraction to violence. These predilections were further nurtured by a political career in which ambition and violence paid off.

Born in 1937, Saddam grew up poor in a village outside the northern city of Tikrit. The death of his father left him in the care of an uncle, Khairallah Tulfah, a local politician. As a thug carrying out dirty work for Khairallah, Saddam learned the value of political violence early, and he is even said to have assassinated one of his uncle's rivals.[12] Khairallah sensed Saddam's promise and convinced his friend—and Saddam's cousin—Ahmed Hassan al-Bakr to take him under his wing.[13]

These were the early days of the Ba'ath Party's role in Iraqi politics. Iraq was ruled by General Abdul Karim Qassem, who seized power in 1958 after his Free Officers assassinated King Faisal II. The Ba'athists initially backed Qassem but soon switched sides. Saddam participated in a Ba'athist attempt to assassinate Qassem in 1959, but when the coup failed he was forced to flee to Damascus, followed by several years in Cairo.[14]

Saddam spent his years abroad supported by the Arab nationalist governments that reigned in Syria and Egypt. He grew close to Michel Aflaq, a key figure in the growing Arab Ba'ath Party.[15] In 1963, a coup supported by al-Bakr finally deposed (and executed) General Qassem, installing the Ba'athist sympathizer Abdul Salam Arif as president and al-Bakr as prime minister. Still in his mid-twenties, Saddam returned to Iraq and soon acquired a seat on the influential Ba'ath Party intelligence committee.

The Ba'ath Party's influence in Arif's government, however, was short-lived. Arif grew frustrated with Ba'athist infighting and fired al-Bakr and many other Ba'athists, using the army to crush the Ba'ath militia. Al-Bakr nonetheless remained influential, and Saddam used al-Bakr's support and his own clan ties to climb the ranks, running a secret Ba'ath security apparatus by 1964. At this point he was detained for suspected involvement in a coup attempt and spent several years in jail. In the meantime, President Arif was succeeded by his brother, Abdul Rahman Arif, in 1966.[16]

Soon after leaving prison, Saddam returned to his coup-plotting, helping to bring about the 1968 coup that carried the Ba'ath Party to power under Saddam's mentor al-Bakr. Al-Bakr's patronage allowed Saddam to become deputy chairman of the Revolutionary Command Council (RCC), a Ba'ath Party apparatus that was to become the primary decision-making group in Iraq. This position provided a springboard for Saddam's stealthy consolidation of personal power over the next decade. The RCC, for instance, had final authority over the army, the budget, treaties, and declarations of war, and as its head Saddam could choose and discharge the most important decision-makers in the country. Over the course of the following years, Saddam slowly stacked the regime's governing bodies (particularly the intelligence agencies) with cronies and family members, started to build a cult of personality, and purged the armed forces of individuals who could threaten the civilian Ba'ath government.[17]

While Saddam had been using political violence since his teenage years, its most dramatic display to date took place in 1979, when, at the age of 32, Saddam forced the aging al-Bakr to resign and formally seized power.[18] One of his first moves was to call a meeting of high-ranking Ba'ath Party members. At the gathering, he announced the names of sixty-six alleged conspirators sitting in the crowd. Each one was hauled off by security personnel and taken into custody. Soon after, Saddam ordered officials who had survived the purges to participate in the executions by firing squad.[19]

Thus, by the time Saddam assumed power in 1979, he had clearly demonstrated a belief in the effectiveness of violence to settle domestic political matters. The violence always had a purpose—for example, signaling to his subordinates that opposition would cost dearly and opening up positions in the party and government for Saddam to fill with friends and relatives.[20] Nevertheless, it is difficult to make the case that his chosen tactics were the *only* ones suitable to the task of achieving political influence or that a leader with less of a stomach for violence would have chosen the same tactics. Numerous scholars have concluded from Saddam's early history as his uncle's henchman, his tutelage under al-Bakr, and his own successful rise to power that he believed that "in the violent Iraqi political world there was no substitute for physical force; that physical force was indispensable both for coming to power and staying there, as well as for subordinating any and all political factions to one's will."[21] Joseph Sassoon, in a detailed evaluation of the Iraqi regime based on documents and tapes recovered after the 2003 invasion, links Saddam's penchant for violence internally to his later choice of violence externally; Saddam, he writes, was "consistent in his belief in coercive power" both domestically and internationally (2012, 6). Former regime insiders reached similar conclusions. The Iraqi head of military intelligence Wafiq al-Samara'i, who defected in 1994, told PBS, "It's very important for you to know something about Saddam's character. We know him because he lived with us. He was a very evil person as early as his childhood. He lived in our district. . . . He always resorted to terrorist methods and tactics." For Saddam, violence was the strategy of first, not last, resort.

Like his willingness to use force, Saddam's *ambitions* were more extreme than those of typical nonpersonalist leaders. He took cues on political strategy from relative contemporaries like Nasser and Stalin, but more broadly, Saddam considered himself the historical heir of both Nebuchadnezzar, the Babylonian leader who ruled Egypt and conquered Jerusalem, and Saladin, who recaptured Jerusalem from the Crusaders in the twelfth century.[22] Drawing on these role models, Saddam "firmly believed that it was Iraq's destiny to be the preeminent force in Middle East politics. . . . Saddam saw himself as . . . a powerful figurehead providing leadership over the entire Arab world."[23] Iraq's successes during Saddam's rise, buoyed by new oil wealth, may have encouraged his belief that he was part of a vast historical narrative.[24] But while most leaders are ambitious, Saddam took that ambition to unusual heights, setting his sights on expanding Iraq's role in the Middle East from very early in his rule. Saddam's ambitions went well beyond reacting to Iraq's security environment to protect its interests: Expansion and glory were goals in and of themselves. This revisionism was born not of necessity but of personal ambition. Combined with Saddam's willingness to use violence and a political system in which no one could constrain him *ex ante* or punish him *ex post*, this was a potent recipe for international conflict.[25]

The Decision to Invade Kuwait

The combination of lack of constraint, a predilection for violence, and personal ambition implies that bosses will initiate conflicts where other leaders would not. Not only are they more motivated to use violence abroad, but they also face fewer consequences if the venture goes poorly.

Saddam's decision to invade Kuwait in 1990 clearly illustrates how the lack of political constraints in boss regimes increases the likelihood of initiating international conflict.[26] Freedom from domestic checks provides bosses—who, I argued above, tend to be more attracted to violent strategies and often have more expansionist motives than leaders of other kinds of regimes—with significant latitude to enact their policy preferences. Moreover, they can do so with little concern for the potential costs that ordinary citizens or even lower-placed political elites would bear. The Iraqi experience also provides a useful baseline for comparing the very different domestic politics of foreign policy in nonpersonalist juntas and machines.

What did Saddam hope to gain from invading Kuwait? The thesis here is that personalist leaders, all else being equal, are more likely to have revisionist ambitions than other kinds of leaders and are more likely to see violence as a necessary and effective way to further those ambitions. This seems to have been the case here. Saddam came to office with a host of regional ambitions, and Kuwait's resources provided a possible solution to the gap between Iraq's economic situation and those aims. The Iran-Iraq War, which lasted from 1980 to 1988 and resulted in half a million battle-related deaths, had left Iraq's economy in shambles.[27] Revenues from Iraqi oil were not enough to cover the cost of Saddam's ambitious military rearmament program and also to cover its debt repayments.[28] By 1990, Iraq owed non-Arab creditors over $50 billion in debt and another $30 to $40 billion to the Gulf States, in particular Kuwait and Saudi Arabia.[29] But Saddam, feeling that Iraq deserved forgiveness on the latter loans because it provided security to its neighbors, requested debt relief.[30] In February of 1990, Iraq was further devastated by a sharp drop in the price of oil. Saddam blamed the price drop on OPEC, believing that its members, in particular Kuwait and the United Arab Emirates, were not adhering to their agreed-upon quotas. Saddam also accused Kuwait of illegally tapping into Iraq's Rumaila oil field through the use of slant drilling near the disputed border.[31] Annexing Kuwait would not only eliminate the Kuwaiti portion of Iraq's debt, but it would also improve Iraq's oil production capabilities and give Saddam greater control over oil markets, providing a solution to his budget constraints.

Strategic factors may also have played a role, although these were again exacerbated by Saddam's regional ambitions. Iraq had only limited port access to the Gulf, hampering both commercial access and its ability to develop a navy. The two points of access—the Shatt al-Arab and the deep water port of Umm Qasr on Iraq's southern Faw Peninsula—were both vulnerable: The Shatt is threatened on one side by Iran, against whom Saddam had just fought a brutal war, and Umm Qasr is effectively surrounded by Kuwaiti territory, including mainland Kuwait and its offshore islands Warbah and Bubiyan. United against a common enemy from 1980 to 1988, Kuwait and Iraq had overlooked these issues. At the same time, however, the conflict with Iran and its deleterious effects on Iraqi shipping convinced Saddam that Iraq needed access routes to the Gulf beyond the Shatt al-Arab. In 1981, therefore, Saddam made ongoing border negotiations contingent on Kuwait leasing of the Warbah and Bubiyan islands to Iraq.[32] Negotiations were inconclusive, and Saddam continued to demand rights to the two strategic islands through 1989, citing Iraqi naval vulnerability.[33]

Many authors argue that Saddam saw expanding into Kuwait as an opportunity to increase Iraq's, meaning his own, prestige.[34] Saddam had long considered military accomplishment the primary source of respect among states. The Kuwaiti emir had been "disrespectful" and not "deferential enough," and Saddam wanted to show the world that he deserved better.[35] Iraqi journalist Saad al-Bazzaz also alleges that Saddam anticipated that the United States would respect him more if he demonstrated his strength in the region.[36] Saddam wanted Iraq to be an Arab superpower, and such a superpower had to unify the Arabs, root out Western influence, and destroy Israel.[37] Consistent with his broader views on the effectiveness of violence described above, Saddam believed that the only way to unite the Arab world was through war.[38] Demonstrating his military strength and, if necessary, standing up to the West would enhance Saddam's prestige and allow him to "go into history as a great leader."[39] More broadly, there is evidence that Saddam saw his invasion of Kuwait as part of Iraq's larger mission to lead the Arab world against the Zionists.[40]

Defenders of the regime later tried to portray the invasion of Kuwait as a defensive maneuver but, again, one rooted in Saddam's violence-oriented mindset. In 1994, Tariq Aziz cast the invasion as the product of a "deliberate conspiracy against Iraq, by Kuwait, organized, [and] devised by the United States."[41] He portrayed the invasion as a "defensive decision" aimed at creating a "balance of power" among Arab states, since George H. W. Bush and the United States were intent on dismantling Iraq by force—regardless of whether Iraq had invaded Kuwait. The ultimate goal of the United States, asserted Aziz, was control of the region's oil reserves. Therefore Iraq had "either to be destroyed . . . or attack the enemy on the outside."[42] While it is unclear whether these motives were genuine, they are plausible given Saddam's belief that violence was the way of the world.

Thus, the end of the Iran-Iraq War left Iraq with a heavy debt burden, a decline in foreign aid, increased unemployment as soldiers returned home, and a lingering dispute over port access.[43] Invading Kuwait could—if the invasion succeeded—potentially alleviate some of these economic and strategic problems. To what extent would a similarly placed leader with different perceptions and ambitions have seen the benefits of invasion in the same way? The evidence suggests that Saddam's personal ambitions as a great Arab leader and his beliefs in the necessity and effectiveness of war played an important role in the decision to invade. It is not at all clear that a less ambitious leader or an individual less focused on violent strategies would have reached the same conclusions.

For a leader with a more tenuous grip on power, the downsides of invading Kuwait would have loomed large. But Saddam was no ordinary leader. In 1990, his position at the top of the regime was undisputed, strengthened by more than a decade of measures that ensured that no rivals could pose a threat. Saddam was therefore unusually insulated from the domestic downsides of war. He also had few concerns about costs being directly imposed from abroad. He had little reason to think that his hold on power would be weakened unless a foreign army ventured all the way to Baghdad, which seemed unlikely. He had elaborate security measures already in place to protect himself against domestic threats, access to numerous underground bunkers in the event of an air assault, and a network of safe houses. Thus, Saddam was free to focus on the upsides of winning—power, glory, influence, and freedom from economic constraints—without fretting about negative consequences.

Accordingly, there is little evidence that Saddam undertook any serious assessment of the costs or consequences of invading Kuwait. There is some dispute as to when Saddam made the final decision to invade, with estimates ranging from March to mid-June 1990.[44] While the lack of records makes it difficult to know for certain, the existing evidence suggests that Saddam made the decision in isolation, or possibly after consulting only with his son-in-law.[45] No evidence suggests that Saddam asked the minister of defense, the chief of staff, or other military and civilian leaders to weigh in on an invasion or to provide a detailed assessment of the costs of fighting. According to Kevin Woods's analysis of the interviews and documents recovered after the U.S.-led invasion of Iraq in 2003, many government officials were "entirely ignorant" of war preparations until the last minute.[46] One advisor has suggested that before August 1, 1990, only six individuals knew that Iraq would soon invade Kuwait.[47] Moreover, the few individuals who were consulted had little incentive to speak out against the plan, for the aforementioned reason that criticism could be taken as a sign of disloyalty with serious consequences.[48]

There is also very little evidence that Saddam commissioned any formal prewar evaluations of the costs and feasibility of occupying Kuwait. According to the chief of staff of the Republican Guard, the Guard was not asked until approximately June to plan for a military operation, an assignment that was carried out by a small and secretive group.[49] Furthermore, nothing suggests that the group was tasked with producing an in-depth evaluation of the wisdom or viability of the operation. Other, less trustworthy, military organs were not even informed until hours before the invasion was to begin, so no planning or consultation occurred there either.[50] The little evaluation that Saddam did commission appears to have come in a series of five reports produced only weeks before the invasion by Iraq's main military intelligence organization, the General Military Intelligence Directorate (GMID).[51] Four of these five reports dealt with details about Kuwait, such as the theater of operations, the Kuwaiti government structure, and vital targets. Only one of these reports approached anything close to a strategic assessment: on July 25 (eight days before the invasion) the GMID delivered an "evaluation on probable foreign military intervention in case of conflict with Kuwait" and noted that the United States would likely intervene. This seems to be the same report that Wafiq Al-Samara'i, the former deputy director of Iraqi military intelligence, says he delivered to Saddam on the eve of the war: a seven-page handwritten document concluding that in the event of an invasion, the United States would probably respond by both air and land.[52]

In sum, Saddam's prewar evaluation of the costs of invading was stunningly meager, and the one formal report whose existence is documented concluded that there was a strong possibility that the United States would intervene. This raises two questions: Did Saddam actually believe that the United States would respond militarily, and if so, why did he proceed with the invasion? The evidence is mixed on the first question. Much has been made of U.S. Ambassador April Glaspie's noncommittal statement that the United States had "no opinion on Arab-Arab conflicts like your border disagreement with Kuwait," which is widely considered to have assuaged Saddam's anxiety about a U.S. intervention.[53] Tariq Aziz, it is argued, also told his boss that Iraq would face little immediate international opposition to its invasion, either from the Gulf States or from the United States.[54] Saddam consistently dismissed the possibility that the United States would enter the conflict, for a variety of reasons: his belief that the United States had learned its lesson in Vietnam and feared engagement on land; his confidence that other Arab states would support him; and his belief that the USSR would stand up to the United States in the UN Security Council (UNSC).[55] For the most part, the incentives of Saddam's yes men gave them little reason to disabuse him of these strongly held beliefs. On the other hand, the GMID report does indicate that Iraqi intelligence believed there was a strong chance of a Western response. Thus it is unlikely that Saddam was completely ignorant of this possibility.

This leads to the second question: Why did Saddam invade Kuwait if there was even a moderate probability that the United States would intervene? The answer appears to be that Saddam thought he could weather a U.S. intervention and perhaps even benefit from it. According to Al-Samara'i, Saddam's only concern was whether U.S. forces would venture all the way to Baghdad, which we can infer was because only a foreign capture or assassination posed a realistic threat to his tenure even in the wake of defeat.[56] At the time, there was little reason to think the United States would send forces to Baghdad, an expectation that was ultimately borne out. Instead, Saddam appears to have thought he could gain personal prestige by standing up to the West. For Saddam personally, even a moderate chance of U.S. intervention was unlikely to be terribly costly.

Digging In

By the spring of 1990, Iraqi rhetoric had publicly turned against Kuwait. Saddam's primary demands were economic, including a $2.4 billion compensation for Kuwait's supposed tapping of the Rumaila field, a $12 billion compensation for Kuwait's alleged depression of world oil prices, and forgiveness of Iraq's $10 billion war debt to Kuwait.[57] As he often did, Saddam turned to history to justify his increasingly hostile stance toward Kuwait, pointing out that Kuwait has historically been part of Iraq and that Western colonialists had intentionally deprived Iraq of its "southern province" Kuwait and the oil resources it possessed.[58] Wafiq al-Samara'i, the former chief of Iraqi military intelligence who defected in 1994, claimed that Saddam's historical rhetoric about a "Great Iraq" that included Kuwait was not mere posturing but was a product of Saddam's genuine belief in Iraq's historical destiny.[59]

The Iraqi Republican Guard was mobilized in July 1990. On August 2, one hundred thousand Iraqi troops started their invasion of Kuwait, quickly conquering the tiny country and its army of sixteen thousand.[60] The UNSC immediately passed a resolution condemning the hostility and demanding that Iraq withdraw. The United States, which already had troops in Saudi Arabia, asked the UN for authorization to use force to liberate Kuwait. The UN granted the authorization and gave Saddam a deadline.

Why didn't Saddam withdraw from Kuwait once it became apparent that Western intervention was imminent? Some evidence suggests that Saddam underestimated American resolve and capabilities, though it is difficult to say whether this was a genuine belief or whether Saddam's statements were intended to keep up morale. In January 1991, Saddam told his military commanders that the U.S.-led coalition "does not have the same level of determination as the Iranian enemy" and asserted that "the enemy we are faced with would collapse if we manage[d] to challenge and confront it in a determined way."[61] Saddam also fired at least one military commander who gave him a pessimistic assessment of Iraq's chances in September 1990.[62] As before, Saddam felt that standing up to the United States would enhance his personal prestige in the Middle East and that even if the United States did invade, he would not personally pay the costs of war.[63] He made his decision even in the face of consistent reports by Iraqi intelligence that the Western forces would pose a formidable threat to Iraq.[64]

The UN deadline passed; the Gulf War began on January 17, 1991. It took less than six weeks for the coalition forces to debilitate the Iraqi military severely. Losses in men and equipment were extreme, with around forty thousand battle-related deaths and many more soldiers and civilians wounded.[65] On March 2, the UNSC passed Resolution 686, outlining the conditions Iraq had to meet in order for a ceasefire to take place. The terms were accepted by Iraq, and a week later the coalition forces withdrew.

Survival after Defeat

To the astonishment of the international community, Saddam survived Iraq's devastating loss in the Gulf War with his power relatively unshaken. How did he do so? One possibility is that Saddam's control over the press would have allowed him to conceal the extent of Iraq's defeat. Indeed, immediately after the coalition forces withdrew, Saddam and his regime attempted to frame the war as a strategic victory for Iraq; Iraq had stood up to thirty-one nations, including the United States, in what Saddam had called "the mother of all battles."[66] The regime also claimed that the coalition forces proposed a ceasefire mainly out of fear of Iraqi military strength.[67]

However, many of the Iraqi people were not fooled. Unrest began in February 1991, when Iraqi soldiers returning from Kuwait defaced portraits of Saddam Hussein. Widespread vandalism and targeting of government personnel ensued, and in March 1991 uprisings spread through Shi'ite areas in southern Iraq and Kurdish areas in the north.[68] An influential Iranian-backed political party in Iraq (which had long been outlawed but enjoyed support among the Shi'a) apparently encouraged the rebellion.[69]

The uprisings, however, were doomed. In about one month, the regime's loyalist elements—headed by the Republican Guard—had restored order in the rebellious regions. Over one hundred thousand Shi'a and Kurdish civilians reportedly lost their lives in the violence. Iraqi forces under the command of Hussein Kamel al-Majid even resorted to chemical attacks against the Shi'ite protesters in the south.[70]

The regime's ability to quash the rebellion can be attributed to several factors. One is that even though many Shi'ites expected that Iran, with a majority Shi'ite population, would support a rebellion, in the end Iran showed little interest in another protracted conflict with its neighbor.[71] Support from other foreign quarters was also absent. President Bush encouraged the Iraqi people to overthrow their dictator, but military or economic support from the United States and other Western powers did not materialize, other than the imposition of a no-fly zone.

Second, and perhaps more important, the uprisings failed because the Iraqi political and military elite remained loyal to Saddam. Although some demoralized soldiers did turn against the regime—for example, the Iraqi tank commander who fired a shell at a large mural of Saddam in Basra, thus sparking the uprising—the vast majority of military leaders stuck by their boss.[72] The structure of punishment and reward that Saddam had so carefully crafted was instrumental in ensuring that officers in the various military organizations remained loyal. This was partly because, unlike in nonpersonalist machines and juntas, so much of the leadership was composed of relatives and other cronies who would have sunk with Saddam had he lost power. It was also partly because of Saddam's ability to monitor his subordinates. Knowing that they lacked the backing of the military leadership, many ordinary soldiers believed that the rebellion would fail and that they would face serious punishment for joining the rebels.[73] Without support from within the military and political elite, Saddam's forces, particularly the Republican Guard, successfully contained the rebellions.

There is also little evidence that regime elites strongly considered ousting Saddam. Cockburn and Cockburn (2002) report that an Iraqi source told them that senior generals were considering a coup before and after the war.[74] However, the generals never carried out their plans. They were not only afraid of detection but also concerned that Saddam's ouster would fuel a Shi'ite uprising against the ruling Sunni minority of which they were a part. To the dismay of the Americans who wished to see Saddam ousted, the generals found it "more expedient . . . to rally around Saddam."[75] After the war, in the summer of 1992, evidence emerged of a plot by two Republican Guard brigades, but it was detected and its supposed planners were executed or arrested. A similar supposed plot was foiled the following year.[76] Saddam, not only because of the fear that his brutal regime instilled in the masses but also through the support and fear he had engendered within the ruling elite, was able to survive arguably the worst military mistake of his leadership.

In sum, the Iraqi case illustrates important implications of the argument about how personalism fosters international conflict. First, Saddam's ambitions greatly exceeded those of the kinds of leaders who are typically selected to rule nonpersonalist regimes. Saddam believed it was his destiny to lead Iraq to the apex of Middle Eastern regional politics, and invading Kuwait was to be a step toward realizing that goal. Second, Saddam consistently believed that violence was the key to his political ambitions, whether domestic or international. Force, rather than diplomacy, was usually his tool of choice. Third, absent domestic actors with the will and ability to restrain or punish him, Saddam was free to enact his plans with little fear of the repercussions. The result was a poorly planned war, an embarrassing defeat, and yet more than another decade of power for Saddam.

Joseph Stalin: A Powerful but Loose Cannon

While few leaders illustrate the consequences of personalism as vividly as Saddam Hussein, the case of Joseph Stalin of the Soviet Union shows how personalism affects decisions to use force in a very different context. The rest of the chapter demonstrates that Stalin made decisions in the manner typical of boss regimes, without fear of direct domestic repercussions. It also shows how the nature of his regime increased the USSR's propensity to initiate international conflict, both by empowering a particularly ambitious leader and by insulating him from the costs of war.

Stalin the Leader

A first similarity between Iraq under Saddam and the Soviet Union under Stalin is that both countries were led by highly ambitious individuals who demonstrated a predilection for political violence at an early stage in their careers. As with Saddam, Stalin's biographers insist that he displayed a penchant for violence as early as boyhood. One reports that Stalin threw a dagger at his father at a young age.[77] Another argues that Stalin's vindictiveness was "extraordinary" and that even in his youth, he had "an unusual attraction to violence in dealing with enemies."[78]

This faith in the effectiveness of violence was reinforced in Stalin's well-documented early political career as a Bolshevik thug. As early as 1918, he was considered one of Lenin's "most ruthless troubleshooters," taking extreme measures to eliminate suspected enemies of the Bolshevik revolution during the Red Terror, even supposedly burning entire villages.[79] It was during this period—well before his rise to power as the leader of the USSR—that Stalin "grasped the convenience of death as the simplest and most effective political tool," supposedly once declaring that "death solves all problems. No man, no problem."[80] Violence was not simply a tool of last resort; according to his biographers, Stalin had a "vast desire to dominate, punish, and butcher."[81] This inherent attraction to violent strategies was a theme in Stalin's policies; one of his cruelest measures was to instigate the death penalty for children as young as 12 in order to fight his political enemies.[82]

Stalin's proclivity for violence was coupled with the other typical characteristic of personalist leaders—extreme ambition. As with Saddam, historians concur that Stalin was a man with unusual aspirations. According to Robert Tucker, the need for power and adulation was deep-seated and not merely a product of the desire to survive politically: "Abundant evidence indicates that Stalin needed a [personality] cult as a prop for his psyche as well as for his power. He craved the hero worship that Lenin found repugnant"; Stalin's supreme goal was "fame and glory."[83] Others have spoken of Stalin's desire to "enforce his will as far as possible."[84] This personal ambition, we shall see, clearly colored Stalin's foreign policy decisions.

The Structure of the Regime

While few leaders reach the extremes of personalized power to the extent of Saddam Hussein, the Soviet Union under Stalin was also characterized by a form of one-man rule. By the middle of the 1930s, Stalin had effectively consolidated his power as a personalist ruler. He perfected many of the classic measures of aspiring dictators, centralizing control over political appointments, subverting the preexisting military hierarchy, and cleverly leaching Party institutions of any real power. In 1934, following Stalin's "suggestion," the 17th Congress abolished the Control Commission, whose duty it had been to supervise the Central Committee and the Politburo. The Congress instead elected a new Politburo consisting of cronies of Stalin.[85]

As in Iraq, the absence of institutions to check the leader soon meant that personal loyalty, rather than competence, seniority, or institutionalized practices, determined the career potential of important regime officials; as one observer put it, "Loyalty to Stalin as a person superseded all other values and loyalties, and the system of rewards and punishments [was] based upon this value system."[86] For example, Marshal Kliment Voroshilov was one of Stalin's most trusted military advisers, yet foreign observers noted his lack of military knowledge, and his own peers seemed to think him incompetent.[87] In contrast, no amount of skill could compensate for Stalin's personal distrust. Mikhail Tukhachevsky was widely acknowledged as one of the Soviet Union's premier military minds and yet Stalin's fear that he could be a potential rival sealed his fate in the Great Purge in 1937.[88]

More generally, to ensure that only the loyal held positions of power and that those in power remained loyal, Stalin relied on terror rather than on the family connections that some personalist dictators employ. The most vivid display of Stalin's eagerness to rid himself of potential rivals was a series of purges in the 1930s. High-ranking army officers, a natural subject of suspicion because they command the loyalty of troops, were targeted with particular ruthlessness; by November 1938, a huge majority of top military officers—marshals, commanders, corps commanders, and commissars—had been shot.[89] Even the NKVD, the secret police organ, was not immune, with tens of thousands of its members killed.[90]

At the apex of his power, Stalin's trusted inner circle was made up of sycophants: "the unambitious paper-pusher Molotov, the slavish but merciless Kaganovich, the unintelligent Voroshilov, the spineless bureaucrat Malenkov, the facelessly agreeable Zhdanov, the unbearable toady Beria, [and] the bumpkin Khrushchev."[91] Stalin implicated them in his policies and ensured that "his enemies were theirs too, and they knew that their fate would be sealed if he tumbled from power."[92]

But even among Stalin's supposedly trusted associates, the all-consuming need to demonstrate loyalty led to a reticence to weigh in on policy advice.[93] Once Stalin had made a decision, very rarely would someone summon the courage to voice his disagreement because disagreeing too much could be "deadly."[94] Subordinates were so deferential to their leader that if Stalin mispronounced a word in a speech, each subsequent speaker would repeat the mistake. Even Stalin's trusted crony Molotov reported that "if I'd said it right . . . Stalin would have felt I was correcting him."[95] Zhdanov and Molotov "each happily changed his opinion if it turned out to differ from Stalin's."[96] Betty Glad attributes Beria's rise and survival in Soviet politics to his willingness to feed "Stalin's intense need for admiration."[97] Kaganovich, Malenkov, and Voroshilov have been described in similar terms, with Voroshilov singled out as particularly mindless.[98] Thus even the "inner circle," instead of speaking their honest opinion, "tried their best to guess Stalin's opinion in advance and to say yes in good time. There were never disagreements of principle with Stalin."[99]

Many anecdotes illustrate the pressure officials faced to agree. A Soviet scientist for example lamented how no one dared to point out flaws in a "dumb" proposal for a tank design once the pitch had been endorsed "from above."[100] Or consider General Konstantin Rokossovsky, who was in charge of the May 1944 Belorussian offensive and preferred a two-pronged approach while Stalin favored a single-pronged approach. The two argued inside Stalin's office, and when General Rokossovsky refused to budge, Stalin suggested he go outside and "think it over." This happened several times, but each time General Rokossovsky maintained his position. During one of these breaks, Molotov and Malenkov approached him. Malenkov said, "Don't forget where you are and with whom you're talking, General." And after a pause he added, "You are disagreeing with Comrade Stalin." Molotov then exclaimed, "You'll have to agree, Rokossovsk[y]. Agree—that's all there is to it!"[101] Rokossovsky's willingness to contradict Stalin was rare. In general, commanders who argued with Stalin too much faced the risk of the "almost inevitable consequences of incarceration and worse."[102] The fear was pervasive, infecting lower-level officials as well. As General Kirill Meretskov reflected on the lack of Soviet preparation for the Winter War, "Our people are afraid to say anything directly, they are afraid to spoil relations or get in an uncomfortable position and are fearful to speak the truth."[103]

Stalin also eschewed an orderly chain of command, both civilian and military, because such a thing might place too much power in the hands of high-ranking officials. For example, Vianno Tanner, Finland's finance minister and then later its foreign minister, says that in the prelude to the Winter War, negotiations between the Soviet Union and Finland were kept from the official Soviet envoy and that the "true" negotiations had been delegated to someone of much lesser rank.[104] A similar pattern occurred in the military sphere. Stalin would frequently "short-circuit the formal process at various points and often issued directives and commands to military units and commanders by phone or in face-to-face oral instructions and orders."[105] In the beginning of the Winter War, Stalin did not appoint an operational commander; once he had, Stalin "continued to bypass levels of command to issue orders directly to subordinate leaders."[106] Similarly, in the Lake Khasan incident against Japan in 1938, Stalin called General Vasily Blyukher directly when the general did not bomb two hills in the early stages of the confrontation; later, Stalin purged him.[107] This lack of institutionalized chain of command kept commanders and high-ranking officials off-balance and made it difficult for anyone to build a power base, because subordinates never knew where the authority really lay.

By the late 1930s, Stalin was the "ultimate center of all power," and the policymaking process "was increasingly reduced to preparing proposals for Stalin, to asking permission from Stalin, to appealing for help to Stalin, and, above all, to implementing the orders of Stalin."[108] Stalin in turn made decisions without seeking input or consent; Aspaturian describes Soviet decision-making at this time as "highly idiosyncratic and intensely personal."[109] Lazar Kaganovich, a high-ranking official and crony of Stalin's, said that by 1939 he rarely assembled the Politburo and instead made decisions informally and in secrecy.[110] Nikita Khrushchev writes in his memoirs about his ignorance of the conflict at Khalkhin Gol in 1939 against the Japanese, claiming that he did not know "what diplomatic steps were taken . . . because the matter was not reported to the Politburo. Stalin and Molotov took care of it." He adds that Stalin "did everything necessary so as not to have to consult with anyone else if that didn't enter into his plans. He didn't report to anyone."[111] Even plans for the Molotov-Ribbentrop Pact were withheld from Khrushchev; it seems that only Molotov, Voroshilov, Beria, Zhadanov, and probably Mikoyan knew of this decision in advance.[112] The lack of any credible opponents inside the regime meant that Stalin could weather even foreign policy disasters, such as his failure to anticipate that Hitler would turn on him. This was "a mistake which could not be hidden from his courtiers who had repeatedly heard him insist there would be no invasion in 1941. But that was only the first part of this disaster: the military collapse had revealed the damage that Stalin had done and his ineptitude as commander. The Emperor had no clothes. Only a dictator who had killed any possible challengers could have survived it. In any other system, this would have brought about a change of government but no such change was available here."[113]

Effects on Decisions about War

The previous section established several aspects of Stalin's Soviet regime. Stalin's personality fit the personalist mold in that he was extremely ambitious (increasing the perceived benefits of winning) and oriented toward violent strategies of conflict resolution (reducing the perceived costs of fighting). The lack of powerful institutions left Stalin free of constraints on his foreign policy decisions (again reducing the costs of fighting as well as the costs of defeat). The final question is whether this combination of factors increased Stalin's propensity for initiating international conflict as argued by the theory.

On the one hand, scholars often characterize Soviet foreign policy as cautious.[114] This was particularly true in the Far East throughout the 1930s, where Stalin generally proceeded carefully.[115] However, recall that it was not until 1937 or 1938 that Stalin's hold on power was completely without constraints.[116] Thus Stalin's "cautious" policy toward Japan unfolded primarily in the era where his rule as boss was not entirely consolidated.

After the Great Terror had fully consolidated Stalin's power, the evidence suggests a pattern of decision-making that fits the model of the belligerent boss who is more prone to using force than other leaders both because he perceives lower costs to himself personally and because he is more likely to crave the personal rewards of international conquest and recognition. While it appears that Stalin was also motivated by genuine concerns for Soviet security, beginning in the late 1930s one can nonetheless detect a pattern of foreign policy decisions that a leader more sensitive to the costs of war would probably have avoided. Not *every* decision Stalin made fits this model, but his lack of costs and desire for personal aggrandizement appear to have tipped the Soviet Union toward greater expansionism and use of force than would have occurred under a different authoritarian political system.

A significant example of these forces at work was Stalin's disastrous adventure in Finland. By 1939, Soviet foreign policy was firmly in the hands of Stalin and his sycophants. Now that the Great Terror had freed Stalin of domestic constraints, he was, according to Politburo member Anastas Mikoyan, "an utterly changed person—absolutely suspicious, ruthless and boundlessly self-confident."[117] Molotov, a particularly obedient Stalinist, had replaced Maxim Litvinov, the Western-oriented foreign minister.[118] The USSR signed a peace treaty with Japan on September 15, thereby officially ending the Battle of Khalkhin Gol, and had signed the Molotov-Ribbentrop Pact with Germany earlier in August. Stalin nonetheless remained concerned about foreign aggressors, particularly Germany, and remained unsure about the intentions of France and the United Kingdom.

Stalin's main concern was an attack on Leningrad by the Germans. The issue was that Leningrad was dangerously close to the Finnish border and the Gulf of Finland.[119] Stalin had therefore initiated negotiations with Finland in April 1938.[120] In mid-August the Soviet envoy Boris Yartsev requested Finland to guarantee that it would "ward off possible attacks"; allow a Soviet advisor to oversee the fortification of the strategically important Åland Islands; and permit the Soviets to erect a Soviet defensive air and naval base on another island. In return, the Soviet Union would guarantee Finland's territorial sovereignty, supply it with cheap arms, and agree to a trade treaty with excellent terms for Finland.[121] Finland demurred, and negotiations paused until November 1938. The Soviets then tried a new approach, inquiring into the possibility of medium-term leases. When Finland declined, Stalin offered to give Finland Soviet territory in exchange for some of the islands. Again Finland refused.

By the time talks resumed in October 1939, much had changed. The Soviet Union had beaten the Japanese at Khalkhin Gol and signed an armistice with Japan. The Molotov-Ribbentrop Pact had removed the German threat for a time. In the fall of 1939 the Baltic states had acceded to Soviet hegemony. And importantly, Stalin's purges were complete and his rule was unchallenged. These victories, both domestic and international, freed Stalin to look more seriously at Finland.[122] Beginning in October, he started to take part in the negotiations with the Finnish, dominating most of the discussions. Stalin once more requested the islands and offered a much larger parcel of land in exchange. On October 31, Molotov made a threatening speech at the Fifth Supreme Soviet to try to put pressure on the Finnish.[123]

The Finns remained obstinate for several reasons. For one, the Soviet proposals violated the Finnish policy of strict neutrality.[124] Furthermore, some prominent officials, including Foreign Minister Eljas Erkko, did not believe that the Soviet Union would carry out its threats and assumed that the Soviets would drop their claims if Finland stood firm. He was convinced that Molotov's threats were merely "a tactical maneuver to frighten us. . . . We are calm. The Russians must be shown a firm front."[125]

In the meantime, Stalin had already begun to plan for military operations, requesting draft plans for war with Finland around June 1939. Commander Boris Shaposhnikov, chief of the General Staff, submitted a plan for a large campaign requiring most of the Red Army.[126] Stalin rejected the plan and asked Kirill Meretskov, the recently appointed commander of the Leningrad military district, to devise a new, leaner one. In July Meretskov submitted a more optimistic proposal that required fewer Soviet troops. Stalin approved it in principle but insisted that the offensive be concluded "within a few weeks," a tall order.[127]

These plans were put on hold until late October, when Stalin convened the Main Military Soviet to update operational plans for the invasion of Finland and set military preparations in motion.[128] Shaposhnikov argued for a cautious and limited invasion that "carried with it no glib assumptions regarding political conditions in Finland."[129] Mocking Shaposhnikov's timidity, Stalin and Voroshilov favored Meretskov's less cautious proposal, which calculated that Finland's "combination of military weakness and internal divisions" made Finland an easy target and that "the Red Army would be liberating rather than fighting."[130] This proposal was based on Stalin's assumption that Finnish domestic opinion would not support resistance and that the victorious Red Army would be "cheered on by hordes of liberated and breathlessly happy Finns, free from the yoke of Fascist oppression."[131] According to the boss, the war would be short and painless, and the one person who dared voice an alternative viewpoint—Shaposhnikov—was ignored.[132]

Why did no one else speak up? By this point, most of Stalin's subordinates knew better than to disagree. The purges had also had a chilling effect on intelligence analysis. According to Chubaryan and Shukman, the purges had "eliminated any possibility that gathered intelligence would receive objective analysis in Moscow: Stalin, a voracious consumer of raw intelligence, determined all aspects of policymaking and a climate of political correctness—backed by the ever-present threat of arrest and incarceration or worse—meant that facts gathered by the agencies could only be interpreted to confirm Stalin's dogmatic beliefs" (2002, xxiv). This may help explain the September 1939 NKVD report that the Finnish working classes would support a communist regime.

A last attempt at diplomacy on November 9 yielded little. On November 26, Molotov sent Finnish Ambassador Aarno Yrjö-Koskinen a note denouncing a (possibly fabricated) Finnish bombardment of Soviet troops.[133] Molotov demanded that all Finnish forces withdraw to roughly fifteen miles from the border. Two days later, another note officially abrogated the nonaggression treaty with Finland in light of "the deep-rooted hostility of the Finnish Government towards the USSR."[134] On November 29 the Soviet Union recalled its diplomats, and Molotov delivered a public address justifying the Soviet invasion. The following morning, the Red Army rumbled into Finnish territory.

The war began inauspiciously; General Yakovlev of the Seventh Army proved incompetent, and was removed from command a week into the conflict. Stalin, Voroshilov, and Mekhlis, who "eagerly but ineffectively assisted," took over.[135] The war continued as dismally as it had started. The Finns put up much stiffer resistance than Stalin had expected, causing enormous Soviet losses. The Soviets were ill equipped for the frigid cold; over the course of the war more than 125,000 Soviet soldiers were killed.[136] Superior Soviet numbers eventually wore down the Finnish resistance, and the Soviets gained 10 percent of Finnish territory, but Finland remained independent.

Beyond the staggering death toll, the debacle also had international political ramifications. Germany was giddy about how "the Red Army . . . had been pleasingly humiliated," and Khrushchev later suggested that the Winter War had emboldened Hitler to launch Operation Barbarossa, Germany's invasion of the Soviet Union.[137] Medvedev believes that "Stalin's irrational foreign policy" buoyed Finnish militarists and "pushed Finland into Hitler's arms."[138] All told, the Winter War was a fiasco.

Returning to the central question, how did the personalist nature of Stalin's regime contribute to the decision to initiate the Winter War? Stalin was insulated from the costs of fighting and the costs to the Soviet Union if the war went poorly, and he overestimated the likelihood of Soviet success. Consistent with the argument of this book, that caused him to initiate a conflict that a leader more concerned with the domestic repercussions would have either avoided or carried out in a much more cautious manner. The war was not "a carefully considered strategy on the part of the Soviet leadership," and the decision "was obviously taken personally by Stalin, without regard for the military or political situation of the respective countries."[139]

While blame for the outbreak of World War II cannot be laid at Stalin's feet, he conducted Soviet involvement in the conflict with much less concern for the domestic costs than other leaders. There was "no evidence that Stalin suffered even the slightest remorse about sending millions of his citizens to death in battle," and at no point—even when Hitler turned on the USSR—was he at risk of losing power.[140]

How consistent with the argument was Stalin's foreign policy *after* World War II? To what extent did the personalist nature of Stalin's regime raise the risk of war via the mechanisms highlighted in this book? One complicating factor is that both Stalin's relatively peaceful behavior *and* the tensions of the Cold War were the product of numerous causes. The USSR had just emerged from an all-out struggle with Germany and, like most countries, was ill equipped to fight another major war. Stalin remained extremely wary of threatening or using military force where he thought that this would spark an outright military confrontation with the United States, perhaps suspecting that his tenure could not weather a defeat directly after a massive world war.[141] Moreover, tensions between the communist and capitalist camps were amplified by ideological differences and distrust between the two blocs. The United States, a democracy with a relatively constrained leader, was itself guilty of stoking tensions. It would therefore be a stretch to attribute the Cold War to Stalin's preferences alone.[142]

On the other hand, many important aspects of Stalin's Cold War foreign policy are consistent with the argument. One is that Stalin continued to make all major foreign policy decisions while his underlings jockeyed for his favor.[143] Little evidence suggests that he ever feared that his foreign policy decisions would cost him office. This gave him much wider latitude over policy than later Soviet leaders. Stalin's ambitions for a vast Soviet empire are also consistent with the argument. With the announcement of the Marshall Plan in 1947, Stalin quickly moved to consolidate Soviet power in Eastern Europe. After a brief contraction after World War II, Stalin soon started to massively increase defense spending and the size of the military and also built a nuclear weapon.[144] While some have attributed the expansion of Soviet power to structurally induced "realist" motivations to maximize power out of the desire for self-defense, others have suggested that Stalin's desire for empire stemmed at least in part from his "hubris about the place that victory should accord the USSR in the postwar world," that he expected "far more recognition and concessions from his partners in the Grand Alliance than he actually received" and that he wanted to avoid any "servility" to the West.[145] Similarly, some have attributed Stalin's tensions with Tito to his desire to "absolutize" his leadership of the Soviet bloc.[146]

More generally, scholars have argued that "the use of military power for political ends is a striking characteristic of Stalin's foreign policy."[147] Stalin repeatedly took actions that were plausibly influenced by this combination of ambition and domestic omnipotence. The decision to blockade Berlin in 1948, while it did not spark outright conflict, certainly raised the risk of war. Stalin's behavior vis-à-vis the Korean War was measured, though this appears to have been because he did not want to trigger a direct armed conflict with the United States until the USSR was more prepared.[148] However, he did assent to the buildup of the North Korean military and ultimately condoned Kim Il Sung's decision to launch the invasion.[149]

It is not at all clear that a less ambitious decision-maker, or one facing fewer domestic constraints, would have chosen the same strategies for the future of the Soviet Union. And as we will see in chapter 6, the Soviet strategy did soften over time as the Stalinist system was replaced by a much more oligarchical system in which leaders were constrained by their peers.

Both the Iraqi and the Soviet cases demonstrate how, in two very different domestic contexts, personalist rule increases the likelihood that a country will initiate international conflict. Both Saddam and Stalin showed signs of ambition and an attraction to violence well before they came to power. And both leaders were shielded by the costs of war because they faced no domestic audience with any power to constrain them, either before or after the fact. These factors combined to allow the leaders to initiate conflict at high rates and yet to escape punishment even when things went poorly. But while the cases of Saddam and Stalin paint a fairly conventional picture of foreign policy decision-making in a dictatorship, the following chapters reveal that matters are quite different in nonpersonalist military juntas and civilian machines.

[5]

Juntas: Using the Only Language They Understand

Why are military dictatorships more belligerent than civilian regimes? In this chapter, I turn to two different countries and time periods to shed light on this question. First, I explore why Argentina invaded the Falkland Islands in 1982, provoking a war with the United Kingdom. The Falklands War is often seen as an archetypal case of diversionary war. Finding scant evidence of diversionary mechanisms in this case would therefore cast doubt on the idea that diversion plays an important role in explaining the belligerent behavior of military juntas documented in this book. I then turn to Japan in the 1930s, where the struggle between military and civilian forces provides a unique opportunity to compare how military and civilian elites approached the same policy decisions from quite different perspectives.

Within these two case studies, I adopt two strategies for assessing why military regimes are at greater risk for initiating international conflict than democracies or machines. First, where possible, I assess the evidence for or against different causal pathways—were decisions the product of a "military mindset"? Or do alternative accounts involving diversionary incentives or the fear of severe punishment explain juntas' belligerence? Second, I ask whether the decisions would have been made differently if the conditions specified by my theory, or the alternative theories, had been different.

As the discussion will show, the evidence from the Argentine case suggests that diversionary motives alone cannot explain the junta's decision-making. First, the timing of key decisions does not match the expectations of a diversionary explanation. Second, the junta made a series of calculations that even a similarly imperiled civilian regime would probably not have made, calculations that closely match patterns typical of "military thinking." Similarly, the Japanese case cannot be explained by diversionary or gambling motives. Rather, major differences in opinion between civilian and military elites suggest that officers' judgments about the wisdom of fighting versus diplomacy were, to a significant extent, a product of their background as military officers buttressed by parochial interests.

ARGENTINA AND THE FALKLANDS/MALVINAS WAR

The 1982 Falklands/Malvinas War between Argentina and the United Kingdom sprang out of an enduring dispute over a sparsely populated collection of islands about three hundred miles off the coast of Argentina. Discovered by Europeans in the 1500s, the islands were controlled by England and then Spain until a newly independent Argentina laid claim to them in 1820.[1] The Argentines failed, however, to establish a stable colony, which facilitated the islands' takeover by Britain in 1833.[2] Despite the nearly eight thousand miles of water separating Britain from the Falklands, the British built a naval base at Port Stanley and encouraged a small settlement.[3] By the latter part of the twentieth century, the settlement had about two thousand residents of mostly British descent, relying primarily on wool exports for its economy and on Britain for its defense and communications.

Over the decades, Argentines—their nationalist feelings often stoked by opportunistic politicians—remained bitter over British control of the islands.[4] Sensing an opportunity during the decolonization movement of the 1960s, Argentina took up its claim with the UN Committee on Decolonization, which in 1964 recognized the Falkland/Malvinas Islands as a territory that should be decolonized and suggested that Argentina and Britain work toward a negotiated settlement. Talks began in 1966 and produced a "Memorandum of Understanding," which outlined an eventual transfer of power to Argentina. However, the Falkland Islands Committee—a group of British citizens supporting the British claim over the islands—successfully lobbied the British government to accept a transfer only if it took into account the "wishes" of the islanders.[5] Unfortunately for the Argentines, the islanders had no wish at all to join Argentina, which was culturally different, economically troubled, and intermittently ruled by military dictatorships.

Negotiations stalled and did not resume seriously until 1976. Tensions rose in February of that year when the *Shackleton*, a British ship sent to investigate the economic potential of the islands (including its potential for oil), was intercepted by an Argentine destroyer about eighty miles off the coast of the Falklands in Argentina's newly claimed territorial waters. Despite warning shots, the British captain refused to stop and headed for Port Stanley. The United Nations General Assembly issued a resolution pressuring Britain to resume negotiations with Argentina.[6]

The following month, for reasons unrelated to the *Shackleton* incident, changes occurred in Argentine domestic politics when the Argentine armed forces toppled the democratic government of Isabel Peron, widow of Juan Peron, on March 24, 1976. To consolidate power, the new military junta banned all political activities and used violent tactics such as political assassination, disappearance, and torture in a "dirty war" to subdue the opposition.[7] The resulting regime was a clear example of a nonpersonalistic military dictatorship. The regime, known as *El Proceso* (National Reorganization Process), was led by three sets of actors: the Junta Militar, the Legislative Consultation Commission (CAL), and the president. The president held executive and legislative powers, but the Junta Militar, consisting of the service commanders of the army, the navy, and the air force, was the "supreme organ" of the state and could override the president. Each service also nominated three members to the CAL, which formally served as a legislative consultant to the president, though in reality it was primarily an extension of the junta. Moreover, each branch of the military extended deeply into the government, holding ministerial and administrative positions at various levels. In sum, the separation of authority among the relatively autonomous branches of the armed forces was designed to prevent any individual leader from centralizing power and personalizing state institutions, including the military itself.[8]

Following these events, the Malvinas dispute stalled for several years. In late 1979 and early 1980, the British Foreign and Commonwealth Office (FCO), which recognized that the islands were economically vulnerable and costly to defend, began quietly to propose a "leaseback" agreement as a middle ground. Under such an arrangement, sovereignty would officially be transferred to Argentina, but Britain would "lease back" the land for a long period of time (ninety-nine years or more) and continue to oversee the islands' administration. However, once the islanders learned of the proposal it became clear that any agreement that would relinquish sovereignty of the Falklands to Argentina—even in name only—was unacceptable to the islanders and their backers in the House of Commons.

Thus, by the time army general Leopoldo Galtieri became President in December 1981, the state of negotiations between Argentina and Britain was bleak.[9] Newly in power, the junta started to discuss military options and ordered plans for a possible invasion drawn up by mid-March.[10] It had apparently set no timetable for the invasion and intended to continue with negotiations; it planned to pursue military options only if negotiations failed by the summer or fall.[11]

[108]

In March, however, these plans were overtaken by events when a crisis arose over South Georgia Island, a remote dependency over which both Argentina and Britain laid claim. The dispute arose when Argentine businessman Constantino Davidoff arrived on the island on March 18 with sixty men—some of them, it is alleged, Argentine marines—to dismantle an old whaling station.[12] After discovering the Argentine party the next day, Britain suspected the workers of collaborating with the Argentine navy to occupy the islands. After some back-and-forth culminating in Argentina's refusal to evacuate the workers, Britain ordered the HMS *Endurance*, an ice patrol ship, to the island in order to put pressure on the Argentines. The Argentines felt that allowing British ships to land on the islands would be conceding sovereignty and would deal a blow to their claims, and on March 23, the Argentines sent a ship of their own to protect the workers. Fearing that the South Georgia crisis would draw a greater British presence to the area, thus weakening the Argentine bargaining position on the Falklands, the junta started to consider an immediate invasion of the Falklands. The Argentine press had by now caught wind of the dispute, making it difficult for the junta to retreat. On March 26, 1982, the junta officially ordered a military intervention.[13] On April 2, Argentine troops landed at Port Stanley and overwhelmed the British garrison.

Unfortunately for the Argentines, the British response to the invasion was not what they had hoped. The British took several weeks to transport their troops to the distant South Atlantic, but once they arrived and started to attack the islands by air and sea on April 25, they quickly overwhelmed the Argentine forces. The Argentine troops at Port Stanley surrendered on June 14, effectively ending the war.

Does the Argentine case provide support for the argument that military officers view conflicts of interest differently than civilian decisionmakers? Or does some other theoretical perspective better explain the decision to invade? Historians agree that the new junta felt pressure to make progress on the Falklands for several reasons. One was that matters were going poorly in Argentina's dispute with Chile over the Beagle Channel. The two countries had agreed to Vatican mediation in 1979, and the initial Vatican ruling had gone in favor of Chile. While the Vatican was considering Argentina's counter-claim, the junta was not optimistic about a reversal.[14] Second, January 3, 1983—one year hence—was going to mark the 150th anniversary of the British occupation of the Falklands, which could provide a focal point for the dispute.[15]

But perhaps the most popular explanation for Argentina's decision is that the junta had diversionary motives. At the time of the invasion, the economy was in shambles, popular discontent was rising, and the opposition was starting to organize. In light of the existence of this widely accepted explanation for Argentina's behavior, the rest of the discussion proceeds as follows. I first review the evidence in favor of the conventional diversionary interpretation of the Falklands War, showing that this explanation leaves crucial aspects of the Argentine decision unexplained. I then show evidence that the predictable beliefs of junta members greatly enhanced the regime's willingness to use force. I then briefly consider two alternative explanations for the junta's behavior: the argument suggested by Debs and Goemans (2010) that military regimes are more conflict-prone because their leaders fear severe punishment for making concessions, and the selectorate theory of Bueno de Mesquita and his colleagues (Bueno de Mesquita et al. 2003).

A Diversionary War?

As reviewed in earlier chapters, some scholars have argued that juntas are especially tempted to engage in conflict in order to divert attention from domestic troubles.[16] In this view, military regimes face few alternatives for shoring up their popularity; lack of a powerful party apparatus, or "infrastructural power," means that juntas have few alternative strategies at their disposal for quelling the public discontent that inevitably arises under any regime.

This interpretation of the incentives of military juntas coincides with the view, shared by several scholars, that the Argentine junta's decision to occupy the Falklands was motivated by the deep political insecurity it faced in the spring of 1982.[17] The essence of the diversionary account is that by early 1982, when Galtieri's new junta started seriously contemplating the use of force, the combination of the regime's human rights abuses and several years of economic hardship had badly undermined the regime's popularity and legitimacy.[18] In March 1980, a financial crash and a public run on the banks had plunged Argentina's economy into disarray, with inflation skyrocketing and GNP decreasing by nearly six percent in 1981.[19] Seizing on the junta's weakness, opposition groups set aside their differences and unified into the umbrella group known as the Multipartidaria, thus posing a more potent challenge to the regime.

In the midst of this turmoil, General Galtieri—head of a powerful hardline faction in the army—had replaced Roberto Viola as president in December 1981.[20] The new junta suspended political activities and enacted new stabilization policies, but the short-term results of these measures were an additional rise in unemployment and a further fall in wages.[21] Even the press, which until this point had generally remained quiet, started critiquing the junta's economic policy.[22] According to a January 1982 *Washington Post* article, the junta was doomed and knew it.[23] The unrest crested on March 30 in the form of a demonstration in which roughly forty thousand members of the major opposition groups took to the streets to demand the end of military rule.[24] The regime responded with violent repression, arresting approximately two thousand demonstrators. On April 2, only three days later, Argentine forces landed on the Falklands, and spontaneous prowar demonstrations broke out. For these reasons, many scholars have interpreted the invasion of the Falklands as a case of diversionary war.

Critics of the diversionary argument paint an alternative interpretation of the events. First, they note that while proponents of the diversionary argument often point to the timing of the invasion, in the midst of escalating domestic unrest and only a couple of days after the famous March 30 demonstrations, in actuality the junta ordered the intervention several days before the demonstrations, on March 26; the Argentinian ships actually left for the Falklands on March 28.[25] Thus, it cannot have been the demonstrations that drove the decision. Moreover, there is evidence that junta officials did not expect a rally in public opinion and that even if there had been such a rally, it would not have helped with the main source of discontent: the economy.[26]

In the critics' account, first, elements within the military had long favored military action in the Falklands, and the regime generated new war plans soon after taking power in 1976. Jorge Anaya, who helped Galtieri maneuver to power, was a longtime advocate of military action, and Galtieri and Anaya in fact discussed the possibility of an invasion immediately after Galtieri took office in December 1981.[27] Their intention was to continue negotiations with the British through the spring, but if that failed, to invade in the summer or fall in order to force Britain back to the negotiating table.

But as Arquilla and Rasmussen (2001) and Fravel (2010) point out, these plans were soon overtaken by the unfolding events in the South Georgia islands. The South Georgia dispute put Argentina in a difficult position: It could either remove its forces—an acknowledgment of British sovereignty over South Georgia—or it could stand firm, in which case the British would likely send naval reinforcement to the region. But an increased British presence in the region would endanger any hopes of a summer or fall invasion. In this view, fear of increased local British strength—not the escalation in domestic unrest in March 1982—explains why the junta decided to carry out its plans as early as it did.

A proponent of a diversionary argument might grant this but nonetheless argue that the junta would not have reacted so forcefully to the South Georgia crisis if its domestic situation had been less dire. More specifically, if the junta had been less embattled domestically, it could have quietly backed off in the South Georgia islands; stood firm and allowed the British to increase its local military presence and pursued the matter in the UN; or perhaps refrained from secretly sending Marines along with Davidoff's party in the first place, assuming it is true that the Argentine landing on South Georgia was part of a navy-backed plot.

Despite the purely indirect evidence, this perspective has some merit: It is plausible that domestic concerns added *urgency* to the Falklands issue. Moreover, it seems true that backing down at this point could potentially have incurred domestic audience costs both within the public and within the junta—costs that would have been less consequential if the regime had not already been so unpopular.

But even a generous reading of the diversionary interpretation leaves crucial questions unexplained. Why did the junta opt for an occupation of the Falklands rather than staying put in South Georgia and then raising the issue in the UN? Why did it not simply stand its ground in South Georgia and force the British to take the next step? One can imagine that the sight of British destroyers forcibly removing Argentine citizens from South Georgia would have provoked a welcome domestic rally effect— but with much less risk. Given that there was ambiguity about whether the Argentine forces on South Georgia were military or civilian, an attack on South Georgia would have made the United Kingdom look like the aggressor, which also could have won the Argentines international support. This option certainly seems less risky than sending an invasion force to the Falklands. And the junta was clearly *not* so embattled that it would have been rational to undertake an action with a low likelihood of success, that is to "gamble for resurrection." Indeed, there are doubts as to whether the junta anticipated a rally at all. Rather, Galtieri and Anaya seem to have thought that a military invasion was the only viable option for recovering the Malvinas: They thought that they were making the optimal move, not engaging in a desperate gambit.

In sum, the diversionary argument cannot explain why Argentina invaded the Falklands rather than choosing a less objectively risky approach and is, at best, incomplete. In order to explain the decision to invade rather than pursue less aggressive strategies, we must turn to the perceptions of the Argentine leaders and understand why they thought a military occupation was the best option.

The Role of the "Military Mindset"

The above arguments leave the most important question about the Falklands war unanswered: Why did the junta choose war over other plausible strategies? Why did Galtieri, Anaya, and other backers of the junta believe an invasion to be the best course of action? Earlier I argued that shared beliefs about the necessity and efficacy of military force mean that military dictatorships—led by military officers—turn to military force in situations where civilian governments would be more likely to choose diplomacy. There is strong evidence that precisely these sorts of beliefs encouraged the junta to choose invasion. Moreover, it seems likely that a civilian government faced with the same domestic and international context would have perceived the situation differently and thus chosen a different option.

First, there is ample evidence that Anaya and other officers who favored seizing the Falklands over diplomacy had long held this preference: Their perception of the utility of using force was not a byproduct of other concerns, such as retaining office.[28] The navy in particular had long agitated for an invasion; the year after the military dictatorship came to power in 1976, the navy drew up plans for military involvement.[29] Indeed, one of the military regime's first foreign policy initiatives in 1976 was to undertake a coercive diplomatic effort, the *Shackleton* incident. Those early plans to retake the Malvinas were revised again in 1980.[30] Galtieri focused his attention on the islands as soon as he came to office in late 1981, with junta colleagues Admiral Anaya and General Basilio Lami Dozo of the air force.[31]

Moreover, decision-making was almost entirely bereft of civilian or diplomatic input. Only a select number of senior military officers played a role in the planning, and more generally, Galtieri's closest advisers and friends tended to stem from the military.[32] In mid-February, Galtieri told civilian foreign minister Costa Mendez that a military invasion was being considered, but he apparently provided no details and did not ask for input from him or other civilians.[33] There is also evidence that the Argentine Ministry of Foreign Affairs was taken by surprise by the "workers" on South Georgia.[34] Soon after the invasion, reports emerged of the junta's total failure to consult diplomats about their views on the wisdom of military operations.[35] In sum, it is clear that the decision was made almost exclusively by career military officers.

There is considerable evidence that these decision-makers were prone to the biases expected by the earlier theoretical discussion. In general terms, analysts speak of the junta's sense of the "inevitability of war" and "alarmist perception of an imminent threat."[36] At every turn, the junta interpreted British intentions in the worst possible light. They viewed the British "stern warning" to remove workers from South Georgia as an ultimatum and believed that Britain was using the South Georgia crisis as an excuse to tighten military control over the region. The junta panicked when it received unsubstantiated reports that British ships, including a submarine, had left for the Falklands on March 25, believing the British had already begun sending reinforcements to the area, even though it later turned out that the British had been seeking to contain the crisis rather than escalate it.[37]

Given these (objectively unwarranted) threat perceptions, the junta's instinct was to react immediately by both fortifying South Georgia and seizing the Falklands before it was too late. "They could see a momentary opportunity to act on an issue that had long been a high priority. If they waited too long the moment could pass."[38] Moreover, "Anaya felt . . . that this was his last opportunity to carry out his life's ambition to retake the Malvinas Islands for Argentina. . . . The window of opportunity was limited."[39]

In addition to these exaggerated threat perceptions and bias toward striking first, there is also evidence that the junta had only the crudest understanding of Britain's domestic political situation or how Britain would react to an invasion. Even though there was clear evidence that powerful interests in Britain—and their representatives in the House of Commons—would not stand for Argentine sovereignty over the Falklands, the junta believed that there was almost no chance that Britain would fight back. Rather, perhaps as a consequence of the junta's belief in the efficacy of military power, it believed that a seizure would force the British to the negotiating table and that negotiations of sovereignty would then resume in a way that was favorable to Argentina.[40]

But the junta did not base this assessment on a serious analysis of the British position, which would surely have involved civilian diplomatic experts in addition to a military analysis. Rather, the analysis seems to have been based primarily on the junta's own reading of the situation, which relied largely on its own assessment of local British capabilities and whether Thatcher would deploy naval forces all the way to the Southern Hemisphere. For example, the junta placed great importance on the fact that Britain had recently slated its only naval ship in the area, the *Endurance*, for withdrawal.[41] More generally, Anaya believed that British naval power was in decline and "lacked the capability to respond eight thousand miles from home."[42] The Argentine military, "with their traditional notions of honour, considered that a decisive stroke would be regarded as a *fait accompli*, much as a military coup would be regarded by the losing party in their own country."[43] In sum, the Argentine leadership perceived that Britain was willing to give up the islands but needed an excuse to do so; as Gamba-Stonehouse has written, "In an extraordinary way, the junta members perceived that they had to provide an 'honorable way out' for the British Foreign Office and that this could be done by increasing the level of threat."[44] Had the junta engaged in a more thorough analysis of the British political position, it would have realized that this was an entirely mistaken assessment given the strength of the Falklands lobby.

The junta was also highly skeptical that diplomatic options were viable absent a military seizure of the islands. The junta seemed genuinely to believe that an invasion would "force a serious negotiation in circumstances favourable to Argentina, so that they would agree to the transfer of sovereignty legitimised through the UN."[45] Absent this type of local military superiority, Argentina thought that success in the UN was unlikely.[46] The official Argentine analysis of the events, the Rattenbach Commission Report, later concluded that in its "obsession" with preserving strategic surprise, the military junta chose the worst moment to invade from the perspective of international politics.[47] The timing was terrible from a diplomatic standpoint: the Argentine representative to the United Nations, Ambassador Eduardo Roca, had arrived to take up his position only a week prior to the invasion and was suffering from failing health. Many influential countries, especially in Europe, were at this time highly critical of Argentina's human rights abuses. Additionally, Argentina lacked support from other Latin American nations due to the revelation that Argentina was training and sending anti-Sandinista Contras to Nicaragua.[48] The invasion had all the hallmarks of a diplomatic and public relations disaster, but the junta did not perceive this because it failed to appreciate the potential utility of diplomacy in solving the Malvinas issue and because of its bias in favor of military strategies.

In sum, Argentine decision-making leading up to the Falklands War closely matches the description of the "military mindset" laid out earlier. The question remains, of course, whether civilian officials would have perceived the costs and benefits of invasion differently. Here, unlike the Japanese case that follows, it is difficult to amass direct evidence. Of course, later civilian governments condemned Galtieri's decision, but these critiques had the benefit of hindsight, and it is difficult to know what a civilian government would have chosen in the moment. In the meantime, the Falklands case confirms the expectations of a "military mindset" explanation for the above-average conflict propensity of military regimes while casting doubt on a purely diversionary interpretation.

Alternative Explanations

Another possibility suggests that Galtieri's motivation for the conflict was a desire to save his own skin. Recall that Debs and Goemans (2010) argue that military leaders are more conflict-prone than civilian leaders because they have more reason to fear serious domestic punishment if they make concessions. This narrows the bargaining range and causes them to fight rather than reach a peaceful bargain. The reasons for this are twofold, according to Debs and Goemans: First, concessions provide a focal point for coordination by the opposition, and second, military dictators expect that they will face exile, imprisonment, or even death upon removal. To evaluate this explanation for the Falklands War, we

[115]

must establish what Galtieri would have expected about his fate if he had reached a compromise that averted war. Would a concession have provided a focal point? Did Galtieri reasonably expect severe punishment upon ouster?

As for the first point, the domestic politics of the Argentine junta highlight the fact that the "technology of coordination" in nonpersonalist military dictatorships does not require focal points of the type described by Debs and Goemans. In Argentina, the experience of virtually all of Galtieri's predecessors (both in his regime and the earlier 1966–1972 regime) showed that high-level military officers were frequently able to oust incumbents simply by presenting a united front; no special coordinating event was required. The cases of presidents Jorge Rafael Videla and Roberto Eduardo Viola indicated that their tenure had little to do with whether or not they continued to negotiate; Videla served out his term, even though he did not make any progress on the Falklands issue, and the removal of Viola stemmed from his domestic policies, not his foreign policies. Galtieri should have known this better than anyone, since he himself forced out Viola.[49]

Moreover, there is little indication that Galtieri should have been particularly worried about "severe punishment" even if he were ousted. There was ample contemporaneous evidence that in Argentina and neighboring countries, even former military dictators could expect a peaceful retirement. For example, Galtieri's direct predecessors Videla and Viola do not appear to have had their freedoms curtailed in any way after losing power. After stepping down from power peacefully at the end of his term, Videla continued to make public appearances, including the swearing-in ceremony of the Falklands' new military governor soon after the Argentine seizure—this despite the fact that the excesses of the Dirty War had made him a controversial figure.[50] Even Viola, who was prematurely forced out by Galtieri and his backers after unpopular domestic policies, appeared in "vacation spots" after being deposed and faced no discernable punishment.[51]

Members of the previous military regime, which held power from 1966 to 1972, had also escaped the dire fate that Debs and Goemans envision. If anything, the fate of these predecessors indicated that ex-leaders would remain safe even after the restoration of democracy (recall that democracy returned to Argentina from 1972 to 1976). For example, General Juan Carlos Ongania, who ruled from 1966 to 1970, remained safe after being ousted by his peers and even continued to be active in politics.[52] His successors Roberto Levingston and Alejandro Lanusse, who were both ousted by the junta before their terms expired, also did not suffer severe punishment.[53] Finally, Generals Emilio Medici and Ernesto Geisel, the former military rulers of neighboring Brazil, also remained safe from punishment after losing office.[54] Even a transition to democracy was not especially threatening—Galtieri was unique among his predecessors in that he had less severe human rights violations on his hands (it was not until 2002 that he was arrested for his role in the Dirty War, which was not as extensive as that of some of the other top leaders). In fact, the one action that did condemn him to the possibility of severe punishment was his decision to invade: He was sentenced for fourteen years of prison for the Falkland Islands debacle, though he was pardoned by the democratic government in 1989.[55]

In sum, there is reason to expect that if Galtieri had continued to repair the economy and had continued to negotiate with the British, eventually taking the matter to the UN, he would have faced a peaceful retirement. Why did he instead make decisions that led to a losing war? And why did other members of his audience of military officers support the invasion? The historical record does not indicate that fear of severe punishment was part of the explanation. While Galtieri may have believed that backing down would cause him to lose power, there is no indication that he feared a worse fate than retirement; indeed, it is not clear why he would have accepted a surrender if that had been the case. And had Galtieri felt that his life was at stake, he would have had ample incentive to put forward such an interpretation to justify his decision in later years.

Finally, it is worth considering whether selectorate theory could explain the junta's behavior. There are two possible ways in which selectorate theory might make sense of the conflict.

The first is that the junta was a regime with a small winning coalition relative to its selectorate, so Galtieri expected he would not be held accountable even for a military defeat. These kinds of regimes, according to selectorate theory, are more willing to risk war when the likelihood of winning is uncertain. But this view is undermined by ample evidence that Galtieri knew that his rule depended on performance and appeared to have thought that inaction would be problematic for his rule as well.

Alternatively, Argentina might be considered a "large-coalition" regime. This could be because the junta was accountable to a relatively large officer corps, or because the junta was temporarily accountable to the mass public due to Argentina's dire economic circumstances, which provided a focal point for coordination. In this view, the Falklands War is an unanticipated, off-the-equilibrium-path outlier: War ensued out of miscalculation, and the military nature of the regime was incidental to the junta's decision to invade. This explanation falls short, however, if one accepts the evidence that the military backgrounds of key officials did play a role in Argentina's decision. The structure of the regime indicates that the junta leadership was indeed accountable to the officer corps but that the military background of both key decision-makers and the relevant audience supported the choice of a military rather than a diplomatic strategy. What would be unexplained, idiosyncratic behavior for selectorate theory is instead anticipated by the arguments developed in this book.

JAPAN'S ROAD TO WORLD WAR II

Over the course of the 1930s and the early 1940s, the government of Japan provoked one of the most violent decades in any country's history. After inciting an extensive and costly war in China and two small wars against the Soviet Union, Japan capped off its decade of bloodshed with an attack on the United States at Pearl Harbor, sealing Japan's entry into World War II on the side of the Axis Powers and paving the way to eventual defeat at the hands of the Allies.

This series of events provides a unique opportunity to compare the preferences and perceptions of civilian and military elites when faced with identical foreign circumstances. The years marked an intense power struggle between military elites and the civilian politicians who had led the country into the 1930s. The decade began with Japan under civilian control, but the military held the informal reins of power as early as 1937 and threw off the facade of civilian rule in October 1941 when General Hideki Tojo replaced civilian prime minister Fumimaro Konoe. Over these years, civilians and military officers publicly and repeatedly espoused competing foreign policies. Moreover, Japan's eventual occupation by Allied forces allowed outsiders to gain wide access to Japanese government archives as well as to carry out interviews with many of the elites involved in Japan's foreign policy decisions. Thus, the Japanese case allows us to trace in some detail the quite different views held by civilian and military elites about the role that military force should play in Japanese foreign policy.

I begin by briefly describing the events that led Japan to the brink of World War II: a lengthy conflict against China, two border wars against the Soviet Union, and the signing of the Tripartite Pact. I then focus in more detail on the decision to attack U.S. forces in Hawaii on December 7, 1941, committing Japan irrevocably to World War II. As space constraints make it impossible to give a comprehensive history of these complex events, I focus my attention on comparing the policy perspectives of military officers and the civilian government. The evidence from Japan confirms the hypothesis that military officers and civilians have differing beliefs about the use of military force, leading to consistently different foreign policy preferences. In Japan, military officers tended to be more fearful of the consequences of delay or inaction than their civilian counterparts, to view diplomacy with deeper skepticism, and to perceive force as an effective and legitimate policy option. They also clearly kept an eye on their parochial interests, which they often believed were furthered by war. Civilian officials, in contrast, had much greater faith in diplomacy, were less likely to exhibit preemptive thinking, and were more likely to see force to be a risky and costly solution to Japan's dilemmas. The following narrative reveals how the domestic ascendance of the military in Japan led that nation to some of the most disastrous policy decisions of the twentieth century.

Intervention in Manchuria (1931)

By the late 1920s, Japan grappled with whether to expand into Asia. Of immediate interest was the status of Manchuria, a territory on the Chinese mainland that was rich in natural resources. Japan had seized southern Manchuria in 1904, but the Soviet Union exerted control over the north and China remained racked by internal conflict. By the late 1920s, parts of Manchuria were under the control of Chinese warlord Zhang Xueliang, a nationalist allied with Chiang Kai-shek's Kuomintang, as they fought other warlords for control over large swaths of China.

The Japanese military high command and the commanders of the Kwantung Army—a wing of the Japanese army garrisoned in Manchuria—had vastly different views about the future of the empire than the civilian leaders in Tokyo. As early as the mid-1920s, the bulk of military opinion, particularly within the Kwantung Army, favored expansion of the Japanese empire into China.[56] The two principal planners of what would become the Manchurian Incident were officers Ishiwara Kanji and Itagaki Seishiro, who believed that Japan could thrive only through expansion.[57] Ishiwara, a lieutenant general in the Kwantung Army, and likeminded thinkers envisioned a closed Japanese-dominated Asian economic bloc that would provide Japan with independence from the West. Ishiwara's theory of "final war" required Japan to acquire resources and develop its industries to the point that it could sustain a war effort without having to trade with Western nations.[58] In 1930, however, this would require major changes to Japan's resource base, because Japan relied heavily on British and American imports of important strategic goods such as oil and steel.

Ishiwara saw resource-rich Manchuria as the key to Japanese economic independence: Manchuria's resources would provide a solution to overpopulation and food shortages and eventually enable Japan to fight a total war on its own terms. Chaos in Manchuria, however, made it difficult for Japan to exploit the region's resource wealth. As early as 1928, Ishiwara began developing plans to intervene directly in order to

[119]

develop Manchuria and control the stream of resources that would ensue.[59]

Not only were military officers in favor of expansion, but they were also scornful of civilian interference in the Manchurian question. They viewed policy toward Manchuria as a military rather than political domain and tended to believe that the civilian government was incapable of solving Japan's security problems.[60] Civilian statesmen, meanwhile, took a much more cautious view of the prospect of using force to secure Japanese expansion.[61] Many civilians had advocated disarmament and internationalism after World War I, and on the specific issue of Manchuria, civilian politicians tended to advocate a cautious and gradual diplomatic course over military force.[62] Prime Minister Shidehara Kijūrō, in office from 1924 to 1927, had emphasized the importance of developing Japan's economy peacefully, because military action would damage international cooperation and jeopardize Japan's ability to import vital resources.[63] The civilian government continued to pursue diplomacy in the region, and favored reaching a settlement with Zhang Xueliang that assured Japanese access to the South Manchurian Railroad, even showing readiness to recognize Chiang Kai-shek's government in Nanking.[64]

In April of 1931, the army's central authorities—the General Staff—developed a policy for Manchuria that took a middle stance between the hardline approach of the Kwantung leadership and the more dovish approach of the civilian government. This "Three Point Plan" called for first negotiating with Zhang, then replacing him with a pro-Japanese puppet if necessary, and turning to military force only as a last resort.[65] But by 1931, the more radical members of the General Staff were fed up with the civilian leadership's inaction. In June 1931, they circulated a policy document that attempted to allay the civilians' fears of a potential international backlash, emphasizing that any military action in Manchuria would be accompanied by a campaign to cultivate international sympathy toward the Japanese cause. Though more cautious than the General Staff, the leadership of the War Ministry adopted the plan, convinced that with careful planning Japan could minimize the economic and diplomatic fallout of an invasion.[66]

Meanwhile, Itagaki, Ishiwara, and other frustrated officers were furtively concocting a new strategy. In May 1931, the General Staff's Russia and China section heads secretly agreed to stage a provocation, finalizing the plot in August.[67] Civilian leaders in Tokyo were aware of escalating tension in Manchuria and started to hear disturbing rumors of a plot. The emperor called a meeting on September 10, ordering the minister of war and the minister of the navy to rein in the military. After the meeting, Major General Tatekawa Yoshitsugu was dispatched to Manchuria to restrain the Kwantung Army.[68] However, Tatekawa was delayed; many believe that he was a secret ally of the plotters and intentionally dallied until it was too late to prevent the plan from being executed.[69]

The plot proceeded, resulting in an explosion under a railroad outside of Mukden on September 18, 1931. Fighting broke out, and the next day Shidehara, now foreign minister, told a cabinet meeting that the conflict must be contained. Shortly afterwards, Prime Minister Wakatsuki Reijir announced that the army was to follow a policy of "non-aggravation." But the civilian government was powerless to stop the army's advance. With the support of both the War Ministry and the General Staff, field commanders repeatedly ignored orders from Tokyo, citing operational necessity. Given the escalation that had already occurred, Tokyo could not refuse to send reinforcements.[70]

In private, Prime Minister Wakatsuki lamented his loss of control over the army.[71] He held more cabinet meetings over the following days, and on September 23 ordered the Kwantung Army not to advance into Northern Manchuria. But the Kwantung officers once again ignored the civilian government. Although Ishiwara had not envisioned a conflict on this scale, his officers plunged on. By spring, Japan had driven the Northeastern Chinese Army out of the region, with the puppet state of Manchukuo established in March.[72] In a great vindication for the more radical factions, an impressed Japanese public swung its support toward the military leaders.[73]

The divergence in opinion between military and civilian actors in Japan is consistent with the argument developed in this book. Military officers were, on balance, more likely than their civilian counterparts to view the international environment as threatening to Japanese security, to discount the benefits of trade and diplomacy, and to see military force as an effective and legitimate option for building a secure Japan. These preferences were not motivated by a desperate "gamble for resurrection" or diversionary motives, as military officers were not in charge of the government at the time and had no reason to think their political power was in desperate peril.

More Fighting in China (1937)

In the years after the Manchurian Incident, skirmishes between Chinese and Japanese forces continued to break out. However, civilian statesmen took a detached view of the fighting, as it was largely being contained by local agreements that were unlikely to provoke the United States. Moreover, civilians were distracted by serious threats to civilian rule. In 1932, Prime Minister Inukai Tsuyoshi, who had tried to rein in the military after the fall of the Wakatsuki government, was murdered by a radical group of junior naval officers frustrated with his opposition to

Japanese expansion in Manchuria. On February 26, 1936, fourteen hundred army soldiers assassinated several top civilian leaders, including a former prime minister, and attempted to stage a military coup. While the coup attempt failed, civilian control of foreign policy—not to mention Japanese democracy—was clearly in jeopardy. With assassination "lurk[ing] in the wings," civilians were now outnumbered by military officers in several important ministries, increasingly excluded from important discussions, and barred from seeing operational plans.[74]

While on average military officers took a more hawkish, expansionist view on Japanese foreign policy than civilians, the military had both expansionist and nonexpansionist factions. The expansionists included many mid-level and senior officers in the Kwantung Army, a group of army bureaucrats in the Operations, Intelligence, and Military Affairs sections of the General Staff and large portions of the navy.[75] Scholars have attributed the motives of these individuals to a combination of genuine concern for Japanese security, the parochial interests of the military, and ideology.[76] From a parochial interest standpoint, the army found expansion into China attractive because conflicts arising from expansion onto the Asian continent would be fought by the army rather than by the navy and therefore would increase its budget.[77] The navy was also oriented toward expansion, though in a more southerly direction because of the greater naval opportunities available there.[78]

There was also convenient ideological support for expansionist attitudes, though it is difficult to separate the ideological considerations from more material ones. First, expansion was "the Imperial Way," the honorable and proper manner in which to serve the emperor and bring him glory.[79] Expansion was also consistent with the principle of *gun no ishin*, or the dignity of the military, in that it would endow the armed forces with honor and prestige.[80] When it came to China, expansionist sentiments were especially strong because of army officers' racism, nationalism, and aversion to Communism.[81]

As in the prelude to the Manchurian Incident, most civilian leaders held nonexpansionist views. Some senior Army and Navy officials, including some members of the General Staff, took that position as well.[82] Interestingly, Ishiwara, one of the architects of the Manchurian conflict who had since become the head of the Operations Division of the General Staff, now sided with the nonexpansionists. In the years since the Manchurian Incident, he had come to fear that entanglement in China would expose Japan to a Soviet threat.[83] He and other nonexpansionists also believed that interference in China could lead to diplomatic problems with the Western Powers, potentially jeopardizing Japan's longer-term security.[84] Until Japan became self-sufficient, it relied on materials from the West. If an invasion of China triggered an embargo,

Japan's ability to achieve longer-term economic autonomy would be endangered.[85]

In the first half of 1937, the Japanese government received reports that the Chinese were making more aggressive demands and might be preparing themselves for a war, possibly in conjunction with the Soviets.[86] Prime Minister Konoe held a cabinet meeting on July 6, which concluded that the Chinese were probably planning some sort of attack but that a preemptive strike was not wise.

The army, however, took matters into its own hands the very next day when serious fighting broke out near the Marco Polo Bridge outside Beijing.[87] While historians disagree about the extent to which the Japanese manufactured the incident as a pretext for war, Kwantung Army generals argued that it marked the beginning of a major Chinese attack, and demanded a strong response. A series of emotional cabinet meetings ensued in Tokyo, with opinion remaining sharply divided among the different groups represented.[88] Prime Minister Konoe initially sided with the nonexpansionists, hoping that the conflict could be settled through local negotiations and that if Japan pursued a nonaggressive policy, the Chinese would respond in kind.[89] Unfortunately, the fighting escalated, both because the Chinese did not show restraint, and because Japanese field commanders were disobeying orders and then demanding reinforcements. Tokyo felt obligated to comply, and with the government's reluctant help, the conflict widened.[90] After several decisions to order and then cancel mobilization, Ishiwara finally authorized the deployment of troops on July 26, 1937, under intense pressure from other sectors of the military.[91]

The Japanese military planners had anticipated that the war would require between three and fifteen divisions, last three months, and cost 100 million yen.[92] In the end almost the whole standing army was required, and at least a quarter of a million soldiers lost their lives.[93] The hawkish beliefs of military officers, buttressed by parochial interests, once again led Japan to war.

The Changkufeng Incident (1938)

Soon after the start of the second Sino-Japanese War, Japan turned its attention back to the Soviet Union. The next in the series of Japanese conflicts with its neighbors was the Changkufeng Incident, lasting from July 29 to August 11 of 1938, over a disputed area at the borders of Manchuria, the Soviet Union, and Korea.[94]

Leading up to the conflict were a series of skirmishes in early July. Several key cabinet members were against escalation, initially including the army minister and the navy minister. Stretched thin by the Chinese conflict, they feared that Japan could not fight a second war and instead wished to focus their efforts on wrapping up the Chinese campaign.[95] The navy minister had another reason to oppose a ground war against the USSR: such a war would privilege the army's budgetary needs over those of the navy.[96]

In a familiar refrain, the leadership of the Kwantung Army and the Army General Staff both supported a military solution. The General Staff had become increasingly fixated on the Soviet threat and had come to oppose the war in China because it drained resources they felt should be used in a buildup against the Soviets. A war with Russia, they believed, would lead to withdrawal from China and a renewed focus on the main enemy, the Soviet Union.[97]

The cabinet's first response was to try to settle the situation diplomatically and avoid escalation. This led to several weeks of attempted negotiation with the Soviets.[98] However, opinion within the upper echelon of the army was moving in favor of a military approach. The High Command decided that Changkufeng's hills would provide a convenient perch from which to view the area, and that it might be worth using force in order to secure it. The broader diplomatic and strategic implications of seizing these hills appeared to play little role in these calculations.

The idea of a "one-shot attack"—a quick and sudden strike—soon gained popularity in the General Staff. Victory would be swift, they thought, because the Russians would not retaliate with a large offensive.[99] Other ideas, including a "reconnaissance by force" mission in which the Japanese Army used the conflict at Changkufeng in order to scope out Russian capabilities and determination, were also gaining traction.[100] With the blessing of the High Command, serious Japanese scouting missions began in mid-July.[101]

Meanwhile, in Tokyo, the cabinet was holding firm to its policy of nonescalation and negotiation. On July 29, however, large-scale fighting erupted at the border.[102] Lieutenant General Suetaka Kamezo decided to strike without an order from Imperial Headquarters, believing that the opportunity would be lost if he waited for permission from Tokyo. The next day, the 19th Division began a major offensive, still without Tokyo's approval.[103] The war had begun.

On July 31, news of the attack reached Tokyo.[104] The next day, War Minister Itagaki went before the emperor, who had little choice but to approve the *fait accompli*, but still insisted on nonenlargement.[105] It soon became apparent Japan would need considerably more troops and resources in order to win. Unwilling to divert men and materiel from China, the Japanese decided to make peace. The agreement reached on August 10 stipulated that both sides would withdraw to their positions as of July 30.[106] A ceasefire took effect at noon on August 11. During the brief conflict, 20,000 Soviet troops and somewhere between 10,000 and 20,000 Japanese soldiers were deployed, with between 900 and 1,200 Japanese soldiers wounded or killed.[107]

The Changkufeng Incident is yet another example of the Japanese military initiating hostilities against the wishes of the civilian government. Again, a combination of sincere and self-serving beliefs of military officers, who believed that Japan faced serious threats that could only be countered by military force, led to war. There is no evidence that this war was a diversionary maneuver or a "gamble for resurrection" of the type suggested by some theorists.

The Nomonhan Incident (1939)

While the lack of success at Changkufeng chastened the Army General Staff, it had just the opposite effect on officers of the Kwantung Army.[108] Almost incredibly, despite the failure of its past policies, the Kwantung Army once again took matters into its own hands. In April 1939, the Kwantung leadership produced a document entitled "General Principles in Dealing with the Manchukuoan-Soviet Border Disputes," giving soldiers in the field the authority to decide the location of borders without consulting their superiors and then to defend the borders as they had determined them.[109] The guideline "amounted to a type of *carte blanche* authority whereby local Japanese military commanders could arbitrarily decide undefined or ill-defined boundaries, and higher headquarters were supposed to back them to the hilt."[110]

In mid-May 1939, Japanese soldiers saw Mongolians crossing the unclear border between Mongolia and Manchuria near the village of Nomonhan. The April directive emboldened them to attack the trespassers. The mutual assistance pact between the USSR and Mongolia ensured that the Soviets were quickly drawn into the conflict.[111] Skirmishes continued throughout the rest of May, with Japan losing most of them.[112] At the end of the month, the civilian government commanded officers in the field to reach a quick local settlement rather than escalating further.

Predictably, the Kwantung Army ignored the order and continued to enlarge the conflict.[113] Central army authorities in Tokyo were split on how to respond, with the Army Ministry thinking the incident was a foolish distraction and the General Staff wanting to support its officers in the field. The latter position prevailed and the Kwantung Army's actions were approved.[114] By the end of June, the Kwantung Army telegrammed army authorities in Tokyo for permission for an airstrike. The request was denied, but commanders in the field went ahead anyway, moving up the date of the strike when they learned that the General Staff had dispatched an envoy to monitor conditions on the ground.[115] This action earned the Kwantung command a harsh rebuke by the General Staff, but both Japanese and Soviet forces reinforced themselves and the fighting continued.[116]

The Kwantung Army continued to press on through July and August. In late July, the Army Ministry called for the Kwantung Army to reach a settlement, even if it meant withdrawing from the disputed territory. By August, the now desperate Kwantung Army was planning another reckless offensive, but this attack was preempted on September 3 by an Imperial Order to cease and desist.[117] Japan and the Soviet Union reached a truce on September 15, and a ceasefire went into effect the next day.[118]

The conflict over Nomonhan left up to fifty thousand Japanese soldiers dead, wounded, or taken prisoner.[119] The political repercussions were significant. Two of the key figures responsible for the debacle, the chief of staff and the commander of the Kwantung Army, were forced into retirement, and many senior commanders and staff officers were transferred to the reserves or to training positions at army schools.[120] There were strategic ramifications as well. The war affirmed that the Soviet Union was a formidable opponent, and Japan's isolation deepened.[121] These factors increased the attractiveness of a pact with the Axis Powers, and opinion about whether to expand northward or southward converged on a southern path.[122]

As with the previous incidents, the clash at Nomonhan was the product of poor civilian control over a Kwantung Army that represented the extremes of "militaristic" thinking. "Decisive action was extolled; deliberation was equated with timidity. Positive, aggressive opinions generally triumphed. Planning was broad, sketchy, opportunistic, and undistracted by detail."[123] Political ramifications were also totally ignored. The Kwantung Army "was making foreign policy at gunpoint, and risking all-out war; it despised pacific solutions and 'weak-kneed' civilian diplomacy."[124] While central army authorities were more moderate than the commanders in the field, they were nonetheless more sympathetic to the Kwantung Army's militaristic thinking than the cowed civilian government.

Toward Pearl Harbor

Thus, by the end of the 1930s, the China War ground on, while military leaders grew ever more concerned about the Soviet threat to the north. The army now increasingly viewed an alliance with Germany as a path out of Japan' isolation.[125] By July of 1940, pro–Axis Alliance fever was at a high, both within the army and among the public, whose views were encouraged by army propagandists.[126] After Hitler's speedy conquests of France and Holland, Germany appeared invincible.[127] Army leaders

[126]

calculated that a German alliance would not only prevent U.S. interference in Japan's China conflict, it would also potentially clear the way for a campaign into resource-rich Southeast Asia.[128] As long as France and the Netherlands were occupied on the continent, their colonies were exposed, and a pact with Germany would position Japan to seize that opportunity.[129]

Unlike their counterparts in the army, some top navy officials were initially hesitant about a pact with Hitler, fearing that it would draw them into a war with the United States or Britain and endanger their imports of vital resources.[130] However, the pact was becoming increasingly popular among mid-level naval officers. One reason was that an alliance with Germany would facilitate the long-anticipated Southward Advance, allowing the navy to demand a large share of the military budget.[131] However, Navy Minister Zengo Yoshida and other senior naval officials remained opposed to the pact out of the desire to avoid war with the United States. Other officials thought chances of a war with the United States were slim.[132] Ultimately, the naval leadership relented.

Three days before the official inception of the second Konoe cabinet in July 1940, the incoming premier met with his ministers to discuss foreign policy.[133] The army had just flexed its political muscle, forcing the dissolution of the previous cabinet under Yonai by refusing to appoint a new war minister.[134] The meeting produced a policy draft that included provisions for a closer relationship with the Axis Powers. The document spoke of Japan's need for independence from the Western Powers and leadership of a Greater East Asia Co-Prosperity Sphere, a self-sufficient Asian economic bloc.[135]

The primary backer of this particular plan was the "enigmatic" and "quixotic" foreign minister Matsuoka Yosuke, a career civilian diplomat.[136] He believed that a balance of powers, which could be achieved through a pact with Germany, would actually allow for world peace by allowing the United States and Japan to interact "as equals," which would improve their relations and thus prevent war.[137] Matsuoka further believed that the millions of Americans with German and Italian ancestry would sway U.S. policy toward Japan if Japan allied with the Axis Powers.[138]

Intimidated by the military, the civilians did not have much choice. The cabinet endorsed Matsuoka's plan in principle in late July.[139] Most civilians, however, including Konoe and President of the Privy Council Hara Yoshimichi, questioned Matsuoka's predictions. At an Imperial Conference on September 19, 1940, Hara voiced concerns that the pact would lead the United States to pressure Japan economically and would have other negative consequences.[140] Matsuoka attempted to assuage Hara's fears, arguing that Japan would be able to obtain resources from

[127]

alternative sources and that the pact would prevent Japan's encirclement. At the end of the conference, Hara reluctantly approved an alliance with Germany on the emperor's behalf.[141]

The Tripartite Pact among Japan, Germany, and Italy was signed eight days later, on September 27, 1940.[142] The pact recognized each country's leadership in its respective sphere of influence, and required the signatories to come to each other's aid in the case of a new attack. Contrary to Matsuoka's predictions, however, the alliance with Germany further soured Japan's relationship with the United States and Britain.[143] It also raised tensions with Stalin after Hitler attacked the Soviet Union the following year.[144]

At the same time, Hitler's success in Europe created great temptations, as Germany's success had left exposed valuable colonies in Southeast Asia that possessed the oil, rubber, and other resources Japan needed. By September 1940, the military had advanced into French-controlled Indochina; with France defeated by Germany, France was in little position to protest.[145] By late 1940, the navy "was committed in principle to advancing south in the fall of 1941 and had begun mobilizing for war."[146] Opposed to any Japanese expansion into the region, the United States initially responded with export restrictions. At the end of July 1941, with Japan now moving into southern Indochina, the United States froze all Japanese assets, and on August 1, the freeze became a full-scale embargo, banning not only the export of oil but most other goods other than food.[147]

The military, however, refused to withdraw troops from China and the South Seas, viewing it as a capitulation to the Western Powers as well as dishonorable and disrespectful to the soldiers who had been fighting for four years. In one meeting between Konoe and General Tojo, the latter "exploded" when the prime minister suggested that Japan should placate the United States by discussing a withdrawal of troops from China. Tojo angrily told Konoe that conceding to the United States would destroy any chance of victory in China and that troop withdrawal would threaten Japan's interests in Manchukuo and Korea.[148]

Japan's resource shortage continued to loom large. Japan imported approximately 90 percent of its oil, with somewhere between 70 and 85 percent coming from the United States.[149] With the U.S. embargo, Japan had no other viable option for oil.[150] The price of oil had spiked because of demand in the European War, and Japan's weak shipping infrastructure further decreased the attractiveness of purchasing oil from abroad.[151] Japanese leaders knew that the country's oil supply was nearly depleted. In August, separate reports from the army and the navy concluded that with the American embargo in place, Japan would run out of oil in two years.[152]

The embargo convinced military leaders that the time for war had arrived. They reasoned that with Japan's ability to fight reduced every

[128]

passing day, it would be better to start a war immediately than to wait until talks had failed.[153] According to Butow, the training of the military leaders contributed to the belief that a decision needed to be made quickly: "Military men, whose training emphasizes the value of decisive action, seem by nature to become impatient when confronted by the slowness which frequently characterizes the progress of diplomatic and political affairs. In the circumstances of the late summer and early autumn of 1941, the time factor, from a military point of view, was becoming ever more compelling" (1961, 243). Maxon in turn argues that the "military mind" predisposed Japan's military leadership to focus on military rather than diplomatic solutions:

> To a [military] mind so conditioned to orderliness and certainty it is understandable that politics in a modern democratic state will sometimes appear to be a form of social disorder. . . . What more natural reaction for the military man than to retreat into the comfortable illusion that "the nation" is an entity that needs only to be unified, organized, and led in order to fulfill its highest potential; that its best defense is a good offense; that by sacrifice and warfare "victory" *can* be achieved; and that the proper coordinating and directing force for all this is the Military? This sort of logic predisposed the leaders of the Japanese armed services to an aggressive, military-directed [policy]. (1957, 30)

Some higher-level naval officials were, like civilian leaders, hesitant to begin a conflict, and resisted their subordinates for a time. Where the navy disagreed with the army, however, it appeared to be due to stark military realities rather than their reading of the broader strategic or diplomatic context. Globally, the United States dominated in every category of naval vessel, with an overall advantage in tonnage of 1.5 to 1.[154] Furthermore, it would have been nearly impossible for Japan to catch up through indigenous building, given America's vast superiority in production and factory workers. However, naval leaders were heartened when they attained parity in the Pacific by the fall of 1941.[155]

On August 27 and 28, bureau and section chiefs from the army and the navy met in an interservice conference to try to resolve the differences between the hawkish army and the more hesitant navy leaders. At the meeting, army officials advocated for beginning a war as soon as possible. Hoping to set a deadline for the conclusion of negotiations with the United States, they asked the navy the earliest date it would be ready to fight. Chief of the Naval Affairs Bureau Oka Takasumi at first refused, saying it was unwise to rush to war while the European situation was unclear. The army, unconvinced, continued to pressure Oka to give a deadline. Eventually he relented. The navy could be ready to fight by

[129]

November, but would need a decision by early October to allow for adequate preparation.[156]

Against this backdrop of interservice tensions, fervent prowar sentiment in much of the military, and growing panic, the Konoe government struggled to reach a solution. However, most important decisions were now made in "Liaison Conferences." The brainchild of mid-level officers in the General Staffs of the army and navy, the Liaison Conferences were often secret and informal, and they effectively placed control of policy into the hands of the military, with the cabinet able to approve decisions only after the fact.[157] According to Maxon, the problem with the Liaison Conferences was that "personnel and its secretariat were heavily weighted on the military side, and in the further fact that the General Staff sections, from which the service members of the conference received the draft plans on which they acted, were wholly military. Hence the practical effect of the Liaison Conference was to place the planning and initiation of foreign policy in the hands of officers whose experience and background, being exclusively military, had ill prepared them for the evaluation of complex nonmilitary factors in the international situation."[158] Butow also asserts that the decision-making power lay in the hands of "little-known but ever-meddling members of the nucleus group within the army and navy general staffs. Such was the nature of their infiltration of the decision-making process that [the prime minister] would not have been able to curtail their power even if he had felt inclined to do so."[159]

By the end of August, there was consensus among officers in the Army and Navy General Staffs, as well as at middle ranks of the officer corps in both service branches, that hostilities should start sooner rather than later. At the Liaison Conference of September 3, Army Chief Hajime Sugiyama argued for a deadline to end talks at the beginning of October.[160] He chose this date not for diplomatic reasons, but because it would take about a month to prepare for hostilities, and November was seen as the ideal time for landing operations in Southeast Asia.[161] Navy Chief of Staff Osami Nagano emphasized the increasing urgency of Japan's oil problem and argued that the military should be allowed to start war preparations while talks continued. If the deadline passed without an agreement, Japan would be ready to fight immediately. He also articulated classic military thinking about the advantages of a first strike: "Although I am confident that at the present time we have a chance to win a war, I fear that this opportunity will disappear with the passage of time. . . . In short, our armed forces have no alternative but to try to avoid being pushed into a corner, to keep in our hands the power to decide when to begin hostilities and thus seize the initiative. There is no alternative but to push forward in this way."[162] Navy Minister Koshirō Oikawa concurred. At the end of the Liaison Conference, the participants had agreed to begin war preparations during negotiations.[163]

On September 5, Prime Minister Konoe met with the emperor to secure his approval.[164] On September 6, a largely ceremonial Imperial Conference ratified the decision of the Liaison Conference.[165] Those present first discussed the major roadblock to an agreement with the United States: the Japanese presence in China and Indochina.[166] The conference turned next to the issue of a deadline for negotiations. Konoe stated that Japan "must try to prevent the disaster of war by resorting to all possible diplomatic measures."[167] Navy Chief of Staff Osami Nagano countered that "the Supreme Command believes, from the standpoint of operations, that [if we delay] we cannot avoid being finally reduced to a crippled condition. . . . Therefore, it must be said that it would be very dangerous for our Empire to remain idle and let the days go by."[168] Army Chief of Staff Hajime Sugiyama argued that Japan should not allow itself to be "trapped in the intrigues of Great Britain and the United States" and that waiting too long would doom Japan in a war against the ABCD (American, British, Chinese, and Dutch) powers.[169] The meeting ended with the emperor approving a deadline of mid-October to make a decision for war if there was no prospect for agreement at that time.[170]

Talks with Washington continued, but neither side was willing to budge on China, and the United States held the card of continuing the oil embargo. Meanwhile, in Japan, the government was in turmoil. Konoe was unable to break the deadlock. The army, and to a lesser extent the navy, remained convinced that talks were useless.[171] On October 12, Konoe called a meeting with War Minister Tojo, Naval Minister Oikawa, Foreign Minister Teijirō Toyoda, and President of the Planning Board Teiichi Suzuki. The navy, still not confident in a victory, apparently favored continuing talks. However, instead of voicing his concern, Oikawa said that it was up to the government to decide and that the navy would do what the government wanted.[172] Maxon attributes this at least in part to military culture: "Oikawa's decision highlights the difficulties that ensue when the bravado which is a natural and perhaps indispensable factor in the morale of a fighting unit influences high-level planning. It is in fact the strongest possible argument for the practice of having civilian heads for the fighting services."[173] The sort of bravado Maxon describes, however, was part of the cultural ideal of "dignity" or "prestige" of the military (*gun no ishin*), which had to be preserved at an extreme cost. By voicing doubts about his service's ability to fight, Oikawa would threaten *gun no ishin*. This concern was also one of the major reasons the Japanese were so stubborn about withdrawing troops from China at the behest of the United States.[174]

[131]

With the army advocating war and the navy remaining equivocal, Konoe (backed by Foreign Minister Toyoda) once again pleaded for diplomacy, saying "having compared both options, I for one choose diplomatic negotiations." He was unable to persuade the military leaders, who thought that negotiations "hold no promise whatsoever."[175] The September 6 Imperial Conference decision was left in place. A defeated Konoe resigned on October 16, 1941, writing "I believe we must not conclude that with more time there would still be no hope for success in negotiations with the United States. I . . . believe there is hope for compromise even now."[176]

He was replaced by General Tojo, ending the facade of civilian rule.[177] During the rest of October 1941, the Tojo cabinet abolished the October deadline and undertook a review of Japanese policy at the behest of the emperor.[178] By early November, an agreement with the United States remained elusive.[179] The Japanese refused to back down on China and Manchuria, arguing that surging prices on essential materials, caused by the war in Europe, made those territories essential to Japanese national security.[180] Tojo personally refused to leave China, because then the 150,000 casualties and 15 billion yen spent on the war would have been for naught.[181]

Another Liaison Conference was called for November 1. Of the twelve men present, only three were civilians.[182] The participants debated whether to hold out for diplomacy as supplies dwindled, to commence hostilities immediately, or to prepare for war while talks continued.[183] Representatives of the army and the navy stressed that oil was running out but were also concerned about Japan's chances in the face of American naval and production superiority.[184] The Army General Staff, led by Sugiyama, argued passionately that Japan needed to set a deadline and prepare for war.[185] At one point, Sugiyama admonished Tojo for siding too much with the civilians.[186]

Toward the end of the meeting, everyone had agreed on setting a deadline and preparing for war except for two civilians: Foreign Minister Togo and Finance Minister Okinori Kaya. Throughout the conference, Togo and Kaya engaged in heated debates with the other participants, questioning the wisdom of initiating a war against the United States on the grounds that war was inevitable and arguing for more time to arrive at a diplomatic solution.[187] However, Army Vice Chief of Staff Tsukada Osamu would not hear of delaying, retorting that "diplomacy must not obstruct military operations. The deadline will not be changed in the light of diplomatic developments."[188] Kaya and Togo asked for a day to think over the decision, but by the end of the meeting they had relented—reluctantly, and out of fear that if they continued to oppose the war, the cabinet would be dissolved and the new cabinet would be even more powerless in the face of military pressure.[189] The final resolution was to set a December 1 deadline for talks with the United States, after which Japan would attack if no agreement had been reached.[190] The emperor approved the decision on November 5.[191]

As the cutoff of December 1 approached, it became clear that the United States would not change its mind on Japanese troops in China. With the Hull Note of November 26 sealing this perception of the American position, another Liaison Conference convened on November 27–29, again with primarily military officers present. The conference agreed, unanimously, to begin a war.[192] On November 29, the emperor gathered together eight former prime ministers to hear their general views on a war against the United States (they had been told nothing specific about Japan's war plans).[193] Of the eight former Japanese premiers present, five explicitly expressed "doubt or caution" about war, and the only one who supported military action said that "as he had no data for his opinion, he could do nothing but believe the decisions of Imperial Headquarters and the Government."[194] On December 1, 1941, another Imperial Conference was held to ratify the decision officially.[195] On December 7, the Japanese navy attacked the U.S. naval base at Pearl Harbor. The following day, the United States declared war on Japan.

In sum, throughout nearly the entire period under study, military officers (particularly in the army but also in the navy) were substantially more enthusiastic about war than their civilian counterparts. Why? Little suggests that war was the product of diversionary motives on the part of a domestically embattled government. Instead, there is ample evidence that a major contributing factor was the specific beliefs held by military officers. Japanese military officers appeared to share the view that Japan faced grave threats—from the United States, from the Soviet Union, and from resource shortages. They believed that Japan was backed into a corner by "ABCD encirclement" and war with the United States was inevitable. Military officers had deep faith in the benefits of preemption and first strikes, which clearly motivated the attack on Pearl Harbor.[196] They repeatedly expressed serious doubts about the efficacy of diplomacy, instead allowing military timetables to dictate the timing of diplomacy. Parochial interests sustained these beliefs and provided a motivation of their own; leaders of both the army and navy were clearly aware that militaristic policies would result in budgetary expansion.

Civilians, in contrast, repeatedly questioned the military's assumptions, even in an environment in which a coup always loomed. In the 1930s, the civilian government repeatedly tried to stop the military from its adventures, only authorizing force when the military had already charged ahead. In 1941, civilians begged for more time to let diplomacy run its course, and were much more skeptical that the United States would attack Japan even in the face of Japanese expansion into Asia. This is not to say that Japanese civilian interests, and society at large, played no role in Japan's path. As many have pointed out, a nationalistic public fell eagerly in line behind the military. Emperor Hirohito facilitated the military's rise to power by yielding at key junctures.[197] Civilian politicians did not stand up to the military (though often out of a not-unreasonable fear of a coup or assassination), and indeed at times supported specific policies.[198] But as Snyder points out, the role of civilians was peripheral.[199] Their fault lay in failing to stay the hand of the military, not in dragging Japan into a confrontation with the United States that was far from inevitable.[200]

[6]

Machines: Looking Before They Leap

The previous two chapters focused on personalist regimes and juntas, showing how domestic politics can push those regimes toward fighting wars that other countries would have tried to avoid. However, not all authoritarian regimes are so quick to pick up arms. This chapter turns to two nonpersonalist, civilian-led machines—North Vietnam and the post-Stalin Soviet Union—exploring in detail how their domestic politics produced both restraint and success in the use of force. These two cases reveal that leaders of machines have strong incentives to heed the preferences of their elite audiences. Like their democratic counterparts, they therefore tend to ensure that key domestic actors support their policy decisions before turning to force. Compared to both personalist leaders and military elites, the civilians who influence policy in machines are equipped with a broader range of experiences and policy options and do not instinctively prioritize military solutions over diplomatic ones. The result is that machines tend to be more selective in their use of military force than other authoritarian regimes, although when they do choose war, they can be formidable opponents.

Focusing on a small number of cases, of course, involves tradeoffs. The previous two chapters opted for selecting cases that fit the hypothesized patterns—personalists and juntas with high rates of conflict initiation. This permitted us to verify whether the processes by which those leaders chose war fit the theoretical arguments. To explore how and why machines are restrained, however, is somewhat more challenging. Military conflict is a relatively rare event; a country whose foreign policy matched the argument would therefore be one that fought few wars or even engaged in few lower-level disputes. The problem, though, is that it is difficult to find historical data about "dogs that did not bark," particularly in closed governments where scholars must carefully sift fact from propaganda. Historians tend not to write books about non-events, particularly in dictatorships.

An alternative, which I adopt here, is to focus on machines that did choose war and study how domestic politics shaped those decisions. But this raises a different challenge: By choosing cases in which leaders initiated war, we highlight situations in which the leader ultimately decided that war was wise. These are, by definition, decisions where the hawks won the day. If domestic politics induce leaders of machines to fight mainly popular and uncontroversial wars, domestic debate and consensus-seeking endeavors could appear muted. Thus, by looking primarily at cases in which leaders opted for war, we stack the deck against finding evidence of prudence and contemplation even in elite-constrained civilian dictatorships. The cases in this chapter therefore provide a harder test of the argument that machines are more likely to avoid risky gambles than personalists, are less likely to have uniformly hawkish views represented in the domestic audience than juntas, tend to seek consensus before initiating a conflict, and can expect punishment when things do go poorly.

From among the relatively small set of machines that fought wars, I selected one case for intensive study—North Vietnam—and one for a briefer investigation—the USSR after Stalin. Studying North Vietnam provides a fascinating opportunity to examine a series of decisions to escalate the war in South Vietnam. Revisiting the USSR, which I considered briefly in the chapter on personalist bosses, allows examination of how Soviet decisions about war and peace changed after Stalin died, when leaders faced greater domestic political constraints.

The North Vietnamese Wars against the United States, South Vietnam, and Cambodia

In 1975, communist forces in Vietnam finally achieved the goal that their leaders had been pursuing for three decades: unification of the country under one government. This was a remarkable achievement by any standard, but particularly for an impoverished nation that had been ruled by external powers for much of its recent history. Vietnam threw off colonialism, built a socialist economy, and drove out a superpower.

These feats, however, required nearly thirty years of armed struggle, including the conflict against South Vietnam and the United States and the war against Cambodia that toppled Pol Pot. Observers at the time often characterized the regime as "dictatorial," "fanatical," "obsessed," and "irrational"—hardly the image of the restrained machine portrayed in this book. But a closer look shows that this stereotypical rendering is inaccurate. Despite Vietnam's resort to arms, its civilian, collective internal structure produced a pattern of restraint and selectivity that greatly contributed to its ultimate victories.

I begin by describing the North Vietnamese regime: an authoritarian "machine" in which the paramount leader was accountable to an elite audience composed mainly of civilians. The discussion then proceeds chronologically, showing that at every major decision point, North Vietnamese leaders (Le Duan, for most of the period under examination) consulted with powerful Politburo and Central Committee members, military commanders in the field, and even the party rank and file. While not democratic, North Vietnam featured a system of accountability in which the leader could not stay in power without prudent and consistent performance in matters of foreign policy.

Civilian Collective Leadership in the DRV

The government of North Vietnam (Democratic Republic of Vietnam, or DRV) provides a clear example of a civilian, nonpersonalist authoritarian regime. Ordinary citizens were excluded from policymaking, but political decision-making at high levels of the regime apparatus was shared among elites. The regime is often characterized as a "bureaucratic socialist system" in which "the determination of major policies [and] the power over the selection of political and governmental leadership is confined to a small group of party officials."[1] The most influential body in the regime was the Politburo, which had authority over top policy measures.[2] Unlike personalistic regimes such as those under Saddam Hussein or Stalin, the collective will of the high-ranking officials of the Politburo mattered more than the personal will of the leader. Neither Ho Chi Minh nor his successor Le Duan had anything like the latitude afforded to their personalistic counterparts. Instead, in North Vietnam, Ho Chi Minh and Le Duan were in a very real sense "first among equals."[3] They did not enjoy untrammeled control over internal and external security forces, nor did they have the ability to cow potential rivals into silence. Promotion within the regime was based not solely on personal ties to the leader but also on merit, seniority, political views, and nonpersonalistic factional ties. As Porter has put it, "Le Duan never had the kind of political power that allowed him to purge members arbitrarily and to stack the Central Committee with personal supporters."[4] As a consequence, debate was relatively open, and top party members often switched factions and policy positions.[5] As the analysis of North Vietnamese decisions will show, the decision to escalate the conflict against South Vietnam and the United States to the point of war had a genuinely collective nature—if only among the elite.

Another important characteristic of the regime—and one that distinguishes it from juntas—was the civilian nature of its top decision-makers. The party's statutes put the Vietnamese People's Army (VPA) "under the party's absolute, direct, comprehensive leadership"; while top generals from the VPA were influential in the regime, their influence was "clearly circumscribed."[6]

War with the French and the Geneva Accords

By the mid-1950s, the Vietnamese had already undergone more than a decade of military and political struggle against foreign powers, particularly France, its former colonizer, and Japan, which had occupied Vietnam during World War II. On September 2, 1945, Ho Chi Minh, the leader of the communist-leaning Viet Minh, declared Vietnamese independence. Despite "poignant cables and letters to President Truman," the United States and other Western powers supported the French position: France should reclaim its former colony.[7] In the spring of 1950, the United States recognized the French-installed regime under former emperor Bao Dai and announced financial support for the French military effort.[8]

The highly motivated Vietnamese, however, defeated the French in 1954 at the battle of Dien Bien Phu.[9] The United States, France, and fellow great powers Britain, the USSR, and China agreed to a conference in Geneva to partition Vietnam. The 1954 Geneva Conference formally ended the war and divided Vietnam at the 17th parallel, with the Viet Minh leading the North and the French-backed regime leading the South. The partition was supposed to be temporary, with elections to reunite the country scheduled for 1956.[10] The Northern leadership took a dim view of the negotiations at Geneva, but Ho Chi Minh and other leaders apparently believed that if they did not accept the compromise, U.S. intervention might ensue.[11]

Prime Minister Ngo Dinh Diem, a Catholic Vietnamese and staunch anticommunist who the United States believed could strengthen democratic forces in the South, led South Vietnam's new government. Diem refused to sign the Geneva agreement, arguing that he was not subject to its provisions as it had been negotiated by the French high command rather than the South Vietnamese government. From there, Diem revealed himself as something of a "Frankenstein's monster" rather than Washington's obedient agent of democratization.[12] He used harsh tactics that stoked opposition among all major sectors of the Southern population, forcibly redistributing land, replacing village leaders with his own appointees, censoring the press, and cracking down on political opponents. Life under Diem was particularly hazardous for communists and nationalists, many of whom remained in the South.[13] In 1955 Diem introduced a "denounce the Communists campaign"; supporters of the communist movement, meanwhile, were under strict instructions to avoid violence and instead to focus on legal and nonviolent activities such as promoting elections.[14] By 1956, it was clear that elections to re-unify Vietnam were not going to take place.

The question for the North Vietnamese government, whose goal remained reunification, was what strategy would best achieve that goal. There were a few competing viewpoints. The dominant view at the time was to continue focusing on political rather than military strategies, even though Hanoi ultimately doubted that Diem and his backers would permit peaceful reunification.[15] But sticking with a political approach appeared to be the best option for the time being. The Southern revolutionary forces were weak, the North needed to focus on implementing communist policies and rebuilding its economy, and there was value in presenting North Vietnam as the wronged party.[16] Indeed, at this point, North Vietnam sought to comply with the Geneva Accords and to make sure that its observance of the agreement was noticed.[17] Both of Hanoi's main international patrons, the USSR under Nikita Khrushchev and China under Mao Zedong, also supported a peaceful political approach at that time.[18]

The most prominent advocate of the more militant approach was the future leader Le Duan, at that time party secretary of the Nam Bo Regional Committee, which was in charge of coordinating and implementing Northern policy toward the revolutionary struggle in the South.[19] In 1956, Le Duan authored a fourteen-point plan (*The Path of Revolution in the South*) for uniting the North and South under communist leadership. Le Duan's proposal called for supporting the South Vietnamese revolutionary forces by creating support bases, consolidating and expanding military organizations, and increasing funding for activities in Cambodia.[20]

Consistent with the collective nature of decision-making in the regime, the question of whether to focus on a more political or military strategy was debated vigorously within the party in a series of Central Committee plenaries in 1956. At the Ninth Plenum in March 1956, the Hanoi leadership met to consider some of the key points of Le Duan's plan but decided to continue focusing on the political approach for the reasons laid out above.[21] In June, the Politburo authorized the use of force in some limited cases of self-defense.[22] The Tenth Plenum of October 1956 witnessed continuing controversy within the party over the appropriate strategy for reunification.[23]

The likelihood of implementing Le Duan's plan improved somewhat in December 1956, when his pamphlet was discussed at the Eleventh Plenum and some of its core tenets were adopted.[24] Le Duan's three-part strategy was to consolidate the North (including political and economic reforms), to continue to support the revolutionary and reunification struggle in the South, and to gain international support for reunification.[25] However, at this stage the focus was still on relatively peaceful modes of pursuing the Southern cause; the plan did propose a more aggressive approach to the revolution in the South, but it did not mark "a major shift toward a more military approach" or authorize armed action other than in self-defense.[26]

Soon after the Central Committee plenary session, Le Duan and Nguyen Van Linh chaired a conference of the Nam Bo Regional Committee. Southern communist militias were pressing the North to support their struggle against the Diem regime. They criticized the Northern government's timid stance on Diem's repressive actions and refusal to hold elections in 1956; some Southerners took up arms against Diem on their own initiative.[27] But despite pleas from the Southern communists, Hanoi stood firm. The Nam Bo conference agreed that Southern forces could organize secret self-defense and armed propaganda forces, but consistent with the policies just discussed in Hanoi, it did not authorize the use of guerrilla warfare.[28] The party would continue to concentrate on the Northern economy while building up and modernizing the capabilities of the People's Army of North Vietnam (PAVN).

Meanwhile, Le Duan's fortunes were on the rise. Soon after the plenary session and the Nam Bo follow-up, he was chosen to aid Ho Chi Minh in running the party and assumed the position of acting secretary general.[29] According to Nguyen, Le Duan was specifically selected because he would not challenge Ho's precedent of sharing power: "The old guard—including Ho, Giap, Pham Van Dong, and the recently demoted Truong Chinh—wanted to promote a new acting head who would respect and practice the Vietnamese communist leadership's long-held tradition of collective decision-making. Le Duan, who remained far from the troubles in the North and who appeared to lack a strong base of power within the party, appeared the ideal candidate."[30]

The debate over strategy continued through 1957 and 1958 in yet more meetings and Central Committee plenaries. The Twelfth Plenum in March 1957 approved a plan to modernize the military by 1959 but also cautioned against overly hasty changes.[31] At the Thirteenth Plenum in December 1957, Ho argued that consolidating socialism in the North was a necessary foundation for reunification, indicating that he did not want the Southern struggle to eclipse efforts in the North.[32] In March 1958, the Central Military Committee (CMC) developed new military plans to delay the completion of modernization until 1960, bringing them into line with the most recent economic plans and funneling more troops toward economic reconstruction. These meetings indicated that "up until

March 1958 a military campaign for reunification was still not in the cards and was not imminent till at least after 1960."[33]

A More Militant Turn: 1959

Meanwhile, Diem's anticommunist activities had continued unabated. Brutal repression and forced resettlements stoked resistance to the Diem regime, and the communists in the South continued to implore Hanoi for permission to fight back. By the summer of 1958, the Southern Vietnamese were already starting to take matters into their own hands.

Until this point, Hanoi had forbidden Southerners from using violence in their struggle except in limited cases of self-defense.[34] However, the Fifteenth Plenum of the Central Committee held in January 1959 proved to be an important milestone in the shift from a primarily political approach to a "revolutionary" approach that incorporated the possibility of violence other than in self-defense.[35] The enlarged meeting was chaired by Ho Chi Minh and included representatives from the Nam Bo Regional Committee and party committees from the provinces in central Vietnam. Representatives from the South once again begged the Central Committee to protect the Southern revolutionary movement against Diem's measures.[36]

Heeding the Southerners' appeals, the Central Committee passed a resolution calling for South Vietnam to be liberated and for the socialist revolution to be completed. The meeting anticipated a difficult, protracted struggle. It declared that mass uprisings would be required to attain these goals and that military force should play only a secondary role.[37] Either way, the North would support the struggle against South Vietnam's government more actively; Le Duan's *The Path of Revolution in the South*, written and only partially accepted in 1956, was finally accepted in full. Details of how exactly the revolution would be achieved were not fleshed out until a meeting in May, before which the resolution went through several drafts.[38] Nonetheless, several preparatory steps followed. The VPA increased activities relevant to the South, and the CMC met to discuss how to speed up the creation of base areas and revolutionary forces in the South.[39] The focus, however, remained on using Southern forces, not the VPA, and the ultimate Central Committee decision (Resolution 15) still did not specifically authorize force other than in self-defense.[40]

Meanwhile in the South, Diem's infamous Law 10/59 represented a new peak in his brutality, authorizing the death penalty for a wide range of political activities. Mobile military courts would now roam the countryside, intimidating peasants and executing suspected communists with a guillotine they often brought along for that very purpose.[41] The

10/59 law set off a chain of responses. The CMC started plans for what would ultimately become the "Ho Chi Minh Trail" linking the North and South, and in 1960, Southern communists staged mass revolts and attacked large South Vietnamese army units for the first time. Despite these developments, the leadership acted with "extreme caution" and hesitated to intensify the military struggle before the time was right to overthrow the Diem regime.[42]

In September 1960, the Third Party Congress decided to step up the modernization of the VPA. Le Duan presented a relatively moderate view to the 576 assembled cadres. He argued that revolution would take time and that the strategies would evolve with the circumstances, but he did not mention any direct involvement from the North. Again consistent with the fact that debate within the elite was permissible, there is evidence of some disagreement within the party at the Congress. Minister of Defense Vo Nguyen Giap obliquely critiqued some within the party, whereas Truong Chinh supported the Russian stance on "peaceful coexistence."[43] Either way, the view—associated with Le Duan—that more forceful measures were on the horizon prevailed. Although some who disagreed with this view were apparently criticized as "revisionists" and "opponents of the party," no major changes took place within high levels of government, and those who opposed the shift in strategy continued to be able to voice their views.[44] The Party leadership also felt the need to explain and justify its policy to the lower-level cadres.[45] The strategy remained a relatively moderate one, with great care being taken not to provoke the United States to intervene or to escalate the conflict into a fully-fledged war.

Shortly after the Third Party Congress, the communists were boosted at a November 1960 international communist conference in Moscow when the Soviets moved closer to the Chinese position and articulated their support for national liberation movements.[46] In December, Hanoi continued its effort to organize the resistance in the South by creating the National Liberation Front (NLF). The NLF included considerable noncommunist membership and leadership, and most of the initial fighting forces were indigenous Southerners motivated by Diem's continued repression, though the North played an important organizational role and directed much of NLF policy.[47] At the Third Plenum of the new Central Committee in January 1961, the party started planning in earnest for an armed struggle.[48]

What drove Hanoi's shift toward a more militarized strategy? Far from being the product of a reckless or unconstrained leadership, the decision was born of intense debate in which a majority of the communist leadership—spurred by exhortations from Southern communists—concluded that Vietnam would be able to free itself from foreign interference only by combining political and military strategies. As a Vietnamese official put it in 1997, "Objectively speaking, Vietnam could not choose whether or not to fight a war. I mean, Vietnam had no choice, to fight or not to fight, unless it was willing to give up its desires for national independence and accepted, instead, the status of an enslaved country."[49]

Most Western research shares this interpretation. Duiker argues that the Vietnamese strategy was the product of circumstance and careful calculation rather than aggression or disregard for the costs of war: "Did Hanoi, as some claim, deliberately set out to destroy the Saigon regime by force? The evidence here suggests that this was not the case. Party strategy had originally hoped that reunification could take place by peaceful, or at least quasi-peaceful means. Only with reluctance was Hanoi compelled to reassess the situation."[50] Writing of Hanoi's general reticence to accept a settlement, not only in the early periods of the conflict but later as well, Pike similarly concludes that "Hanoi's refusal to accept a political settlement was not the result of rigid unreasonable stubbornness in the Vietnamese character or some fanatic intransigence. It was simply a product of Hanoi's objective—unification."[51]

The Death of Diem

In 1962 Hanoi undertook a brief respite from escalation in the form of a "Neutrality Offensive" in which it tried to pursue negotiations. The proposals, which envisioned a "neutral" South Vietnam, were crafted with the hope of giving the United States a face-saving way out of the conflict that would avoid war.[52] The negotiations came to nothing, and during 1962 and early 1963 the conflict escalated gradually. Hanoi was building up the People's Liberation Armed Forces (the PLAF, the armed wing of the NLF); the Diem regime embarked on an ambitious program of "strategic hamlets" to secure villages against insurgent infiltration; and U.S. President John F. Kennedy had sent several hundred aircraft and thousands more military advisers to South Vietnam by the end of 1962. In early 1963, PLAF forces attacked and defeated a South Vietnamese (ARVN) army garrison at Ap Bac. This marked one of the first times that the PLAF had gone on the offensive; the communist defeat of the much more numerous and better-equipped ARVN soldiers provided an important psychological victory.

The other major development during these two years was a rising tide of South Vietnamese resentment against the oppressive Diem regime. Tensions reached a climax in May of 1963 when Diem's brother Ngo Dinh Nhu sent his special ARVN forces to the ancient city of Hue to force Buddhists to take down their flag in a march on a Buddhist holy day. Ngo's use of violence sparked riots in Saigon, which in turn provoked a brutal reaction by Diem. The situation peaked when a Buddhist monk set himself ablaze in downtown Saigon, with more monks following suit in the coming months. Ngo's wife, South Vietnam's unofficial first lady, exemplified the regime's attitude by referring to the protests as "barbecues" and telling reporters, "Let them burn, and we shall all clap our hands."[53] These events not only deepened the rift between the United States and the Diem regime but ultimately led to the end of the Diem brothers as well. In November 1963, ARVN generals, with (at a minimum) tacit American approval, assassinated them both. General Van Minh led the Revolutionary Council that now ruled South Vietnam.

Hanoi struggled with how to respond to this unexpected toppling of the hated Diem regime. On the one hand, the crisis might provide an opportunity to consolidate communist progress if Hanoi could negotiate with the new South Vietnamese regime from a position of relative strength. On the other hand, North Vietnamese leaders viewed Diem's assassination with unease because they thought it increased the probability that the Americans would intervene in even greater strength than before.[54]

These matters were discussed at a "stormy" Ninth Plenum in November and December 1963 in which the party elite engaged in lengthy debates over the correct strategy.[55] While it appears that they agreed that the immediate task was to prevail in the anticommunist "special war," they disagreed over broader strategic questions.[56] The first point of contention was whether to escalate military activities or to retain more of a balance between military and political activities. The Central Committee also disagreed over whether or not to send regular troops or to stick with the PLAF forces. Those who opposed sending regular Northern units feared it would provoke the United States and give it a pretext for further intervention, while those who supported using official Northern forces thought that escalating quickly might either deter further U.S. intervention or result in victory before the United States had time to gather itself.[57] The Committee also paid careful attention to the international diplomatic situation, especially the growing rift between the USSR and China. Although the Soviets had recently voiced some support for national liberation struggles, the Soviet strategy still focused on peaceful coexistence, while the Chinese supported more vigorous armed measures.[58]

These disagreements over strategy led to a division between the "North Firsters" and "South Firsters." The "North Firsters," led by respected general Vo Nguyen Giap and former party secretary Truong Chinh, advocated a somewhat more dovish approach that emphasized political struggle in the South and economic development in the North and more closely resembled Moscow's view. The "South Firsters," led by Le Duan, Chen Nguyen Thi Thanh (commander of forces in South Vietnam), and

Le Duc Tho (party organizational secretary) supported a more hawkish approach closer to the Chinese position. Many in this camp were themselves of Southern origin and advocated a rapid escalation.

Ultimately, less than half of the Central Committee supported the more dovish line, and the Ninth Plenary Session decided to further escalate the war.[59] The escalation included sending men and material down the Ho Chi Minh trail and devoting greater Northern economic resources to the war effort. Some scholars have wondered at the excessive optimism inherent in Hanoi's belief that escalation would encourage the United States to extricate itself given that sixteen thousand advisers were already in South Vietnam. As Duiker puts it, "To many observers, Hanoi's decision to escalate was somewhat of a puzzle. Given the risk of U.S. intervention and the progressive disintegration of the RVN, why did the Party feel compelled to take the gamble?"[60] The answer appears to be twofold. First, the North Vietnamese hoped that communist progress in the South would lead the United States to disengage. Second, their experience against the French indicated that war was inevitable; only military force would persuade foreign powers to leave Indochina.[61] The disorientation in South Vietnam might therefore provide a window of opportunity to achieve victory before the United States undertook its inevitable intervention.[62]

Most historians agree that the differences were hammered out in a peaceful and relatively open elite-level debate in which a majority of the Central Committee sided with the South-first approach out of a combination of genuine belief that this was the superior strategy[63] and concern about being labeled a "revisionist."[64] A smaller number of Vietnam scholars have framed the events surrounding the Ninth Plenum in a more ominous light, including Nguyen (2012), who argues that Le Duan and his supporters used "threats and blackmail," not persuasion, to silence critics of escalation.[65] There is some evidence that several months *after* the Ninth Plenum, the DRV military security forces investigated and put under house arrest certain cadres who were deemed "Pro-Soviet."[66] But these investigations, which occurred months after the Ninth Plenum, were aimed at mid-level cadres, and did not target any of the many party elites who had spoken out against escalation. If anything, the evidence highlights the fact that many party officials felt free to express their skepticism of escalation.[67]

1964–1965: The Gulf of Tonkin Incident and Operation Rolling Thunder

Unfortunately for the North Vietnamese, escalation failed to deter the United States: While the insurgency made some inroads and South

Vietnam seemed unable to maintain a stable government, the United States continued to step up its military involvement. The situation came to a head on August 2, 1964, when the U.S. destroyer *Maddox* became involved in a skirmish with three North Vietnamese torpedo boats, sinking one and damaging two. From the North Vietnamese perspective, the *Maddox* had trespassed several miles inside its territorial waters (though the United States did not recognize that boundary). Moreover, the incursion came directly on the heels of attacks by South Vietnamese naval vessels on North Vietnamese islands on July 30 and 31. To the local North Vietnamese commander, this timing indicated that the two events were coordinated, and he ordered an attack on the *Maddox*, possibly without consulting Hanoi first.[68] The matter escalated on August 4, when the *Maddox* and another American destroyer radioed that they were under attack in international waters by North Vietnamese torpedo boats. While later evidence established that, as the Vietnamese had always claimed, the alleged attacks of August 4 never took place, President Lyndon B. Johnson did not wait for the incident to be verified and ordered retaliatory air strikes within hours.[69] Later that night, he declared to the American public that "the determination of all Americans to carry out our full commitment to the people and to the government of South Vietnam will be redoubled by this outrage." Less than two hours later, American planes were dropping bombs on North Vietnamese territory, and on August 7 Congress passed the Gulf of Tonkin Resolution authorizing the president "to take all necessary steps, including the use of armed force, to assist any member or protocol state of the Southeast Asia Collective Defense Treaty requesting assistance in defense of its freedom."

To many in the North Vietnamese leadership, it seemed clear that the United States had fabricated claims of the August 4 incident as a pretext to attack North Vietnam directly. This greatly strengthened the hand of the "pro-escalation" camp, as it was now even more difficult to argue that a slower, more peaceful strategy would reap dividends, given American eagerness to intervene.[70] A week after the incident, Party leaders called a special session of the Central Committee to discuss the implications of the incident and how to respond. Fearing that the U.S. bombing indicated that the United States intended to send in combat troops, the leadership concluded that they would need to take steps to send regular DRV forces to the South.[71] The event also helped solidify Chinese support and led to an improvement in relations with the Soviets, who were forced to reassess their position as well.[72]

The Politburo convened in late September to discuss the situation further. Its members did not want to give the Americans any pretext to escalate from a limited "special war" to a larger-scale war that might implicate North Vietnamese territory and disrupt efforts to rebuild the Northern economy. But they had reason to believe that U.S. intervention was inevitable and that if they did not take some action to consolidate communist progress, they would be in a worse position when that day eventually came.[73] There was also reason to fear that appearing to back down to the United States would hurt morale in the South and embolden the Americans. Hanoi therefore finally started preparations to send regular PAVN units to the South and instructed the Southern communists to step up their efforts.[74]

These instructions resulted in a series of attacks by the PLAF—the Viet Cong, not regular Northern Forces—throughout the fall and winter. This included attacks on a U.S. airbase at Bien Hoa, on a South Vietnamese battalion in predominately Catholic Binh Gia near Saigon, and perhaps most dramatically, on U.S. bases at Pleiku, Camp Holloway and Qui Nhon; more than thirty U.S. soldiers were killed in all.[75] The Pleiku and Camp Holloway attacks coincided with U.S. National Security Advisor McGeorge Bundy's visit to Saigon, and the Americans therefore interpreted them as a deliberate signal that Hanoi wished to escalate the war. The Vietnamese, however, contend that the Pleiku and Camp Holloway attacks were ordered by local commanders who had not communicated with Hanoi, which was completely unaware of Bundy's presence in Saigon.[76]

Convinced of the meaning behind Pleiku and Camp Holloway, Johnson ordered the bombing of North Vietnam, first operation "Flaming Dart I" and then operation "Rolling Thunder," which had the goal of crippling the North Vietnamese economy and making it more difficult to transport troops and supplies from the North to the South. Soon after, Johnson sent two Marine battalions to South Vietnam, marking the beginning of a massive U.S. presence and the onset of full-fledged interstate war.[77] As Pierre Asselin puts it, "In the spring of 1965, it was only reluctantly that the VWP committed the DRVN to a wider war with the United States."[78]

The 1975 Invasion of South Vietnam and the 1979 War Against Cambodia

As the above discussion indicates, Vietnam's decision to enter a war against the United States differs sharply from the decision-making processes we examined in personalist regimes such as Saddam Hussein's Iraq and Stalin's Soviet Union. While it appears—based on the available evidence—that Le Duan and his backers became more dominant after 1968, the nonpersonalist nature of elite-level politics endured.[79]

Over the course of Le Duan's continued tenure, Vietnam became involved in several more wars, all connected in some way to the reunification struggle. While the ultimate decision to initiate some of these conflicts rested with other countries (for example, China's brief punitive war against Vietnam in 1979), two Vietnamese decisions in particular bear investigation: the decision to invade the South in 1975 and the decision to topple Pol Pot's genocidal regime by force in 1978 and 1979.[80] As with the decision to escalate the conflict against the United States in the 1960s, these later wars could cast doubt on the claim that Vietnam's "machine" regime type led to a generally cautious pattern of decision-making in which leaders turned to force only after careful evaluation of alternative strategies, typically in pursuit of a broad-based national interest.

Before proceeding, it is worth noting that this period poses greater challenges to inference than the pre-1965 era because of the even greater scarcity of credible source material. As Asselin (2011), Nguyen (2012) and others have argued, decision-making in the DRV became more secretive after 1968, making it difficult to know in any detail exactly how decisions were reached. Nonetheless, while the limited evidence should be taken with a grain of salt, the evidence that does exist is consistent with the pattern of collective decision-making outlined in the earlier period.

The 1975 Invasion of the South

The road to the 1975 North Vietnamese invasion of the South began with the close of hostilities against the United States. After eight years of fighting and enormous human and economic costs, both sides were ready to negotiate. The communists concluded that while they had the long-term military advantage, switching to a strategy of negotiation might provide an opportunity for the Americans to withdraw, allowing Hanoi and the PLAF to regroup. Moscow and Beijing also wished to settle the Vietnam problem due to their own interests in improving their relations with the United States, which further encouraged the Vietnamese to negotiate.[81] On the American side, President Richard M. Nixon phrased his rationale for an agreement thus: "We cannot keep this child sucking at the tit when the child is four years old."[82] The election year of 1972 provided a promising opportunity for reaching agreement.

On January 27, 1973, not long after the U.S. election, the DRV, the Provisional Revolutionary Government (PRG) of South Vietnam, the Republic of Vietnam, and the United States signed the Paris Peace Accords. The bargain included a ceasefire in Vietnam, Cambodia, and Laos; the return of prisoners of war; the withdrawal of U.S. forces; and permission for the DRV to continue to station troops in South Vietnam until a coalition government could be established.[83] The PRG and the Thieu administration would each hold power in the geographic areas they currently held, and a Council of National Reconciliation and Concord would eventually organize elections in the South. While the agreement did not represent an unequivocal victory for the DRV, as Vietnam was not unified and Thieu remained in office, it did achieve the crucial goal of getting the United States out of Vietnam and was portrayed as a major victory in the North.[84]

On March 29, 1973, the United States pulled its remaining military forces from Vietnam, leaving behind a North Vietnam that was exhausted both economically and militarily. While the American bombings had not led to a communist defeat, the bombs had achieved their objective of stalling the Northern economy and sapping morale.[85] Revolutionary forces in the South were also weakened and suffering severe shortages of food and ammunition. The South Vietnamese government, still under the leadership of Thieu, eyed the North and the NLF warily.

While the Paris Accords brought a temporary lull to the fighting, they by no means heralded the end of the communists' long-term goal of reunification. What remained uncertain was which strategy would best achieve this goal. Most agreed that in the short term, the North should abide by the Paris agreement and take advantage of the end of American bombing to resume building its economy and strengthening its military capacity.[86] The renewal of all-out war was seen as a last resort, but decades of conflict had taught the communists that peace without victory was unlikely.[87] Indeed, Thieu, taking advantage of the communists' indecision in the immediate aftermath of the American withdrawal, used the ARVN to seize NLF-held territory.[88]

Throughout 1973 and most of 1974, North Vietnamese political and military authorities, the PRG/NLF, and revolutionary commanders in the South debated whether to continue the struggle on primarily political terms or to resume war, possibly using Northern troops.[89] The "vigorous" debate within the leadership ultimately homed in on two possible strategies. First, the communist side would work on all fronts (political, military, diplomatic, and legal) to pressure the Thieu government to adhere to the Paris Peace Accords. Failing that, the communists would continue the armed struggle until victory was complete. While the leadership preferred the first option, it would prepare for the second and decided that the immediate tasks were to develop the armed forces, to win over the population, to reinforce the liberated areas, and to push ahead with the diplomatic struggle.[90]

The endless series of meetings eventually led to a draft report for the Twenty-First Plenary Session, ultimately issued as a resolution in October 1973.[91] The process of reaching a workable consensus reflected a process of at times "heated debate" and tense disagreement.[92] "Despite the objections of the PRG/NLF and some PAVN field commanders who urged the resumption of all-out warfare, the Politburo ultimately heeded the advice of the Central Committee. . . . Hanoi believed that victory could be achieved through a struggle that remained essentially political and legal"—at least in the near term.[93] This approach had the advantage of lending the Southern communists legitimacy, reducing the likelihood that American forces would return.[94]

The debates continued in 1974, with countless sessions analyzing past events and discussing strategy.[95] In January 1974, Hanoi resisted pressure to escalate quickly, with moderates securing a promise to work on reconstructing the economy.[96] The military plan was to build up supplies and readiness during 1974, to start engaging in medium-sized battles in 1975, and to escalate to fully fledged war in 1976.[97] An important meeting of the CMC in March 1974 did not set a target date but indicated an expectation that victory would not be possible until 1976 to 1977.[98] The Central Office for South Vietnam held meetings of its own in which it concluded that victory should be pursued in 1975 and 1976.[99]

As the meetings went on during the summer and fall of 1974, however, a much more ambitious strategic plan emerged. A Politburo meeting in late September or early October of 1974 concluded that the enemy was finding it difficult to withstand the communist offenses due to economic difficulties, low morale, and the weakness of the Thieu regime.[100] In addition, Southern forces had completed a network of roads deep within enemy territory. The leadership thought the return of U.S. troops unlikely but believed that intervention by air or naval forces was not beyond the realm of possibility.[101] The Politburo therefore switched gears and approved a strategy of launching medium-scale offenses from December 1974 to February 1975 and larger attacks from March until June 1975. August and October 1975 would be used for consolidating progress, and the final general offensive and insurrection would occur in 1976.[102]

In the middle of December, communist forces attacked Phuoc Long Province, a main line of the defense of Saigon. The campaign had been a trial run, but it was a dramatic success. While the offensive was going on, the Politburo conducted another expanded meeting from December 18, 1974, to January 8, 1975, in which it agreed to step up mobilization.[103] The decision to press ahead, however, "did not mean that the communists had thrown caution to the wind or that they had an unrealistic sense of their own abilities."[104] Le Duan discussed the communists' "handicaps" and stressed the need for contingency planning in case the United States resumed its attacks.[105] The decision was a result of the realization that Thieu would never give up power unless forcibly removed and the growing certainty that the American people and Congress would not allow a new involvement in Vietnam; Nixon had resigned, and Congress had slashed military aid. Moreover, the Phuoc Long campaign was doing well, and the lack of intervention by the United States emboldened Hanoi.[106] When it was clear that Thieu either could not or would not defend the province and that President Gerald Ford would not return U.S. forces to Vietnam, Hanoi decided to plan a larger offensive, to begin in March.[107]

From here, things proceeded quickly. North Vietnamese units went into action in mid-March 1975, but no U.S. retaliation materialized. The Politburo continued to meet regularly and, pleasantly surprised by the developments, adjusted its forecasts several times that month.[108] In a March 29 message, the Politburo said that the communists should "seize every opportunity and act with determination and boldness."[109] On April 19, the Politburo approved a military plan for an attack on Saigon, and on April 22, it gave the green light. Thieu fled the country on April 21. Hanoi began its final offensive on April 26, and Saigon fell on April 30, 1975.[110]

The available evidence suggests that, as with the decision to escalate to the point of war in the first place, the North Vietnamese decision to invade the South was reached through a process of open discussion (at the elite level, of course) that included vigorous debates of policy alternatives. None of the evidence suggests that the decision to invade was shoved down the throats of frightened colleagues by a hawkish, personalistic leader or that regime insiders were afraid to discuss their "wide divergence of views."[111] The product was a "highly cerebral strategy" that culminated in communist victory, the realization of a decades-long ambition of reuniting North and South Vietnam, and the reward of a long tenure for Le Duan.[112]

The Vietnamese-Cambodian War

The year 1975 marked the close of the war to reunify Vietnam, but it marked the beginning of a new struggle against neighboring Cambodia and its patron, China. At the end of 1978, Vietnam launched an invasion of Cambodia, ousting Pol Pot's brutal Khmer Rouge regime. While the Vietnamese intervention ended a Khmer Rouge genocide that had killed up to 25 percent of the Cambodian population, it nonetheless left Vietnam a pariah in the international community.[113] An incensed China reacted with a small retaliatory war in 1979. The United States, scarred by its withdrawal from Vietnam only a few years earlier and eager to court China, cast Vietnam as an expansionist power with hegemonic designs on Indochina and supported the Khmer Rouge in the United Nations.[114] With the exception of the Soviet bloc, the international community shared this condemnation of Vietnam's overthrow of Pol Pot, despite that leader's genocidal "excesses."[115] These views are echoed even in some relatively recent scholarly treatments of the topic. Stephen Morris, for example, claims that the background cause of the war was "the imperial ambition of Vietnam's communist leadership, which had always wished to dominate the entire region of what was formerly French Indochina," and argues that the decision was based in part on Vietnam's "irrationality" and "paranoia."[116]

These depictions of Vietnam as an excessively ambitious power willing to use force at any cost seem at odds with the argument that nonpersonalist machines tend to be more cautious in their decisions to use force. However, a different reading of the story, based on sources less colored by Cold War lenses, casts the Vietnamese decision in a light that is in fact quite consistent with the argument in this book.[117] The evidence suggests that Vietnam's actions were not a brazen attempt to create an Indochinese empire but rather a reluctant response against a (personalist) tyrant who, under the protection of his Chinese patron, had expelled about 150,000 Cambodian citizens of Vietnamese origin, killed at least 20,000 more, and attacked Vietnamese territory repeatedly over a two-year period.[118]

Tensions between Vietnam and Cambodia had existed for centuries, as Vietnam's precolonial expansion into Indochina led to racial antagonisms and competing territorial claims between the Khmer and Vietnamese peoples.[119] These historical animosities were fueled in the 1970s by Pol Pot and the extremist Khmer Rouge, who viewed themselves as the legitimate leaders of communist Southeast Asia because of their adherence to the "true" Maoist mold, unlike the Vietnamese "lackeys" of the "revisionist" USSR.[120] Pol Pot also had designs on part of Vietnam's Mekong Delta, also known as "Kampuchea Krom" or "Lower Cambodia," which he viewed as Cambodia's rightful territory.[121]

A combination of racist beliefs and political expediency led the Khmer Rouge to foster this antipathy toward Vietnam. Despite extensive cooperation between the Cambodian and Vietnamese communists during the Vietnam War, there were already signs of Cambodian animosity by September 1971, when the Khmer Rouge declared Vietnam the "acute enemy" of Cambodia at a Party Congress.[122] The Khmer Rouge had already started harassing members of the Vietnamese community living in Cambodia, including intimidation, kidnapping, and assassinations.[123] Throughout the first half of the decade, the Khmer Rouge organized anti-Vietnamese demonstrations and distributed propaganda alleging, among other things, that the Vietnamese liked to cook tea on Cambodian heads.[124] By 1973, the Khmer Rouge were driving Vietnamese farmers and fishermen out of Cambodia and herding the remaining Vietnamese residents into "cooperatives" that, according to some observers, quickly came to resemble concentration camps. They were also attacking Vietnamese army installations inside Cambodia, including hospitals, though these attacks were explained as being the fault of undisciplined, low-ranking soldiers.[125] By the following year, the Khmer Rouge were executing its Vietnam-trained members.[126] Despite the two communist parties' alliance, the Khmer Rouge even attacked Vietnam directly along its borders. From 1970 to 1975, records count 174 military incidents provoked by the Khmer Rouge, including attacks on Vietnamese munitions depots, land border clashes, and maritime border clashes.[127]

Still, common external threats and strategic interests kept the fragile alliance afloat until 1975. But Pol Pot's policy toward Vietnam took an aggressive turn in April and May 1975, immediately after Phnom Penh (like Saigon) fell to the communists. Pol Pot quickly issued a secret eight-point directive to expel the entire Vietnamese minority from Cambodia and to send troops to the Vietnamese border.[128] The Khmer Rouge also attempted to seize several Vietnamese-held islands in the Gulf of Thailand by force, sparking clashes and a serious maritime dispute.[129] By September 1975, the Khmer Rouge had expelled more than 150,000 of the approximately 170,000 ethnic Vietnamese living in Cambodia.[130]

The next year brought further ominous moves when the Khmer Rouge carried out massive purges, specifically targeting moderates, those sympathetic to Vietnam, and those whose loyalty to Pol Pot's ultra-leftist policies were suspect.[131] Interestingly, while he was purging those sympathetic to Vietnam at home, Pol Pot attempted to maintain the appearance of normal relations with Vietnam itself.[132] Indeed, the Vietnamese did not seem to have known much of the purges at this point, though they grew concerned when they stopped hearing from former Cambodian diplomats.[133]

External forces also pitted the two neighbors against each other. In the immediate aftermath of the capture of Saigon in 1975, the Vietnamese communist leadership turned its attention to economic challenges such as how to rebuild the Northern economy and how to move the Southern economy toward a socialist model. But like the war effort, economic reconstruction required foreign support. Throughout the long war against the United States, the North Vietnamese had taken advantage of Chinese and Soviet competition for influence in Indochina and carefully attempted to extract resources from each without alienating either. But the Sino-Vietnamese relationship had grown increasingly strained even before Vietnam's 1975 victory due to disagreements over how to handle military and diplomatic strategy. Once the war drew to a close, China returned to its long-held position that a strong Vietnam was undesirable.[134] The two countries clashed on several other issues, such as ideology (including the speed of revolutionary change) and border issues, notably the Spratly and Paracel Islands in the South China Sea. The Chinese responded to these developments by reducing aid to Vietnam and ramping up aid to Cambodia.

As the Chinese cut their aid, the Soviets stepped in, promising large amounts of economic and military aid.[135] In response, by December 1976,

the Vietnamese Workers' Party adopted a policy calling for closer relations with the USSR.[136] The Vietnamese did not take the decision to align
with the Soviets lightly and did not intend it as a belligerent action
against China.[137] While direct evidence is lacking, most scholars believe
that Hanoi knew that depending on the Soviet Union would come at a
cost to its relations with China and the United States but had little
choice.[138] Different factions within the party reportedly debated whether
to cooperate with the West or to turn toward other socialist countries.[139]
Eventually, the American refusal to deliver the reconstruction aid that
Nixon had secretly promised and Chinese reticence about providing aid
forced the resource-hungry Vietnamese toward the Soviets. After much
persuasion and internal handwringing, and seeing few other options
given that the United States and China were unwilling to provide aid,
Vietnam aligned itself with the Soviets, eventually joining Comecon in
June 1978 and signing a friendship treaty later that year.[140]

As the Vietnamese feared, these developments increased tensions with
China, as did Vietnam's poor treatment of the Chinese diaspora in Vietnam. Ethnic Chinese in Vietnam tended to be members of the bourgeoi-
sie. They were targeted during the period of socialist reform that followed
the end of the war, both out of ideological principle and because Vietnam
saw that the concentration of domestic wealth in the hands of ethnic Chinese could provide China with leverage. A large number of ethnic Chinese started to flee the country, angering China and providing bad press
for Vietnam.[141] Together, these complex issues meant that despite the
death of Mao and the fall of the Gang of Four, Deng Xiaoping's new
policy would be strongly anti-Vietnamese.

At the same time, China saw that strengthening the new Cambodian
regime and encouraging its hostility toward Vietnam could provide a
bulwark against Vietnamese leadership in Indochina. Chinese support
for Cambodia would also balance against the Soviet influence on China's
borders. Thus, as China grew cold toward Vietnam, it lavished aid on the
Khmer Rouge.[142]

Bolstered by Chinese support, the Khmer Rouge's anti-Vietnamese attitude now became more public. In January 1977, the Khmer Rouge
launched its largest attack on Vietnamese territory to date, targeting six
Vietnamese provinces.[143] Another attack took place in late April, and the
Vietnamese responded with aerial bombing and deploying troops along
the border.[144] These actions coincided with announcements by members
of the Khmer Rouge of their ambition to retake Kampuchea Krom.[145]
Moreover, that spring the Khmer Rouge unleashed a brutal campaign
with the goal of exterminating the entire remaining Vietnamese population in Cambodia (10,000), though it would take some time for Hanoi to
understand the full extent of Cambodian designs. The campaign lasted

through 1978 and affected ethnic Vietnamese as well as other minority groups.[146]

Despite these provocations, Hanoi attempted to contain the conflict. The Vietnamese made peaceful overtures, sending a letter on June 7 requesting a meeting between both sides (the Cambodians declined), and also refrained from publicizing the attacks among the domestic population.[147] In July, Cambodia said that compromise was not possible, asserting that it could no longer negotiate with a state that clearly had "a dark scheme to conquer our land and destroy the Khmer race"—an ironic position given its extermination of both its own population and the Vietnamese living in Cambodia.[148]

The summer of 1977 was marked by escalating clashes. In September, the Khmer Rouge launched a series of attacks that killed hundreds of civilians—some say more than a thousand—in Vietnam's Tay Ninh Province.[149] The Khmer Rouge also started informing the Cambodian population of its intentions to attack and seize portions of Vietnam.[150] The Vietnamese response was at first extremely cautious, with the Politburo taking pains not to publicize the brutality of the slaughter of villagers and prohibiting the local commander from planning retaliatory measures.[151] Only after "months of planning" did the Vietnamese respond with quiet counterattacks inside Cambodia's borders.[152] These events coincided with a visit by Pol Pot to Beijing, where the Cambodian leader received a warm welcome.[153] During Pol Pot's visit, the Chinese set up a meeting with Vietnam's deputy foreign minister, but the meeting didn't come to much.[154] China's warmth toward the Khmer Rouge, even as Pol Pot's forces were directly attacking Vietnamese territory, sent ominous signals to Hanoi.

The end of 1977 brought no respite from Khmer Rouge attacks on Vietnam's borders.[155] Vietnam finally launched a large-scale attack on December 16 with the intention of spurring negotiations.[156] The Khmer Rouge leapt to publicize the attacks, painting Vietnam as the aggressor and making no mention of the months of Khmer attacks that the Vietnamese had quietly tolerated.[157] Hoping to contain the conflict, Vietnam withdrew its troops in early January 1978. In January and February, meanwhile, the Khmer Rouge made repeated incursions into border areas, "massacring villagers, burning houses, and disrupting commercial life," all the while rebuffing Vietnamese offers to negotiate.[158]

With these security concerns in mind, the Vietnamese leaders met with the Khmer head of the eastern zone of Cambodia in early 1978 and discussed overthrowing Pol Pot through a Vietnamese-backed uprising.[159] At the end of January, the Politburo convened for a secret meeting to assess the situation and consider military options.[160] In early February, the DRV proposed a peaceful solution involving a ceasefire with international supervision. But Pol Pot rejected the offer, even though some analysts consider the deal a credible one that would have likely prevented a Vietnamese invasion.[161] In mid-February, at the Fourth Plenum, the Central Committee met to approve a proposal to oust Pol Pot through popular uprising, and Vietnam soon began training and arming Cambodian defectors into a secret guerilla army, though the plot was later foiled.[162] The same meeting also produced, according to some sources, a decision to invade Cambodia if a popular uprising failed.[163] Later that summer, the Fifth Plenum approved a new plan to invade Cambodia and overthrow the Khmer Rouge regime.[164] By the summer of 1978, 750,000 Vietnamese living near the border had fled, and by late 1978 over 400,000 refugees had escaped from Cambodia into Vietnam.[165]

With no respite from Cambodian border attacks and the success of a guerrilla-style uprising seeming remote, the Central Committee finally agreed to launch an invasion to remove Pol Pot.[166] The "meticulously planned" attack was launched in December 1978, and the regime fell in early 1979.[167] The "vast majority of Cambodians applauded" the new Hanoi-backed regime that took its place.[168]

What explains Vietnam's decision to invade Cambodia and overthrow its government? First, Vietnam's *motives* in invading Cambodia seem to conform to those of a typical machine. The Vietnamese decision to oust Pol Pot was clearly within the broader national Vietnamese interest, since Cambodia had been attacking Vietnamese territory for years. The Khmer Rouge had produced massive refugee flows into and within Vietnam. Pol Pot's violent provocations against Vietnamese citizens and territory and rejection of repeated peaceful overtures suggest that Vietnam had little choice other than to remove him by force. While some have claimed that Vietnam had expansionist designs on Indochina, it seems that establishing a sphere of influence was at most a secondary goal born of security concerns rather than the desire for glory or prestige.[169] It is certainly a stretch to characterize Vietnam as the "expansionist" power that observers such as Henry Kissinger described in 1979.[170] Vietnam's primary goal, rather, was to protect itself from the repeated cross-border attacks that had terrorized the population and thrown into question the government's ability to protect its own territory.[171] Vietnam's leaders, faced with evidence of escalating attacks and increasing cooperation between China and Cambodia, had no reason to believe that its security situation would improve without some kind of drastic change.[172]

This leads to a related question: Was the decision to invade Cambodia the product of a biased focus on military solutions, or could Vietnam have taken steps other than war to shore up its security? The balance of recent historical analysis indicates that Hanoi drew a reasonable conclusion that ousting Pol Pot and his regime was the only way to stop Cambodian attacks. Aggression against Vietnam was, in fact, a core part of the Khmer Rouge ideology and Pol Pot's own thinking, and Cambodia had repeatedly rebuffed Vietnamese attempts at peace. Westad, for example, concludes that there were not any solutions to the Cambodian problem short of war:

> At the core of any argument about peaceful solutions must be an argument about how Hanoi could have handled the Pol Pot regime in any way short of war in 1978. Punishing the Khmer Rouge through short-term military incursions, airborne operations, or even the setting up of a Vietnamese-controlled buffer zone on Cambodian territory would almost certainly not have prevented further attacks on Vietnam. What is more, it would not have stopped the Khmer Rouge's genocide against its own people. It is very hard not to conclude that Vietnam's reasons for going to war against Pol Pot's regime were as good as any *casus belli* in history.[173]

Quinn-Judge similarly casts Vietnam's decision as born out of necessity, not a pro-military bias, and points out that it was not reached until Pol Pot had shown ample evidence of his willingness to use violence to see out his "virulent irredentism"[174] and seize Vietnamese territory:

> For the Vietnamese to have done nothing would have been interpreted by the KR as a sign of weakness and invited further incursions, if the declarations of the KR leadership are to be taken at face value. Even so, Vietnam did not implement its plan of 'regime change' in Cambodia until its diplomatic options, in particular normalization of relations with the United States, were closed off and it had secured a friendship treaty with the USSR in November 1978. The Vietnamese moved ahead with their invasion with plenty of indications that they would be welcomed as liberators by much of the Khmer populace, as was indeed the case. Thus one could conclude that their decision to invade was a desperate but carefully calculated choice.[175]

Other historians echo these analyses. Khoo argues that Hanoi "would have preferred to achieve [security] through means other than war," but Cambodian antagonism made this impossible.[176] According to Chanda, the Vietnamese made repeated attempts to shore up the relationship with China and requested that it stop supporting the Khmer Rouge; Vietnam also took conciliatory measures even in the face of Khmer Rouge attacks.[177]

Unfortunately, there is not as much detailed evidence available about the decision-making *process* or the precise nature of the internal political situation (such as Le Duan's potential vulnerability if the invasion had been botched) as there is for the earlier period of the Vietnam War. The information that is available, however, is consistent with the earlier depiction of the cautious, deliberate politics of a machine. For example, there is a clear record of a long series of Central Committee and Politburo meetings to discuss the matter, of a type that simply did not take place in the personalist regimes studied earlier. Moreover, Hanoi's many diplomatic overtures indicate that the decision to resort to force was not the only option considered. The DRV also showed great forbearance in the early years of Cambodian attacks, indicating that the decision to use force was not a hasty or reflexive one. There is also evidence that the party weighed the costs of defeat: "the VCP was a ruling party with great confidence in the skill of its military, willing to take risks for the good of the revolution (as it had done in 1968 and 1972), but usually possessed of enough realism to try to avoid entering battles which it could not win."[178] Finally, scholars have concluded that the invasion itself was planned with great care, which would seem impossible without extensive internal consultation.[179]

In sum, the motives behind the Vietnamese invasion of Cambodia appear quite different from those of the typical boss, strongman, or junta, and the resort to military rather than diplomatic options appears to have been the consequence of serious deliberation and realistic calculations of the efficacy of various policy options, rather than a reflexive turn to war.[180]

THE SOVIET UNION IN THE POST-STALIN ERA

In the previous chapter, I showed how the personalist nature of Stalin's Soviet regime fostered its willingness to resort to war. This raises the question, however, of what happened when Stalin died and subsequent leaders faced greater constraints. Did the Soviet Union moderate its behavior in any way, as the argument of this book would expect?

Below, I show how increased constraints on leaders in the post-Stalin Soviet Union at the hands of a civilian audience resulted in an appreciably more cautious approach to the use of force. After Stalin's death in 1953, a new principle of "collective decision making" replaced Stalin's personal monopoly on power. Khrushchev initially abided by these new constraints, though as his tenure progressed he attempted to centralize power by appointing cronies to key positions. However, his neglect of some of the principles of collectivity and a series of domestic and foreign policy failures led Khrushchev's colleagues in the Politburo and Central Committee to jettison him in 1964 in favor of the cautious and consensus-oriented Leonid Brezhnev. Brezhnev learned from his predecessor's mistakes and carefully observed the new rules of elite-level Soviet politics. The changed nature of the post-Stalin regime, in turn, had significant implications for how the Soviet Union made decisions about using force.

When leaders did resort to major interstate conflict, it was after extensive internal debate, attempts at diplomacy, with the backing of Politburo colleagues, and with realistic expectations of success. In other words, constraints on leaders at the hands of an elite civilian audience contributed to the more cautious, and ultimately more peaceful, Soviet foreign policy that characterized the post-Stalin era.

The Evolution of Elite Constraints from Stalin to Khrushchev to Brezhnev

The death of Stalin ushered in dramatic changes to elite-level politics in the Soviet Union. Eager to prevent the rise of a new tyrant, Soviet elites ensured that no leader was ever able to replicate Stalin's iron grip on power, curtailing the role of the KGB and attempting to institute new practices of "collective decision making."[181] Without the help of an obedient KGB, and with a new understanding of the limits of the power of the general secretary, it became much more difficult for the leader to continue Stalin's practices of spying on rivals and packing the apex of the regime with cronies.

As a result, the Politburo took on new importance under both Khrushchev and Brezhnev. This elite subset of the Central Committee consisted of the highest party and government officials in the regime,[182] mostly drawn from the civilian ranks.[183] An important effect of the leader's reduced power was the "gradual broadening of open policy debates by those who are willing to work within the system."[184] According to observers, "The fact that disagreements could no longer be suppressed by police violence, as they were under Stalin, placed a distinct limit upon the leader's power because he was subject to criticism from other members of the elite."[185] In general, debate over policy at the top level of the regime became significantly more open and less imbued with fear,[186] and "decisions often were taken only after stormy controversies and agile maneuvering among the various factions."[187] Politburo members debated for long hours until they could agree on a decision, and when they could not reach consensus, the body would take an overnight recess to allow leaders to sleep on the ideas or to bargain with other officials.[188]

These changes had important implications for Soviet leaders' freedom of maneuver in both domestic and foreign policy. Valenta writes, "With the restoration of collective leadership after Stalin's death, coalition politics reemerged as an important instrument in the Soviet decision-making process. The most crucial decisions of the post-Stalin era have been made by coalitions of senior Soviet leaders."[189] Or, as Richter puts it, "After Stalin died, differences on foreign policy had to be resolved through conflict and compromise. In such an environment, leaders had to justify

[159]

policies by demonstrating the policies' effectiveness in achieving objectives."[190] Moreover, "Although the office of Party secretary general theoretically constitute[d] a base of enormous personal authority and power, the reemergence of the collective leadership as the normal pattern of Soviet decision making in the post-Stalin era restrain[ed] the incumbent from becoming a personal ruler."[191]

Nonetheless, as time wore on, Khrushchev appeared to chafe more and more against his lack of freedom of maneuver. He began to push the envelope on his power and authority, consulting less with his colleagues and taking greater personal initiative. Sakwa attributes this tendency to Khrushchev's "personality and schooling in the shadow of Stalin[, which] encouraged elements of charismatic leadership, giving rise to 'harebrained schemes' and lack of consultation with colleagues."[192]

This tendency toward ignoring the constraints on his rule became more evident after the Anti-Party affair of 1957, when Khrushchev drew on his support in the Central Committee to withstand an attempt by powerful members of the Politburo to oust him. Some of Khrushchev's contemporaries went so far as to say that his rule involved two distinct periods, before and after 1958. According to Taubman, "After 1958 Khrushchev stopped listening and surrounded himself with 'yes-men.'" He quotes Khrushchev's daughter as reporting: "At an earlier stage, he would hear you out even if you were telling him something that included criticism. But at a certain stage, he said, 'That's enough! Don't tell me that sort of thing. I'm sick and tired of it. I don't want to hear it.'"[193] Oleg Troyanovsky, Khrushchev's foreign policy aide starting in 1958, writes, "The trouble was that as time went on, and especially after Molotov and Kaganovich were expelled from the Presidium in June 1957, the other members of the leadership group became more and more reluctant to argue with him, particularly regarding his ideas and proposals."[194] Fursenko and Naftali describe the loyalties of Presidium members in 1958: "Ten of the sixteen full members of the Presidium had been elevated since 1955 and felt various degrees of gratitude to Khrushchev."[195] Taubman explains, "No longer constrained by powerful critics like Molotov, he was free to pronounce on subjects of which he knew nothing, to consult or not as he pleased."[196]

This trend became even more pronounced after a few more years of Khrushchev's reign. As Taubman writes, "By 1962 the most influential of Khrushchev's colleagues were his own men, longtime associates he had promoted to high office, protégés who had rallied to his side in 1957. Yet as his miseries multiplied, he withdrew into an inner circle of personal aides and advisers, avoiding his colleagues, acting without informing them."[197] Dmitri Shepilov argues in his memoirs that "Later, under Khrushchev's one-man rule, all these procedural conventions were tossed aside, and the whole storehouse of diplomatic discourse was turned upside down. Things reached a point where any statement on any question, large or small, was left almost exclusively to Khrushchev."[198] Anatoly Dobrynin recalls that he had to phrase his criticism of Khrushchev's policies with care: "It was not always easy to persuade him how unreal some of his ideas were, especially in the presence of other Politburo members. I had to make him understand diplomatically."[199]

Thus, collective decision-making in the Khrushchev era weakened as time passed. But in the end, Khrushchev's unwillingness to abide by the new rules of the game—or his failure to perceive what those rules really were—proved fatal to his hold on power. Khrushchev's attempts to concentrate decision-making into his own hands and the policy failures that ensued had consequences; by 1964, his colleagues concluded that he "had become uncontrollable in his emotions and willful in making decisions."[200] In making the case for Khrushchev's ouster in 1964, Brezhnev enumerated examples of unilateral action on Khrushchev's part, and other colleagues charged Khrushchev with failing to respect the principles of collective leadership.[201] Some scholars have also emphasized the role that Khrushchev's foreign policy failures played in his ouster, which according to one scholar was in large part "because of his responsibility for two major and humiliating failures"—the Cuban Missile Crisis and the terrible 1963 harvest that resulted in the purchase of wheat from the United States and Canada.[202]

After Khrushchev was ousted, it was clear to everyone within the regime that the general secretary served at the pleasure of his peers. Indeed, as Khrushchev himself put it in the midst of his removal, "Could anyone have dreamed of telling Stalin that he didn't suit us anymore and suggesting he retire? Not even a wet spot would have remained where we had been standing. Now everything is different. The fear is gone, and we can talk as equals. That's my contribution. I won't put up a fight."[203] Dobrynin observed that after Stalin and especially after Khrushchev, "A general secretary of course had many ways of persuasion to carry his ideas through the Politburo, but he was always careful not to antagonize the other members unnecessarily. After all, they could always revolt and replace him, as they did with Khrushchev."[204] This resulted in what Simes calls a "consensus style of leadership" in which the Politburo was "transformed from a group of personal associates and aides to the dictator, as it was under Stalin and to a lesser extent under Khrushchev, into a kind of supreme legislative-executive committee of the Soviet elite, representing all principal power groups."[205]

As a consequence, Brezhnev was even more susceptible to domestic political concerns in making foreign policy decisions than Khrushchev.[206] According to Dobrynin, "True, he was number one among the leadership, but even as first among equals he could not always impose his views on the other members of the Politburo. Each of them had a right to express his opinion on any subject on the agenda of the regular weekly meeting."[207] Hough and Fainsod write, "Whether he had the ability to do so or not, Brezhnev obviously did not force through many major policy initiatives over the resistance of his colleagues."[208] Brezhnev's subordinates in fact praised him for his commitment to collective decision-making and his ability to work with others.[209]

How Political Constraints Affected the Use of Force

Thus, the post-Stalin era resulted in the tightening of constraints on the leader. Khrushchev began his rule by respecting the new focus on collective decision-making, but after 1958 his respect for collectivity waned somewhat. This, along with a series of policy failures, led to his ouster in 1964. He was replaced by Brezhnev, who clearly knew that the Politburo could remove him from office if he strayed from the collective will or presided over too many policy failures.

The constraints faced by Khrushchev and especially Brezhnev meant that successes and failures in foreign and domestic policies affected the leaders' hold on power and ability to govern effectively. As Richter (1989) puts it, "a successful foreign policy may cushion a leader from domestic failures," whereas foreign policy setbacks—particularly for an already weak leader—"would confirm any doubts or suspicions others might have about a leader whose authority was already shaky."[210] Anderson similarly notes that foreign policy failures "reduced sponsoring leaders' credibility."[211] As a consequence, even Khrushchev rarely "disrupted the unity of the collective" and instead sought consensus for most of his major decisions.[212]

One of the theses of this book is that when an authoritarian leader is constrained by a civilian domestic audience such as the post-Stalin Soviet Politburo, this should (all else being equal) have a dampening effect on his willingness to use force abroad. Instead, the leader should resort to military force only when the goals of the operation enjoy the backing of his peers and when the chances of success are high.

To test this argument, we would ideally show that Khrushchev, and to an even greater extent Brezhnev, eschewed the use of force where a boss such as Stalin would have been freer to resort to military means. Broadly consistent with this idea is the fact that Khrushchev and especially Brezhnev pursued much more conciliatory policies toward the United States than Stalin had, resulting in the relaxing of superpower tensions commonly known as "détente." Indeed, some scholars have argued that on the Soviet side, détente was primarily the result of domestic politics rather than international circumstances.[213] Establishing that domestic politics "caused" détente or indeed affected any decision not to engage in conflict, is however, challenging for several reasons. Establishing a causal link between domestic regime type and a broad policy such as détente would require us to account for and isolate the multitude of other factors that contributed to that decision. And when it comes to specific decisions not to use force, historians tend not to write detailed histories about non-events and "dogs that did not bark." It is difficult to demonstrate that a leader decided *against* force because of a fear of punishment, precisely because those conflicts never materialized and thus failed to become a focus of historical attention.

A different approach, as before, is to focus on the times that the leader *did* resort to force. When the leader did use force, was it in the pursuit of goals shared by the relevant accountability group? Did the leader carefully weigh the costs and benefits of using force and seek domestic support for his policies from the actors who had the power to punish him? Of course, it is important to keep in mind that the times that the leader did use force may include off-the-equilibrium-path instances when he acted unilaterally for idiosyncratic reasons despite the importance of constraints. This creates a bias against finding evidence of constraints but also allows us to observe whether the leader was punished for those deviations from the collective will.

Decisions to Use Force under Khrushchev

During his time in office, Khrushchev initiated only one conflict that rose to the level of interstate war—the 1956 invasion of Hungary. To what extent is Khrushchev's decision-making in 1956 consistent with the arguments about machines laid out earlier? Did he make the decision to invade Hungary in the shadow of domestic accountability? The answer is clearly yes.

In October of 1956, emboldened by Khrushchev's policies of de-Stalinization and led by reform-minded Imre Nagy, a popular rebellion broke out against the Soviet-backed Hungarian regime. The situation quickly deteriorated into a chaotic revolt, including clashes between popular militias and Soviet troops already stationed in Hungary. The secretary of the Hungarian Workers' Party appealed to Moscow for military assistance, fearing that otherwise Hungary would slip out of communist control.

Meanwhile, Khrushchev's own position in the Soviet Politburo was rather precarious. He had only recently emerged as the party leader and successor to Stalin, and the Politburo contained both supporters of Khrushchev (such as Anastas Mikoyan and Alexei Kirichenko) and "hardline opponents" (such as Kliment Voroshilov, Lazar Kaganovich, and Vyacheslav Molotov).[214] Medvedev argues that by 1956, "in the Presidium of the Central Committee and elsewhere, opposition to [Khrushchev] had begun to take shape that exploited any blunder or failure on his part."[215] Moreover, Khrushchev's own de-Stalinization initiatives were blamed for creating the conditions that sparked the crisis in Hungary and similar demonstrations that had occurred months before in Poznań, Poland.[216]

Khrushchev and the other Presidium members had several reasons to fear the developments in Hungary. First, they were worried about potential spillover into nearby states; demonstrations had already broken out in Poland, Romania, and Czechoslovakia, and there was reason to fear ripple effects in East Germany as well.[217] In the eyes of many, "the Soviet bloc threatened to crumble."[218] Moreover, if Hungary withdrew from the newly formed Warsaw Pact, this would provide a troubling precedent and weaken the alliance in the eyes of the West.[219] The Western powers would assist Hungary in democratizing, they feared, and use Hungary as a means of gaining more influence in Eastern Europe. Thus, in an October 23 Politburo meeting, all except Mikoyan agreed that military force would be necessary.[220] The following week, Khrushchev announced to his colleagues, "If we depart from Hungary, it will give a great boost to the Americans, English, and French—the imperialists. They will perceive it as weakness on our part and will go onto the offensive. We would then be exposing the weakness of our positions. Our party will not accept it if we do this. To Egypt they will then add Hungary. We have no other choice."[221] Even Mikoyan, the one Presidium member opposed to invasion, admitted, "We simply cannot allow Hungary to be removed from our camp."[222]

Fortuitously for the Soviets, the timing of the crisis in Hungary coincided with the Suez crisis, which focused Western attention in Egypt rather than Eastern Europe.[223] While at least one Politburo member raised the issue of NATO's response to intervention in Hungary, few Presidium members were especially concerned that NATO or the Western powers would become involved.[224]

Although the Soviets had been monitoring the situation in Hungary for months and had even developed contingency plans for an invasion, the final decision to invade developed over two days of Presidium meetings. On October 30, the Presidium met to discuss the deteriorating situation in Hungary and Soviet policy toward satellite states more generally.[225] The Presidium decided to issue a declaration on a new approach to Soviet foreign policy toward satellite states, which it believed would bring the Hungarian rebels back into the fold.[226]

Meanwhile, Nagy began calling for Hungary to leave the Warsaw Pact and for all Soviet troops to be withdrawn.[227] Realizing that its softer approach would not work, the Presidium therefore met again on October 31. By this point Khrushchev was "aware that his own chances of remaining in power would have been slender indeed had he not crushed the Hungarian revolution."[228] Declassified notes taken by Vladimir Malin during meetings of the Presidium indicate that Mikoyan, a supporter of Khrushchev's, was the only Presidium member to oppose the decision to invade.[229] While he agreed that the Hungarian uprising had to be put down, he thought it more politically sound to let the Hungarians attempt to resolve the crisis and only then to reevaluate the situation.[230] The rest of the Presidium, however, was in agreement. Due to Mikoyan's absence, the decision to invade Hungary was unanimous, and there is no evidence that Politburo members were coerced into this position. More than two hundred thousand Soviet troops entered Hungary on November 4, 1956, and quickly extinguished the rebellion.

Despite the military success of the Hungarian intervention, the 1956 crises in Hungary, Poland, and the Suez Canal severely undermined Khrushchev's authority.[231] Ross argues that "Khrushchev's leading position on de-Stalinization and the linkage between de-Stalinization and the subsequent turmoil in Eastern Europe in the fall of 1956 clearly was a major blow to Khrushchev. Not only was he put on the defensive on all the major issues he was identified with and forced to retreat, but his major rivals made remarkable comebacks."[232] Similarly, Richter suggests that the fallout from the 1956 crises encouraged the anti-party group to execute their (ultimately unsuccessful) attempt to remove Khrushchev from power.[233] Thus, the invasion of Hungary demonstrates both the intimate role of the post-Stalin Politburo in Soviet decisions to use force and the extent to which foreign policy reversals could damage the prestige of the incumbent leader.

In other situations, Khrushchev's behavior poses a conundrum for the thesis of this book. Despite the constraints he faced at the hands of the Politburo, Khrushchev was often faulted by his contemporaries for his "penchant for taking risks" and "his various errors in judgment and unjustified risk-taking" in the domain of foreign policy.[234] Others have noted Khrushchev's "remarkable tendency for sudden moves and ill-advised initiatives," both in domestic and foreign matters.[235]

Both scholars and Khrushchev's political contemporaries have often invoked the Cuban Missile Crisis as an example of Khrushchev's recklessness and risk-taking in matters of foreign policy. While there was a valuable prize to be gained by deploying nuclear missiles in Cuba—greater strategic balance with the United States—the risks were also large if the plans were detected before the missiles were fully deployed.[236] Goldgeier argues that Khrushchev formulated the plan mostly on his own and that the decision to deploy missiles in Cuba secretly was "a personal decision to seek a quick fix."[237] Recall, however, that by the early 1960s, Khrushchev had managed to stack the Politburo with supporters and was flouting some of the principles of collective decision-making. It is therefore difficult to know what to make of the fact that all of the Presidium members in 1962 favored deployment (though Mikoyan did have reservations concerning the secrecy of the proposed operation).[238]

In the end, Khrushchev either was unlucky or underestimated the risks involved. But his behavior represents the exception that proves the rule. Khrushchev's "adventuristic behavior" in sending the missiles meant that his "authority was never the same after Cuba."[239] Taubman calls the Cuban crisis "an unmitigated disaster for the Soviet leader."[240] In 1964, Khrushchev's hasty decision-making and foreign adventurism played a large role in bringing about his downfall at the hands of his colleagues.[241]

The Use of Force under Brezhnev

The unambiguous message of Khrushchev's ouster meant that Brezhnev was even more aware of the political constraints he faced than Khrushchev had been. This was evident in his foreign policy. While Brezhnev did not initiate any conflicts that rose to the level of an interstate war, he deployed large numbers of Soviet troops to quell the 1968 unrest in Czechoslovakia. This conflict did not rise to the level of a war because unlike the Hungarians, Czechoslovakian citizens put up little resistance and fatalities were low; nevertheless it merits attention as the most significant interstate use of force of the Brezhnev era. The Soviet Union also invaded Afghanistan in 1979, but researchers typically treat this as an external intervention in a civil war since the Soviets interceded at the invitation of the Afghan government. As the empirical focus of earlier chapters is on strictly interstate conflicts, I do not take up the Afghan case here, though one would expect similar dynamics to apply.

Both in foreign and domestic policy, Brezhnev is universally seen as a cautious leader who played by the rules of collective decision-making.[242] Scholars characterize Brezhnev as "a team player" who was "cautious and unhurried";[243] a man whose "personal style had always been accommodative and nonconfrontational";[244] and "averse to taking risks in foreign policy."[245] Others claim that "he moved with caution, seeking to balance bold initiatives in one area with concessions in another or to coopt his critics and their programs rather than opting for confrontation."[246] This caution led Brezhnev to seek "full concurrence by the Politburo before acting."[247]

Brezhnev's cautious behavior illustrates both the effects of constraints and the tendency of leaders of machines to be selected on the basis of quite different traits than their more risk-acceptant, violence-prone personalist counterparts. On the one hand, the disappointing lessons of Khrushchev's tenure had driven home the importance of choosing a more sober replacement. But constraints appear to have reinforced what may have been an innate tendency in Brezhnev's nature. Scholars have often explicitly drawn a link between Brezhnev's cautious behavior and his awareness of the domestic costs of acting without the consent of his peers. Writing about Soviet foreign policy, Ross argues that after Khrushchev's ouster, the caution displayed by subsequent leaders evolved out of Khrushchev's loss of power and a new awareness of the constraints they faced. He argues that "the character and dynamics of the Soviet decision-making process, as it has evolved, dictate a kind of general caution and relatively low risktaking propensity."[248] Similarly, he argues that the Khrushchev experiences "must have given the members of the current leadership a very powerful stake in not putting themselves in a position where a mistake, blunder, or obvious failure can be pinned on them—the potential costs are simply too high. . . . It must also make them prone toward caution and not eager to pursue paths that carry high risks and potential failure."[249]

These tendencies clearly affected Politburo decision-making during the 1968 crisis in Czechoslovakia, Brezhnev's most unambiguous use of interstate force. The crisis began soon after Antonín Novotný, the first secretary and president of the Communist Party of Czechoslovakia, was ousted by his own regime in late 1967.[250] At first, Novotný's downfall was welcomed by the Soviet leadership, due to Novotný's apparent mishandling of economic issues, attempts to concentrate power in his own hands, and difficulty finalizing the status of Slovakia.[251] Brezhnev recognized Novotný's failures and supported his removal in the hopes that it would reunite Czechoslovakia's leadership, which was split between reformers and conservatives.

But under Novotný's successor Alexander Dubček, reformers gained the advantage. Soon after coming to power, Dubček launched a "dizzying period" of economic reform and political liberalization, including discontinuing press censorship and widening the sphere of permissible political activity, a period that would come to be known as the Prague Spring.[252] Additionally, Czechoslovakia began to open up economic negotiations with capitalist West Germany.[253]

While Dubček had been cautious in implementing these reforms and had attempted not to provoke Soviet ire, the USSR nonetheless felt threatened as the thaw unleashed pressure for more far-reaching political change and once again raised the possibility that a Warsaw Pact country would slip from the communist fold.[254]

These challenges to orthodox communism soon began to worry the Soviet Politburo.[255] As in the case of Hungary, Czech liberalization

[167]

threatened to spark similar activity in Poland and East Germany, whose leaders began to express concerns.[256] Fears started to arise about contagion to Ukraine, Moldavia, Georgia, and the Baltic states. Hence, starting in mid-March of 1968, the Czechoslovak issue "was constantly at the top of the Politburo's agenda."[257] Brezhnev's fear of the effect of the Prague reforms on the cohesion of the Soviet bloc was shared by several other prominent Politburo members, including Prime Minister Aleksei Kosygin, Ukrainian party leader Petro Shelest, Aleksandr Shelepin, Mikhail Solomentsev, and Yuri Andropov.[258]

Brezhnev initially turned to peaceful diplomacy to halt the reforms, meeting with Dubček repeatedly and pressing him to rein in the situation.[259] In July, the Soviet Union and the other Warsaw Pact nations wrote the "Warsaw Letter," which reminded the Czechoslovakian leaders that other communist nations were deeply concerned about the fate of communism in Czechoslovakia and demanded a crackdown on non-orthodox political activity. The Soviets also tried to signal their resolve, conducting military exercises in the country in the late spring "in an effort to intimidate the [Czech] reformers."[260] In a last attempt at peaceful diplomacy, a summit between USSR and Czechoslovak leadership took place on July 29 in Čierna nad Tisou, Hungary. Brezhnev hoped the summit would produce enough pressure to split the Czechoslovak leadership and reinforce the Soviet influence on Czechoslovakia, but the result was a hazy agreement that at most delayed the invasion.

How did the Politburo react to these developments? The evidence suggests that all of the members of the Politburo agreed that the changes in Czechoslovakia were detrimental to Soviet interests and the cause of communism abroad. Where there was disagreement, it was about tactics; diaries and transcripts from Politburo meetings indicate that "some [Politburo] members, such as Andropov, Podgorny, and Shelest, were consistent proponents of military intervention, whereas others, particularly Suslov, were far more circumspect." The transcripts also demonstrate that "a substantial number, including Kosygin, Aleksandr Shelepin, and Pyotr Demichev, fluctuated markedly during the crisis, at times favoring 'extreme measures' . . . and at other times seeking a political solution."[261]

Indeed, Brezhnev and the Politburo carefully considered the risks of military intervention. They had good reason to believe that an invasion of Czechoslovakia was not especially risky. The Soviets had massive local military superiority, and the regime had carried out extensive political and military preparations to minimize the chances of military failure. In fact, it was due only to these extensive preparations that Brezhnev was willing to authorize the military action.[262] Moreover, because the United States was itself bogged down in Vietnam, it was very unlikely that the United States would become involved or that a Soviet action would seriously damage U.S.-Soviet relations.[263]

Brezhnev actively encouraged members of the Politburo to voice their opinions on the matter, himself remaining undecided throughout much of the deliberations.[264] By the middle of 1968, however, the Politburo reached a consensus. "The necessity of countering that threat was no longer in doubt . . . the only question remaining for Soviet leaders was not whether—but when—an external military solution would be required."[265] Brezhnev himself seems to have felt that domestic political considerations required him to support the intervention, reportedly explaining to a Czechoslovak reformer in Moscow in November 1968: "You thought that because you were in a position of power you could do as you pleased. This was your basic mistake. I also cannot do what I desire. I can actually realize perhaps only a third of what I could like to do. If I had not cast my vote in the Politburo in favor of military intervention— what do you suppose would have happened? Certainly you would not be sitting here. And *perhaps even I would not be sitting here either!*"[266]

On August 6, the Politburo reached a consensus to go ahead with a major military intervention unless the Czechoslovakian regime took radical steps to comply with Soviet demands. At an ad hoc session of the Politburo on August 13 through 15, the members "acknowledged that a military solution 'would be fraught with complications,' but they all agreed that a failure to act 'would lead to civil war in Czechoslovakia and the loss of it as a socialist country.' "[267] In sum, "the Soviet decision to intervene in Czechoslovakia was a collective decision that resulted from consensus building."[268]

On August 20, Warsaw Pact forces invaded Czechoslovakia and put an end to the Prague Spring. Six hundred thousand troops from the USSR, Poland, Hungary, Bulgaria, and East Germany occupied the country. By the spring of 1969, the reforms had been rolled back, Dubček and fellow reformers had been replaced by a new Moscow-backed government, and Czechoslovakia was firmly back in the orthodox communist camp.[269]

Thus, despite the biases that arise when focusing only on situations in which force was actually used, the Soviet decision to invade Czechoslovakia is consistent with the argument about how military interventions emerge in nonpersonalist, civilian dictatorships. Brezhnev consulted extensively with colleagues to ensure their support for the invasion's goals and to ensure that it would be militarily successful. Only when diplomatic options had been exhausted, and only when he had received the full consent of his peers after extensive internal debate, did Brezhnev order military action.[270]

Together, the cases of North Vietnam and the post-Stalin Soviet Union clearly illustrate how dictatorships in which leaders are constrained by

[169]

civilian elites adopt a much more cautious approach to the use of force internationally than personalist regimes or military juntas. Unlike leaders of personalist regimes, leaders of machines face powerful incentives to engage fellow elites in debate about the relative merits of competing policy options and to avoid using force unless there is a consensus that the cause is worthy and the likelihood of defeat is low. Compared to juntas, the civilian nature of that elite audience contributes to a more careful and accurate consideration of alternatives to using force or, if force is to be used, of the political and diplomatic ramifications of fighting. In these respects, even though ordinary citizens are largely excluded from the policymaking process, machines more closely resemble democracies than they do their autocratic brethren.

Conclusion

DICTATORSHIP, WAR, AND PEACE

As this book has shown, there are vast differences in dictatorships' decisions about war and peace. All leaders contemplating the use of force must weigh the costs and benefits of fighting compared to the status quo, and authoritarian regime type affects these calculations. Both the perceptions and often the reality of these costs and benefits depend on whether the leader is accountable to a powerful domestic audience. But the composition of that audience matters as well, particularly whether the accountability group is civilian or military in nature, because civilians and military officers have different preconceptions about the necessity and utility of force relative to diplomacy. Finally, the leader's personal attributes and predispositions matter. This is especially true when the leader does not face a significant domestic audience, though leader-specific characteristics can matter even when leaders face accountability; this is because leaders must sometimes make decisions quickly and without the benefit of substantial domestic consultation.

Building on these insights, I classified authoritarian regimes into four distinct types: civilian machines in which the leader faces a powerful elite audience, military juntas in which an elite audience is composed of military officers, civilian personalist boss regimes in which the leader faces no powerful domestic audience, and military personalist strongman regimes (though the discussion noted that boss and strongman regimes share many of the same attributes).

Chapters 2 and 3 assessed three broad implications of these arguments. Chapter 2 showed that personalist bosses and strongmen and nonpersonalist military juntas are substantially more likely to initiate conflicts than civilian nonpersonalist machines, which, surprisingly, initiate conflict no more frequently than democracies. Moreover, in most analyses, strongmen are more likely to initiate conflict than juntas and bosses, indicating that both personalism and the military backgrounds of key decision-makers play a role in conflict initiation. The chapter also explained how these results are inconsistent with other possible theoretical explanations.

Chapter 3 turned to the outcomes of wars and the fates of leaders in the aftermath of defeat. Civilian nonpersonalist machines are no more likely to lose wars than democracies, with juntas trailing not far behind. Bosses and strongmen, in contrast, are much more likely to be defeated in war. As in the case of conflict initiation, the differences among different types of authoritarian regimes are at least as important as those between democracies and nondemocracies. As for the fates of leaders after defeat, personalist bosses and strongmen usually survived in office even when they were defeated on the battlefield. Leaders of juntas and machines, on the other hand, like leaders of democracies, usually were punished for defeat in war with loss of office. These patterns do not seem to be explained by alternative theories, such as the possibility that variation among authoritarian regimes is attributable to variation in the fear of severe punishment.

Next, a series of historical case studies probed the causal mechanisms behind the theory. Chapter 4 studied two personalist bosses—Saddam Hussein and Joseph Stalin. The analysis of Saddam's decision-making in the prelude to the Gulf War demonstrated how his relative lack of domestic accountability allowed him to make risky and aggressive decisions that a more constrained leader would have avoided. The same was true, though to a less extreme degree, for Stalin, as was evident in the decisions surrounding the invasion of Finland. Neither leader undertook any serious assessment of the costs of invasion, and both were surrounded by eager sycophants hesitant to voice the slightest apprehension about their plans. Both Saddam and Stalin survived embarrassing defeats that would surely have unseated a leader who faced a more formidable domestic audience.

Chapter 5 turned to two nonpersonalist military regimes: Argentina in 1982, when it invaded the British-held Falkland Islands, and Japan in the long prelude to World War II. I first demonstrated that the common diversionary interpretation of the Falklands War cannot explain the junta's decision unless one takes into account the particular perceptions, biases, and preferences of the military leadership and its domestic audience of military officers. The case also shows how the risk of being deposed makes leaders of military juntas far more "accountable" than commonly thought. Next, the analysis of Japan in the 1930s and early 1940s provided a unique opportunity to examine the very different ways in which military officers and civilian officials viewed Japan's international position. Military officers, as hypothesized, tended to view force as a necessary and legitimate means to ensuring Japanese security. They saw it as inevitable that the United States would attack Japan given Japan's expansion into the Pacific and therefore pressed for a preemptive first strike on a strict military timetable. Civilians, in contrast, were less likely to see war as inevitable and showed greater confidence in diplomacy. The military hawks won the day, and Pearl Harbor provoked a devastating war in the Pacific.

Chapter 6 turned to nonpersonalist civilian machines. Much of the chapter investigated the intriguing case of North Vietnam in the 1960s and 1970s as it fought for the reunification of Vietnam and later became embroiled in a war against the fanatical Pol Pot. I showed that the domestic politics of the regime, in which the leader answered to a powerful group of high-level regime officials, most of them civilians, encouraged serious debate of alternative strategies. The result was a surprisingly prudent and effective set of decisions that, while violent, was ultimately successful in defeating both the United States and Cambodia. I then turned back to the Soviet Union and assessed how the foreign policy process changed after Stalin's death ushered in a new era of "collective decision making." The discussion demonstrated how Khrushchev was punished for a series of domestic and foreign policy debacles, the lessons learned by the much more cautious and consensual Brezhnev, and the decisions to use force that resulted.

IMPLICATIONS FOR THEORY

The findings in this book have a series of important implications for theorists of international relations. Most generally, I show that rather than focusing only on differences *between* democracies and dictatorships, much can be learned by investigating the important differences *among* authoritarian regimes. Authoritarian leaders can be answerable to domestic audiences to an extent that has not been fully appreciated. Turning our focus to the politics of dictatorships promises to reveal many insights about the causes of war and the determinants of conflict and cooperation more generally, for example why some authoritarian states have "greedy" or expansionist preferences while others seem content to focus on a more narrow definition of national security.[1]

The book also has implications for democratic peace theory, which predicts that pairs of democratic countries are less likely to fight armed conflicts. The argument in this book is "monadic," in that it does not take into account the regime type of the *opponent*, a central feature of many variants of democratic peace theory and also many variants of constructivist theorizing. The findings suggest a monadic "democracy and machine" peace in which domestic politics in these kinds of countries make leaders more cautious about resorting to force.

Future studies could take these insights a step further to explore how different kinds of authoritarian regimes relate to each other and to democracies, developing a dyadic theory of regime type and conflict.[2] Are cautious tendencies of machines amplified or muted against opponents with certain regime types? Are personalists more or less likely to use force depending on political institutions in the potential target state? Can democracies and machines build trust and enjoy peaceful relations based on mutual restraint, despite differences in views about the importance of civil liberties and free economic exchange? These are important questions for future research.

While the focus of the book is on war, the argument also provides possible avenues for answering a host of other questions about how authoritarian regime type matters in international relations. Just as leader constraints and audience and leader preferences affect decisions to use force, they could prove important for questions such as why some authoritarian leaders open their countries to trade whereas others do not; why some countries forge durable alliances whereas others remain friendless (Lai and Reiter 2000; Leeds 2003); how countries respond to foreign aid and international sanctions (Wright 2009, 2010; Escribà-Folch and Wright 2010); why some countries cooperate more freely than others (Leeds and Davis 1999; Mattes and Rodriguez 2014); why some kinds of regimes are more likely to break down into civil war (Fjelde 2010); why some countries choose to pursue nuclear weapons while others do not (Way and Weeks n.d.); and many other questions.

Another set of implications concerns policy change more generally. While the focus of the book was on the circumstances under which leaders choose war, in particular objectively foolish wars, the same logic could explain why some countries seize on opportunities and make daring reforms, while others suffer from policy stagnation or, at best, incremental policy change. Just as personalist leaders are freer to fight, they are also freer to compromise, innovate, and implement bold initiatives. Machines and juntas, in contrast, must please a constituency made up of more than one person. It is therefore possible that these regimes are less likely to innovate or seize on short-term opportunities. On the other hand, the relative openness to new information in machines could encourage reform by making it more likely that the leadership will be confronted with sound new ideas. Future scholarship could investigate which tendency prevails.

Regime type aside, the findings also suggest some more general insights for explaining international behavior. In this book I argue that we cannot simply deduce how decision-makers will behave by focusing on the presence or absence of "institutional constraints."[3] Rather, the impact of institutions depends on the preferences and beliefs of the individuals who populate and lead those institutions. To understand their preferences and perceptions, in turn, scholars need to recognize that in foreign policy, the optimal course of action is rarely obvious. This is particularly true when it comes to the use of military force. Since war is infrequent, military technology is constantly changing, and decisions are made under duress with limited information, rules of thumb and personal experiences have the potential to color how individuals perceive a situation. In other words, even if individuals make decisions about using force in order to maximize their own welfare, their perceptions of what constitutes that welfare and how best to ensure it are influenced by their own histories, personal characteristics, and background experiences. This approach of blending objective features of institutions with psychological, sociological, and constructivist insights about the sources of foreign policy perceptions and preferences suggests productive lines of future research, moving beyond the typical "rationalist/constructivist" divide toward a more empirically-grounded "behavioral" theory of war.[4]

Furthermore, the analysis suggests a way to integrate "first-image" theories, which focus on the behavior of individuals, with "second-image" theories about the importance of domestic political institutions.[5] For example, I argue that the background experiences of individual leaders may be especially important for understanding behavior under specific institutional conditions.[6] The precise characteristics of a leader are most important when the leader faces few domestic constraints and least important (though still potentially consequential) when the leader is answerable to other domestic actors. This claim leads to an array of propositions that can potentially be tested with new data sources.[7]

The book also brings to the forefront several questions not answered here. For example, how do the insights here shed light on the conflict behavior of states with hybrid forms of authoritarianism, such as "competitive authoritarianism," in which the leader is subject to elections even though these elections are not fully free or fair?[8] Why do different kinds of dictatorships emerge in different places and times?[9] I treated domestic institutions as arising independently of a state's external threat environment and focused on how domestic politics affect war rather than the other way around. Future scholarship could investigate in more depth whether certain international environments are more likely to foster transitions to, and the survival of, certain kinds of authoritarianism.

Implications for Policy

In addition to producing important insights for academic scholarship, the findings suggest policy-relevant lessons for diplomacy with dictatorships by painting different pictures of the conflict behavior of machines, juntas, and personalistic bosses and strongmen. For example, China's civilian, elite-constrained government has been the quintessential "machine" for at least two decades. The evidence here suggests that, although countries like China repress public participation in politics, they tend to be more cautious than other authoritarian regime types when it comes to international conflict. Like democratic leaders, leaders of machines face domestic audiences that are not inherently predisposed toward using force and can punish the leader for costly or foolish decisions. This could be good news for deterrent strategies, because like democracies, these regimes tend to avoid starting fights that they cannot win. However, this view of machines also implies that when they do resort to military force or stake a public claim, their efforts will be intense because their leaders cannot afford failure. Policymakers should know that when they are facing an elite-constrained dictatorship that has already escalated a conflict, they must be extremely careful to provide a graceful de-escalation. Like democratic leaders, this type of authoritarian leader faces a domestic audience (of elites) that may punish him for failures in international politics. Moreover, as in democracies, foreign policy decisions in these regimes tend to be carefully vetted and are the product of careful strategic thought (unlike those in personalist regimes, where the policies are more likely to reflect the leader's temporary whims). Once roused, machines can therefore be rather formidable opponents.

The implications for juntas are somewhat different. If the arguments laid out here are correct, policymakers should consider that military leaders in elite-constrained juntas often use force not because they necessarily desire expansion for its own sake but because the military officers staffing these governments are selected and socialized to see military force as standard operating procedure, to view powerful countries as inherently hostile, and to fear the costs of compromise. In other words, policymakers should consider the possibility that for military regimes, force is often "the only language they understand." These leaders will reach for the sword, sometimes preemptively, where civilian leaders might first try diplomacy. Another issue is that the most important constituency in juntas—military officers—may see military force as serving narrow parochial interests, adding to the allure of war. But policymakers must also understand that verbal threats or minor uses of military force by military dictators do not necessarily carry the same escalatory connotations for these leaders, who sometimes reach for force as much out of habit as out of calculation. Diplomats who encounter foreign policy disputes with military dictators must therefore be particularly careful to strike the right balance between deterrence and reassurance; they must convince military juntas that force will be met with force, while not creating a self-fulfilling prophecy.

Personalist bosses like Kim Jong Il and Saddam Hussein, as well as strongmen like Idi Amin and Gamal Abdel Nasser, have also been especially belligerent, although for slightly different reasons. Personalist regimes tend to select for leaders with extreme international ambitions, and because personalist leaders are unusually insulated from the consequences of policy failures, they can act on these preferences and take risky gambles that more constrained leaders would eschew. Policymakers dealing with such dictatorships must accept that they are likely facing an overconfident adversary with the freedom to take major risks. Moreover, personalist dictators are surrounded by yes men who have incentives to echo their leader's often-flawed interpretations of ambiguous facts. The leader is highly unlikely to trust adverse information provided by subordinates, and those subordinates have their own incentives to downplay the severity of a situation.

The findings suggest that one way to deter personalists is to emphasize that conflict may lead to regime change, whereas peace will reduce the likelihood of external interference. Given that personalist dictators are typically surrounded by sycophants who are afraid to communicate unwelcome news, however, it may be important for foreign leaders to engage with them *directly*, rather than through back channels that leave more room for ambiguity. For example, when communicating with the North Korean regime, it may be important for top-level foreign officials to engage face to face with its paramount leader. Foreign leaders must also leave no room for ambiguity about the possible consequences of hostile actions (such as missile tests). On the other hand, the dynamics of personalist dictatorships also provide opportunities for diplomacy. Because these leaders do not have effective domestic audiences, there may be wider latitude in the types of bargains they will be willing to strike. The relative about-face concerning nuclear weapons in Libya under Gaddafi might not have been possible in a regime in which the leader had narrower powers.

Finally, understanding what aspects of authoritarianism are most detrimental to peace could help guide policymakers toward promoting reform in cases where democratization seems unlikely. Of course, there are substantial tradeoffs when it comes to choosing what types of government arrangements to promote abroad, and policymakers must balance stability, human rights considerations, and practicality with foreign policy objectives. But my findings suggest that when it comes to promoting

international peace, mass-level democratization may be no more important than making sure that the government is led by civilians and that no
single all-powerful leader emerges. For example, foreign countries might
instead make aid conditional on the leader allowing collective, civilian
oversight of appointments and security organs (although they should
expect stiff resistance from the leader). Indeed, given their greater sensi-
tivity to the downsides of defeat, even juntas may be more desirable than
personalist dictatorships on national security grounds. Either way, the
evidence here suggests that scholars should pay careful attention to the
type of regime most likely to emerge after foreign intervention or regime
change, designing their activities to lower the likelihood that belligerent
regimes emerge from the rubble.

Appendix

Regime Type Coding Rules
for Data Collection in Chapter 3

This appendix provides further detail on the procedures used for coding the regime type of war participants.

IDENTIFYING NEW/UNSTABLE REGIMES

Countries (whether democratic or not) were considered "new or unstable" if they met one of the following two criteria:

1. The regime had experienced a three-point or more change in its aggregate Polity score within two years of the start of the war.

2. The regime had experienced other major changes in the institutional structure of the regime not picked up by Polity (for example, the change from Diem's personalist rule to a new authoritarian regime in South Vietnam in 1963) within two years of the start of the war.

I did not further classify the regime type of these countries and instead placed them in the "other" category.

CODING PERSONALISM

I considered a regime to be personalist if the leader received a "yes" coding on one of the following indicators (details on the numerous components of those indicators is below).

- Did the leader personally control access to high office?

- Did the leader undermine the military hierarchy and/or create new military forces loyal to himself personally?

In determining whether a leader "personally controlled access to high office," research assistants collected information about the following series of questions. First, the researchers gathered information on background and contextual factors, including:

1. What are the "high offices" or main positions of power within the regime? Please list them.

2. Who holds these offices, and how are the people in these positions related to the leader?

3. How were these individuals selected/who appointed or elected them?

4. What does it take for the leader to fire these individuals?

5. What proportion of people who hold high office have a "personal" relationship to the leader (kinship, marriage, clan affiliation, and so on)?

Researchers then moved on to a second series of yes/no questions. A clear "yes" to any of the questions below led to a "no" coding on the access to high office question. Research assistants rigorously documented the exact sources used for each answer.

1. Can a legislative body or legal system effectively block the leader's chosen or preferred appointments?

2. Are there de facto limitations/restrictions in the appointment process that effectively limit whom the leader can appoint?

3. Can other members of the leader's political party or junta, or other members of the ruling elite (including family members), effectively limit the leader's options for high-level appointments?

Based on this information, I then asked research assistants to write narratives defending their ultimate coding decision about whether the leader controlled appointments or not. The process of writing narratives and then defending them seemed to allow the research team to reach defensible conclusions in disparate contexts while remaining as transparent as possible about the rationales behind coding decisions.

I used an analogous process for determining whether the leader had undermined the military hierarchy and/or created new military forces loyal to himself personally. In this case, research assistants first collected information about the following background questions:

1. What is the general structure of the military? Provide some background on its formation (particularly if recent).

2. What is the leader's involvement in the day-to-day affairs of the military, such as promotions and tactical decisions?

Research assistants were then asked to provide yes/no answers to the following sub-questions. A clear "yes" on any of these sub-questions led to a "yes" on the overall military hierarchy question.

1. Did the leader retire large groups of officers or conduct large purges of the army for reasons other than nationalization of the armed forces?

2. Are promotions within the armed forces based primarily on individuals' "personal" relationship to the leader (kinship, marriage, clan affiliation, and so on) rather than merit or seniority?

3. Did the leader create completely new military forces loyal to himself personally? If so, what/when/how?

4. Has the leader eliminated top positions within the military or taken on important positions himself (in practice, not just in name)?

5. Has the leader reorganized the military to create parallel chains of command in addition to "regular" chains of command?

As before, after answering each question, students summarized their research and defended their overall coding on the military hierarchy variable.

Coding the Military Background of the Leader and Audience

Coding the military vs. civilian nature of the regime was more straightforward. If the leader was constrained by a domestic audience, I assessed whether that audience was composed primarily of civilians (machines) or stemmed from the military ranks (juntas).

Among unconstrained regimes, I coded leaders as civilian bosses if they did not have an extensive professional military career (typically rising to the rank of general or equivalent) prior to taking power. If the leader had an extensive career in formal military service, I coded the regime as a strongman regime.

Ensuring Validity and Reliability

For all of these measures, I also took steps to ensure inter-coder reliability. For each observation, three researchers worked independently to collect information and to answer the questions based on their own research. I then engaged in an iterative process of critiquing the students' narratives, proposing counterarguments and conflicting evidence, until differences were reconciled according to the historical evidence.

I also took steps to attempt to avoid being influenced by biased judgments about a regime's political institutions. For example, Ido Oren argues that a country's own interests might influence its perception of another country's political regime.[1] Observers might perceive a country as "more autocratic" (and hence "bad") if it behaves counter to the observer's interests or acts especially belligerently. Alternatively, observers might misperceive a leader as being more inclusive, and less despotic, if his country acts in accordance with the leader's values. Observers might also assign attributes to a regime for consciously instrumental reasons. For example, one way to discredit a leader would be to call him a "despot" who terrorizes his own people, whereas one might be tempted to attribute more benign and democratic qualities to a friendly regime. In order to guard against this possibility, the research team compared and cross-referenced as many sources as possible, paying careful attention to whether individual sources might be biased (for example, not putting too much emphasis on authors who might have an unconscious or conscious political agenda, such as regime exiles or retired regime insiders, while placing greater emphasis on research by professional scholars and published by respected university presses). Most importantly, however, I relied on *tangible patterns of behavior*—for example, evidence that the leader had purged the military or had fired a succession of top officials and replaced them with family members—rather than relying on observers' perceptions of a leader's behavior or intentions.

Another possible problem with the procedures described above is that they cannot prevent "hindsight" bias. When leaders are ultimately ousted, observers may infer that the leader must have been insecure throughout his entire regime, even if there was no reason to believe that this was the case *ex ante*. One way to solve this problem is to use newspaper sources to track statements about domestic politics in the country on a yearly basis. A surprising amount of information related to the two indicators above can be found in newspaper accounts. This information can be used either as corroboration of the retrospective evaluations of regime characteristics or as the main basis of the regime type codings.

For a sample of the regimes I coded, I therefore had researchers take a second, complementary approach: Collecting all possible newspaper coverage of the regime *before the leader even declared war*. While obviously this method has drawbacks of its own, such as the limitations inherent in relying primarily on information that is in the public record, contemporary news reports allow insight into how observers characterized the regime before being tainted by knowledge about how the leader ultimately lost office. While the information available through newspaper accounts was significantly less detailed than the information available in scholarly sources, the conclusions reached were nonetheless quite similar to the conclusions reached using secondary sources. In the few cases where there were discrepancies in the portrayal of the regime by contemporaries versus historians, I did not see clear patterns in how or why the accounts varied, offering some confidence that the information I collected was not biased in systematic ways.

Notes

INTRODUCTION

1. See, for example, Reiter and Stam 2002.

2. Kant [1795] 1991. Among many more recent examples, see Doyle 1986; Maoz and Russett 1993; Goemans 2000; Schultz 2001a; Reiter and Stam 2002.

3. See, for example, McGillivray and Smith 2000, which argues that "ousting authoritarian leaders is more costly [than ousting democratic leaders], often requiring social unrest and possibly even civil war" (815).

4. Hao and Su 2005; Shirk 2007; Ross 2009; Roy 2009.

5. See, for example, Medeiros and Fravel 2003; Kleine-Ahlbrandt and Small 2008; Green, Wehrey, and Wolf 2009; Medeiros 2009; Milani 2009; Christian Caryl, "The Hermit Kingdom," *Foreign Policy*, October 19, 2009, available at www.foreignpolicy. com/articles/2009/10/19/the_hermit_kingdom, accessed January 8, 2014.

6. Given the historical rarity of female dictators, I use the male pronoun throughout the book.

7. McNamara, Blight, and Brigham 1999, 7.

8. These labels draw on Slater 2003. My four categories are similar to Barbara Geddes's well-known classification of authoritarian regimes (Geddes 2003), although, as I explain in chapter 1, they differ in important ways.

9. Geddes 2003.

10. Peceny, Beer, and Sanchez-Terry 2002; Peceny and Beer 2003; Peceny and Butler 2004.

11. For additional critiques of selectorate theory and the evidence supporting it, see also Haber 2006; Magaloni 2006; Clarke and Stone 2008; Kennedy 2009; Ezrow and Frantz 2011.

12. In selectorate theory, the probability of being part of the successor's winning coalition is w/s, which is smaller when the winning coalition is small relative to the selectorate (66).

13. See Magaloni 2008; Svolik 2009.

14. In fact, actors in the regime (leaders, members of the winning coalition, and so on) are assumed to be identical on every important dimension. Bueno de Mesquita et al. 2003, 75.

15. Lai and Slater 2006, 115.

16. Gelpi 1997. Other research finds that only mature democracies and "consolidating" autocracies show evidence of diversion. Pickering and Kisangani 2005; Kisangani and Pickering 2009. On regime type and diversion, see also Chiozza and Goemans 2003, 2004. Moreover, potential targets of diversionary attacks may deliberately avoid conflict, short-circuiting the diversionary mechanism. Smith 1996; Leeds and Davis 1997; Clark 2003. Perhaps for these reasons, empirical evidence that diversionary or gambling motives drive patterns of conflict initiation is at best mixed. See, for example, James 1987; Chiozza and Goemans 2003. Tir 2010 suggests that diversionary arguments may apply only to the subset of conflicts with high public salience.

17. Pickering and Kisangani 2010.

18. See also Goemans 2008; Chiozza and Goemans 2011.

19. Downs and Rocke 1994.

20. See for example Croco and Weeks (n.d.), who find evidence that democratic leaders are as a whole more sensitive to war outcomes than nondemocratic leaders.

21. On inference in qualitative research, see King, Keohane, and Verba 1994; Lustick 1996; Van Evera 1997; Brady and Collier 2004; George and Bennett 2005; Lieberman 2005; Bennett and Elman 2006; Brady, Collier, and Seawright 2006; Trachtenberg 2006; Bennett and Elman 2007; Seawright and Gerring 2008. Case studies may be able to rule in or rule out arguments when they can evaluate necessary or sufficient conditions rather than looking for evidence of a probabilistic argument, as is the case here.

22. Given that similar mechanisms apply to bosses and personalist strongmen and that the chapter on juntas demonstrates how the "military mindset" contributes to the initiation of international conflict, I choose not to focus on strongmen in the case studies.

23. Known in Spanish as the *Guerra de las Malvinas*.

1. AUTHORITARIAN REGIMES AND THE DOMESTIC POLITICS OF WAR AND PEACE

1. Morgan and Campbell 1991; Reiter and Stam 2002.

2. See, for example, Morgan and Campbell 1991; Schultz 1999. On the United States, see Howell and Pevehouse 2007.

3. I use the word *preferences* here to refer to both preferences over outcomes (such as international expansion, personal wealth, etc.) and preferences over whether to take the more specific action of using military force. Others might consider using military force to be a strategy rather than an outcome of inherent interest, using the term preferences to refer only to the latter. For more on preferences, see Powell 1994; Moravscik 1997; Frieden 1999; Gartzke 2000. It should also be noted that this theory is monadic, in that it focuses on the constraints, preferences, and perceptions of one state at a time without taking into account characteristics of the target. Developing a dyadic theory is a fruitful topic for future work.

4. For an argument about autocratic domestic audiences drawing on "poliheuristic theory," see Kinne 2005. On mass audiences in authoritarian regimes, see Weiss 2013, 2014. On financial elites, see Kirshner 2007.

5. Below, I discuss why elites in autocracies may be motivated to mete out retrospective punishment.

6. For the classic text on perception in international politics, see Jervis 1976.

7. On expansionist motives, see Snyder 1991; Lake 1992. On revisionist states, see Schweller 1994. On "greedy" states, see Glaser 2010.

8. Goemans 2000.

9. See, for example, Fearon 1995; Powell 1996, 2002; Reiter 2003; Slantchev 2003.

10. See, for example, Colgan 2013b, 666.

11. Future research could investigate whether authoritarian regime type fosters certain kinds of bargaining failures once a dispute has arisen.

12. Geddes 1999, 2003. Space does not permit exploring the merits of alternative ways of differentiating among authoritarian regimes, but see Arendt 1951; Friedrich and Brzezinski 1956; O'Donnell 1978; Linz 2000; Brooker 2000; Wintrobe 2000; Gandhi and Przeworski 2006; Magaloni 2006, 2008; Brownlee 2007; Hadenius and Teorell 2007; Gandhi 2008; Wright 2008; Pepinsky 2009; Cheibub, Gandhi, and Vreeland 2010; Levitsky and Way 2010; Ezrow and Frantz 2011; Svolik 2012; Wahman, Teorell, and Hadenius 2013; Geddes, Wright, and Frantz 2014.

13. Most previous work has used a three-part typology that does not allow separate examination of the military and personalist dimensions; for example, Peceny and Beer 2003 groups strongmen and bosses together as "personalists."

14. See also Lai and Slater 2006. A possible point of confusion is that although I use Slater's (2003) labels (the same as Lai and Slater 2006), I use subtly different criteria to assign regimes to those categories. Slater and Lai and Slater focus on "infrastructural power" or whether the regime is supported by military versus civilian institutions, while I focus on the military versus civilian backgrounds of key decision-makers.

15. Svolik 2009.

16. Weber [1947] 1997; Chehabi and Linz 1998; Geddes 2003. Similarly, Svolik 2012 distinguishes between "contested" autocracies in which "the dictator's allies are genuine political players who share power with him and constrain his choices," and "established autocracies" in which regime insiders "are in a position of fully subservient administrators and do not share power with the dictator in any meaningful sense" (78).

17. Bratton and Van de Walle 1994.

18. See also Frantz 2008; Ezrow and Frantz 2011. The constraints on leaders can be formal or informal. Often, the degree of constraints in authoritarian regimes does not reflect the letter of the law. On how legislatures can constrain authoritarian rulers, see also Wright 2008.

19. Arquilla and Rasmussen 2001, 762.

20. See, for example, Fearon 1994; Downs and Rocke 1994.

21. Guisinger and Smith 2002.

22. Richards, Morgan, Wilson, Schwebach, and Young 1993; Smith 1996; Smith 1998; Fearon 1999; Johns 2006. Lee 2011 has a fascinating discussion of the Iroquoi ousting war chiefs who presided over too many deaths because those deaths revealed the leader's "impurity," which would cause problems in the future. The threat of punishment in turn encouraged chiefs to avoid risky strategies (150).

23. One important question is whether leaders' post-tenure fates could affect their calculations. Goemans 2000, 2008; Debs and Goemans 2010; Chiozza and Goemans 2011. In the empirical chapters of this book, I consider whether the anticipation of severe punishment explains the variation among authoritarian regimes that I document, and conclude that it is unlikely.

24. While most argue that dictators, whether personalist or not, tend to be more secure in office than democratic leaders (Frantz 2008), others argue that nondemocratic leaders are typically *more* sensitive to war outcomes (Chiozza and Goemans 2003, 2004, 2011; Debs and Goemans 2010).

25. As I mentioned above, I use the word "preferences" to refer to preferences over outcomes as well as preferences over strategies such as the use of force. This makes sense in the current context given that different actors have different values for military force as opposed to alternate strategies.

26. Bueno de Mesquita et al. 2003.

27. Lake 1992.

28. Some regimes also take explicit steps to reduce the costs to citizens. See for example Valentino, Huth, and Croco 2010.

29. Holsti 1991.

30. In fact, Flores-Macías and Kreps 2013 argues that in democracies such as the United States, leaders often finance wars in ways that conceal the true costs from citizens, or distribute the costs away from their core supporters. The financial costs to ordinary citizens may therefore not be as high, or as evenly distributed, as commonly assumed.

31. See, for example, Kirshner 2007.

32. I define norms broadly as standards of appropriate behavior shared by a particular community—in this case, a domestic community of policymakers. The norms could either involve moral beliefs about what is right or could refer simply to standard behaviors. See Wendt 1992; Goldstein and Keohane 1993; Mercer 1995; Risse-Kappen 1995; Katzenstein 1996; Kahl 1998.

33. Maoz and Russett 1993; Dixon 1994; Downes 2008; Tomz and Weeks 2013.

34. Wallace 2010.

35. Downs 1957.

36. Kull, Ramsay, and Lewis 2003.

37. From the perspective of bargaining models of war, not only are these states more satisfied with the status quo, but even when there is a conflict of interest, their high perceived costs of war should open up a bargaining range, reducing the likelihood of war. Fearon 1995, 404.

38. See Tangerås 2009, which derives formally the intuitive implication that leaders who are likely to be punished for "bad" outcomes will start fewer conflicts and also win a higher proportion of the conflicts that they do start.

39. In chapter 3 I discuss how selection effects might mute differences among regimes.

40. On military regimes, see Andreski 1954; Nordlinger 1977; Remmer 1989; Geddes 2003; Gandhi and Przeworski 2006.

41. One might argue that military officers are poor at judging the political consequences of war, and indeed the case studies in later chapters suggest this, but it is

not clear whether this would result in systematically overestimating the likelihood of victory.

42. For example, Holsti 2004.

43. E.g. Saunders 2009, 2011; Colgan 2013a; Horowitz and Stam 2014.

44. See, for example, Elkins and Simeon 1979; Snyder 1984; Adler 1992; Goldstein and Keohane 1993; Johnston 1995; Finnemore 1996; Legro 1996; Lake 2010; Saunders 2011; Dafoe and Caughey 2011; Horowitz and Stam 2014.

45. Sechser 2004.

46. Lovell 1964.

47. Note that this argument reaches a similar conclusion as Debs and Goemans 2010, which argues that military officers are often punished for making peaceful concessions. However, their mechanism relies on the technology of leadership removal rather than officers' perceptions of the necessity of using force.

48. Huntington 1957, 64; see also Snyder 1984, 28 and Sagan 2000, 19–20. See Lovell 1964 and Abrahamsson 1969 on selection and socialization into military organizations.

49. Levy 1987, 104.

50. Posen 1984, 57; Snyder 1984, 28.

51. Posen 1984; Snyder 1984. Vagts 1956 expresses a similar view (263). Snyder 1991, citing Van Evera 1984a, argues that military organizations may not favor war directly, but that their organizational interests may lead to war indirectly.

52. Posen 1984 and Sagan 2000; though see also Kier 1997.

53. Jervis 1978; Van Evera 1984b; Snyder 1991.

54. For a helpful overview of this literature, see Sechser 2004. Moreover, see Kier 1997 and Legro 1996, who argue that different military organizations have different "cultures" and that not all military organizations are prone toward the offensive in the way that I describe above. But two points bear noting. First, their argument is that military organizations do not *deterministically* favor the use of force; my argument is probabilistic. Second, Kier and Legro focused disproportionately on wealthy and economically advanced countries. It is possible that the military organizations they studied, in which the military did not automatically hold offensive doctrines, share certain features that make them unlikely to mount military coups.

55. Andreski 1992 reaches a similar conclusion, arguing that sending the army abroad for military adventures renders it unavailable for internal policing (105) and that politicizing the army undermines its war-fighting effectiveness. However, Andreski's evidence is anecdotal, and his argument should apply to any regime in which the military is important to the stability of the country, not only military dictatorships.

56. Though, note that Betts's conclusion was actually that military opinion was often divided and that the hawkish military officers rarely influenced U.S. policy. In fact, Betts's own data showed that during Cold War crises, military officers advocated more hawkish policy positions than civilians 21% of the time, equally hawkish positions 65% of the time, and were less hawkish only 14% of the time (216). When it came to tactical escalation decisions after an intervention, military officers were *never* less aggressive than civilians. Author's calculations from table A in Betts 1977.

Moreover, one might simply dismiss the military conservatism view on the grounds that it is U.S.-centric: most of this work is based on data from military officers in democracies, particularly the United States. In democracies, military officers are usually drawn from a wide swath of society, typically have broad educations that include not only military science but also other subjects, and are inculcated with strong normative beliefs about the situations in which violence is appropriate. Any differences between officers and civilians would therefore likely be muted compared to authoritarian regimes.

57. The civilian sample I analyze here includes random samples of individuals from the 1998 *Who's Who in America*, State Department staff, editorial writers, foreign affairs experts, labor union officials, and students at Duke University. The military sample is drawn primarily from military officers undergoing training at institutions such as the Army and Naval War Colleges and the National Defense University.

58. Other questions considered a host of nonmilitary threats, such as economic competition, threats to American values, immigration, and so on.

59. The margins for the Chinese threat are even larger if one pools together those who thought the threat was very or moderately serious.

60. There are two possible cross-cutting effects here. On the one hand, audiences in juntas might be more forgiving *ex post* because they agreed that military action was necessary. On the other hand, they may judge the leader more harshly for failure because the outcome will be inconsistent with their prewar view of the likelihood of winning. They may therefore be even more likely to attribute the failure to the leader's incompetence.

61. For a similar conclusion, see Snyder 1991 on unitary systems dominated by a single actor.

62. See, for example, Glad 2002; Post 2004. Moreover, many personalist dictators are revolutionary leaders who wish to change the status quo both domestically and internationally. Walt 1996; Colgan 2013a and 2013b.

63. Glad 2002, 26; Rosen 2005, 156–57.

64. Woods et al. 2006.

65. See Schweller 1998.

66. Gurr 1988; Colgan 2010; Horowitz and Stam 2014.

67. Jerrold Post argues that "the certainty of ultimate success to which narcissists feel entitled leads to both a sense of omnipotence and a feeling of invulnerability, that they cannot go wrong." Post 1993, 103.

68. See, for example, 197–98.

69. For example, Geddes 2004; Haber 2006; Frantz 2008; Ezrow and Frantz 2011.

70. For example, Finer 1962; Janowitz 1964; O'Donnell 1973; Nordlinger 1977; Perlmutter 1977; Stepan 1988; Remmer 1989.

71. As I mentioned earlier, I do not focus on strongmen in the case studies because it is difficult to isolate the effects of personalism and military background when the two coincide.

2. Initiating International Conflict

1. Indeed, studies such as Oren and Hays 1997 have noted that single-party states seem more peaceful than other authoritarian regime types. Weart 1994 shows that oligarchies are also relatively peaceful. See also Sobek 2005.

2. For a related analysis, see Weeks 2012.

3. Marshall and Jaggers 2002; Banks 2007, Variable S20F7—"Type of Regime."

4. Marshall and Jaggers 2002, 23. In fact, of the four examples Lai and Slater provide of juntas—Burma, Algeria, Greece (pre-1974), and Argentina (pre-1983)—their empirical analysis counts all four as strongmen because these regimes score low on formal "institutional constraints" according to the *xconst* measure.

5. For a critique of the Geddes typology, which points out that her classification is not mutually exclusive or collectively exhaustive, see also Svolik 2012, 30–31.

6. I use the indicator in Cheibub, Gandhi, and Vreeland 2010 for the effective leader's military background.

7. I code the index as "missing" when I have data on fewer than four of the subquestions.

8. In constructing the personalist dummy variable, I used the following rules to deal with missing values. If there were at least four non-missing answers, I counted a country as personalist if it received a "yes" on more than 50% of the questions. In the few cases where two or three of the questions were answered, I counted a country as personalist if it scored yes on *all* of those answers and as not personalist if it scored no on *all* of those answers. Otherwise, I coded nondemocratic observations as missing on the personalist dummy variable. I also experimented with other cutoffs, basing the cutoffs on a weighted version of the index, and increasing the threshold for coding an observation as "missing"; such changes did not affect the substantive results. I coded democracies as nonpersonalist. I followed similar procedures for the military dummy variable.

9. This dummy variable receives a value of 1 if the regime had undergone a change in Polity score of 3 points or more within the last three years, based on the updated Polity IV dataset in Gleditsch 2013.

10. Note that since I lag the regime type data by one year, the empirical analyses can be extended through 2000.

11. Jones, Bremer, and Singer 1996, 168. For the data analysis, I use the dyadic version of the dataset recoded in Maoz 2005.

12. Lai and Slater 2006.

13. Most and Starr 1989; Oneal and Tir 2006.

14. Green, Kim, and Yoon 2001; Schultz 2001a.

15. These measures rely on Version 4.0 of the Correlates of War (COW) CINC data. Singer, Bremer, and Stuckey 1972.

16. Gowa 1999.

17. Schultz 2001a.

18. Data for these variables came from EUGene. The United States was the system leader in this time period.

19. Stinnett et al. 2002.

20. For each member of the dyad, I measure trade dependence as country A's total trade with country B as a proportion of its GDP, and vice versa. For the analyses reported later, I follow Russett and Oneal 2001 and Oneal, Russett, and Berbaum 2003 and include the trade dependence of the less dependent country. The results do not change if each country's trade dependence is entered separately.

21. The one exception is that juntas are not more likely to initiate than democracies in the bare-bones model in column 1, though they are significantly more likely to initiate once control variables are included.

22. Green, Kim, and Yoon 2001; Schultz 2001a.

23. Beck and Katz 2001.

24. Tomz, Wittenberg, and King 2003.

25. I also excluded new/unstable regimes from the analysis to be consistent with the earlier models.

26. Brambor, Clark, and Golder 2006. Note that because the indices for personalism and militarism range from 0 to 1, the coefficient on the interaction term is multiplied by an even smaller number; for example, if personalism and militarism are each .25, personalism*militarism is only .0625. The coefficient listed in the table therefore appears large until one realizes that it is multiplied by a very small number to calculate the full interaction effect.

27. Both are based on the pooled analysis shown in column 1 of table 2.3, which codes democracies as missing.

28. Available in the replication materials.

29. Lai and Slater report monadic analyses in which the country-year is the unit of analysis, whereas I analyze directed dyad-years because of the greater measurement precision that doing so allows.

30. Indeed, Bueno de Mesquita et al. 2003 suggests this finding (245).

31. See, for example, Bueno de Mesquita et al. 2003, 440.

32. For a discussion of selectorate size and authoritarian regime type, see Peceny and Butler 2004. Although Peceny and colleagues 2002, 2003, 2004 and Reiter and Stam 2002 operationalized regime type dyadically, my findings appear consistent with theirs in that personalist regimes (roughly comparable to my bosses and strongmen) or military regimes (roughly comparable to my juntas) are more belligerent against some types of targets than single-party regimes (roughly comparable to my machines) or democracies.

33. Another question is whether these findings are consistent with Weeks 2008, in which I found that personalist regimes are the least able to signal their resolve credibly, whereas nonpersonalist regimes—including juntas—tend to be no different from democracies. If the costs of war are lower for strongmen, bosses, and juntas, as I have argued, then we might expect them to do better in crisis bargaining because it is credible that they will use force. On the other hand, the extremely low accountability of personalist leaders may offset their greater "inherent" credibility due to their lower costs for war. As for juntas, the combination of lower costs for war and high accountability of the leader to a domestic audience could imply a signaling advantage, which was not evident in the analysis presented in Weeks 2008. Future research could attempt to reconcile these findings, perhaps by considering whether the commitment problems created by the anticipation of future military conflict affect reciprocation rates in the present.

34. Available on the author's personal web site.

3. Winners, Losers, and Survival

1. Desch 2002; Desch 2003; Desch 2008; Downes 2008. For related discussions see Brooks 2003; Biddle and Long 2004; Kaufmann 2004.

2. Lake 1992; Reiter and Stam 2002.

3. Lake 1992.

4. Choi 2004.

5. Reiter and Stam 2002.

6. Quinlivan 1999, 131–65; see also Biddle and Zirkle 1996, 171–212, and Biddle 2004 (50).

7. See, for example, Brooks 1998; Woods et al. 2006. Talmadge points out however, that when motivated, even personalist leaders like Saddam can modify their war-fighting practices for greater success (2013).

8. Fearon 1994.

9. Bueno de Mesquita et al. 2003.

10. I found this to be the earliest date that authoritarian regime type could be coded reliably and consistently. It also coincides with the end of the aftermath from World War I.

11. Sarkees and Wayman 2010. Each participant counts as one observation, regardless of the length of the war.

12. States commit resources to wars to varying degrees, from fighting an all-out war to sending a token brigade or two as a gesture to an ally. For example, the Philippines and Ethiopia in the Korean War and Italy and Morocco in the 1991 Gulf War are listed as war participants by COW even though their contribution to those wars was so minimal that the conflict's outcome was unlikely to pose a major domestic political issue for them. Many of these minor war participants join wars as part of large coalitions that either won or at least tied the war. Including these cases could distort our inferences if, due to chance, states of certain regime types have had more frequent opportunities to bandwagon on their allies' victories.

Moreover, some scholars disaggregate World War II into ten or more smaller conflicts. Reiter and Stam 2002; Downes 2009. This approach credits eight individual victories to autocratic Germany (bilateral victories against Poland, France, Belgium, Holland, Denmark, Norway, Yugoslavia, and Greece), while only attributing two defeats to Germany (the Eastern and Western fronts of World War II). I choose not to disaggregate World War II in this way because it does not seem likely that Hitler would have viewed these as ten separate decisions—they were part of one larger decision to start World War II, a gamble that ultimately failed. Including these wars would inflate the number of victories by bosses, since this is how Hitler is coded.

The data on whether a state was a major combatant come from Valentino, Huth, and Croco 2010. For the few COW 4.0 wars not in their dataset, I utilized their coding rules.

13. This also served as a validity check on the data used in chapter 2; I found extremely high concordance between my independent codings of regime type and the classifications generated using the procedures described in chapter 2. The one exception is the Democratic Republic of the Congo in 1975, which is probably best considered a boss (as I do in this chapter) but was classified as a strongman according to the data sources used for chapter 2.

14. Croco 2011 builds on Valentino, Huth, and Croco 2006. The data are updated by Croco and Weeks n.d. to be consistent with the most recent Version 4.0 of the COW dataset. This included coding outcomes for sixteen war participants for which COW Version 4.0 codes the outcome as transforming into an intrastate war (for example, the recent Afghanistan and Iraq wars).

15. See Croco 2011. Of course, since leaders have some latitude in how they portray the war outcome, the scheme does not rely on leaders' own assessments of whether those objectives were ultimately met. Johnson and Tierney 2006.

16. Unlike COW, the scheme also does not require that all coalition members in a war have the same outcome. COW codes Belgium and the Netherlands as winning World War II, despite German occupation and the fact that it was mostly other states' fighting that produced the Allied victory. Croco's coding scheme counts them as losses because during the phase in which the country's army was fighting, the war resulted in defeat. Similarly, Croco codes Kuwait as losing the Gulf War in 1990, whereas COW counts this as a win.

17. As described earlier, I focus on stable regimes; the democracies counted here therefore include only regimes that had not undergone significant institutional change for at least two years before the war's start. As for grouping together wins and draws, later in the chapter I carry out an ordered logit analysis of all three war outcomes.

18. Note that Croco combines the Changkufeng and Nomonhan incidents, whereas COW treats them as two separate conflicts. I adopt her coding of a "draw" for Japan in both conflicts, because the result involved no change in the status quo for Japan.

19. See Gelman and Hill 2006; Angrist and Pischke 2008. As an analogy, consider a study that tries to assess the causal effect of education on earnings: One cannot accurately assess how education affects earnings if one also controls for occupation, because education causes occupation; in other words, occupation is post-treatment. It should therefore not be included in a study attempting to uncover the causal effect of education. Angrist and Pischke 2008. (Importantly, controlling for post-treatment variables may either reduce *or* inflate the estimated effect of the variable of interest.) In this example, rather than add in more controls, "we would do better to control only for variables that are not themselves caused by education." Angrist and Pischke 2008, 66.

20. An approximate likelihood-ratio test using the "omodel" command in STATA indicates that the proportional odds assumption is appropriate.

21. These variables are culled from standard sources. The online supplemental appendix at https://users.polisci.wisc.edu/jweeks details the source of each variable and how it was operationalized.

22. Bosses are different from democracies at the $p < 0.0706$ and $p < 0.052$ level for Models 1 and 2, respectively. Strongmen are different at the $p < 0.0015$ and $p < 0.0104$ levels, respectively.

23. Marshall and Jaggers 2002, 25.

24. I consider as initiators countries that were on the attacking side and participated in the war from the first day, and I follow Downes 2009 in also including states that shared a preexisting alliance with the initiator and joined the war within one week. Joiners are countries such as Italy and Japan in World War II or China and the United States in the Korean War, countries that did not initiate the broader conflict and did not have a defense pact with the target of the war but joined either side more than a week after the war began. To code these variables, I relied on Downes 2009, COW 4.0, and the Horowitz and Stam 2014 update of the COW 4 data. Of the 120 war participants in the sample, 53 initiated, 6 joined, and the remaining 61 are considered targets. The role of each state in the conflict (initiator, joiner, or target) is listed in table 3.5.

25. Jones, Bremer, and Singer 1996, 168.

26. There are a few MIDs in which very large coalitions (of more than 10 participants) banded together on the initiating side: 3551, 4137, 4186 (all against Yugosla-

via), and 4273 (against Iraq). These observations are potentially influential (because there are so many initiators) and the dependent variable does not vary by dispute. So I drop participants in coalitions from MIDs if their highest action in the MID was only to threaten, but not to show or to use, force. Dropping them does not however affect the substantive results shown in table 3.3.

27. For a similar treatment, see Gelpi and Griesdorf 2001.

28. The coefficient on boss is unexpectedly more negative than that on strongmen, but the difference between the two is not significant. Control variables are from the same sources as in chapter 2. As in chapter 2, regime type and control variables are lagged by one year. Replication data available on the author's personal website.

29. See the replication files for code to carry out these analyses.

30. Schultz 2001b.

31. Croco and Weeks, n.d.

32. Goemans, Gleditsch, and Chiozza 2009.

33. This drops 13 observations. The patterns are nearly identical when these observations are not treated as censored and are instead included in the analysis.

34. The skeptical reader might wonder whether, given the inherent difficulty of forming objective judgments about leaders' true constraints in closed authoritarian regimes, the coding procedures might be biased in ways that favor my hypotheses about the rate of ouster after defeat. For example, perhaps the coding procedures increase the likelihood of considering leaders who were ousted after wars as "constrained," whereas leaders who survived losing wars are more likely to be viewed as "unconstrained." In other words, I could be attributing certain characteristics to the ousted leaders *ex post*, rather than showing true evidence that the hypothesized constraints predict whether leaders will be ousted *ex ante*. I took various steps to attempt to ensure that the codings were not influenced by leaders' postwar fates. For example, I focused only on tangible or demonstrated constraints on the leader that were evident before the war started, rather than focusing on the perceptions of observers whose judgments could have been influenced by later events. I also coded all recently transitioned or unstable regimes as "other" to avoid basing judgments on little information.

35. One stable democratic leader officially survived a "defeat": Richard Nixon, who was president when the United States lost the War of the Communist Coalition (COW Interstate War #176), a 1970–1971 portion of the larger Vietnam conflict in which the United States failed to prevent communist forces from gaining control over large parts of Cambodia. Of course, he soon resigned for other reasons.

36. Replication code available at https://users.polisci.wisc.edu/jweeks.

37. Croco and Weeks, n.d.

4. Personalist Dictators: Shooting from the Hip

1. Coughlin 2005, 151.

2. See, for example, Karsh and Rautsi 1991, 119. Sassoon 2011 demonstrates how officials and ministers almost never disagreed with him (171–72).

3. Sassoon 2011 provides an excellent analysis of the various security agencies (95–128). On how these agencies were used to protect Saddam's rule, see Coughlin 2005, 115; Duelfer 2005; Woods et al. 2006, 3–7.

4. Saddam was obsessed with loyalty and hoped to ensure that the internal security agencies were "dedicated to him personally, rather than to the party, to Ba'athist ideology or to the President." Baram 2003, 99–100.

5. Mansfield 1982, 65; Coughlin 2005, 123; Woods et al. 2006, 53, 56.

6. Woods et al. 2006 and Sassoon 2011 (esp. 129–61) provide extensive detail on how Saddam controlled the military, with Sassoon placing emphasis on how Saddam used the Ba'ath Party apparatus to achieve this. See also Makiya 1989; Baram 2003; Al-Marashi and Salama 2008 (e.g., 99–102), as well as Brooks 1998, which identified other personalist regimes using the same measures.

7. Woods et al. 2006, 56. Sassoon 2011 describes such patterns in military promotions (e.g., 140).

8. Woods et al. 2006, 8, 13–14. On military officers' incentives to report favorable information, see Sassoon 2011, 136.

9. Woods et al. 2006, 39.

10. Duelfer 2005, 11.

11. Sassoon 2011, 163.

12. Coughlin 2005, 21.

13. Coughlin 2005, 27.

14. Coughlin 2005, 33; Sassoon 2011, 21.

15. Coughlin 2005, 33.

16. Coughlin 2005, 50–51, 66; Sassoon 2011, 28, 30.

17. Chubin and Tripp 1988, 114–15; Marr 1988, 197; Coughlin 2005, 87.

18. Karsh and Rautsi 1991, 109, 111; Coughlin 2005, 152; Lando 2007, 46; Gause 2010, 51.

19. Makiya 1989, 70–71; Coughlin 2005, 156–61.

20. Tripp 1987, 63.

21. Karsh and Rautsi 1991, 24.

22. Coughlin 2005, 183–84. See also Sassoon 2011, which indicates that Saddam likened himself to great leaders such as Charles de Gaulle and Nelson Mandela (174).

23. Renshon 1993, 51; Coughlin 2005, 125.

24. Makiya 1989, 270–71; Rezun 1992, 51.

25. This is not to say that Saddam was insane. Numerous accounts emphasize his patience and caution in certain contexts; see for example Sassoon 2011, 164.

26. I do not focus on the Iran-Iraq War because by the time of the war's start (1980), Saddam had been in power only for a year, and the institutional structure of the regime was still consolidating. That said, Iraq's decision to initiate the Iran-Iraq War does appear to be consistent with the argument here.

27. Karsh and Rautsi 1991, 201.

28. Karsh and Rautsi 1991, 202, 209–11; Simpson 2003, 116.

29. Marr 2004, 202–3.

30. Karsh and Rautsi 1991, 212; Simpson 2003, 118; Marr 2004, 215.

31. Rahman 1997, 296.

32. Rahman 1997, 288.

33. Rahman 1997, 289–90. In fact, at the outset of the conflict, many expected Saddam to limit his actions to seizing these islands and some of the oil fields along the border. Had he done so, he might well have been successful.

34. Renshon 1993, 80. Woods 2008 argues that Saddam "often conflated the concept of self and state" (33).

35. Al-Bazzaz 1995, 67; Woods 2008, 47.

36. Al-Bazzaz 1995, 72.

37. Woods 2008, 32, 35. See also Coughlin 2005, 257–58.

38. Woods 2008, 34.

39. Al-Samara'i 1996.

40. Woods 2008, 104. See also 56–57 for a speech by Saddam soon after the invasion characterizing it as achieving "Arab unity" and a speech by one of Saddam's ministers in a small meeting with him a few days after the invasion, characterizing it as Saddam carrying the "Saladin mission from Iraq in order to liberate Jerusalem and Arab occupied lands" (56). This speech was likely carefully tailored to reflect Saddam's own views.

41. Aziz 1996.

42. Aziz 1996.

43. Gause 2001, 6–7.

44. Gause 2001, 10–11.

45. Woods et al. 2006, 12. According to Woods 2008, Saddam's "compartmented" mode of decision-making explains why there are no records of when exactly he reached the decision (53).

46. Woods 2008, 62, 80.

47. Al-Bazzaz 1995, 67.

48. Woods 2008, 213. Some argue that Tariq Aziz in fact told his boss that Iraq would face little international opposition to its invasion, either from the Gulf States or from the United States. Gause 2001, 12.

49. Woods 2008, 60.

50. Woods 2008, 62.

51. Woods 2008, 62.

52. Al Samara'i 1996, in an interview with PBS after defecting.

53. Rahman 1997, 298–99.

54. Gause 2001, 12.

55. Renshon 1993, 54; Al Samara'i 1996.

56. Al-Samara'i 1996.

57. Rahman 1997, 294–96; Woods 2008, 47–52.

58. Renshon 1993, 79, 294.

59. Al-Samara'i 1996.

60. Karsh and Rautsi 1991, 217–18.

61. Woods 2008, 17–18.

62. Hashim 2003; Woods et al. 2006, 13–14.

63. Renshon 1993, 140; on gaining prestige in the Middle East, 142; "Address to the Jordanian National Democratic Alliance," *FBIS Daily Report* 1990. Saddam also tried to link the Kuwait invasion to the Israeli/Palestinian conflict, offering to withdraw from Kuwait if Israel withdrew from Palestinian territory. Woods 2008, 104.

64. Woods 2008, 126–30.

65. Sarkees and Wayman 2010, 176–77.

66. Cockburn and Cockburn 2002, 9.

67. Marr 1985, 240.

68. Marr 1985, 241–43.

69. Gause 2010, 115.

70. Duelfer 2005, 25.

71. Marr 1985, 246.

72. Marr 1985, 243–46.

73. Marr 1985, 247.

74. Cockburn and Cockburn 2002, 38.

75. Cockburn and Cockburn 2002, 38.

76. Coughlin 2005, 287.

77. Montefiore 2004, 26.

78. Service 2005, 27, 30. Conquest 1991 also stresses Stalin's appetite for violence, and Tucker 1990 also alludes to Stalin's legendary vindictiveness (3).

79. Montefiore 2004, 32; Service 2005, 337.

80. Montefiore 2004, 33.

81. Service 2005, 12.

82. Montefiore 2004, 179.

83. Tucker 1990, 3.

84. Conquest 1991, 82.

85. Volkogonov 1991, 219; Watson 2004, 152.

86. Aspaturian 1984, 33.

87. Erickson [1962] 2001, 286; Bialer 1969, 442.

88. Montefiore 2004, 225.

89. Montefiore 2004, 226.

90. Volkogonov 1991, 332.

91. Boterbloem 2004, 340. On the composition of this inner circle, which is often described as including Mikoyan and Malenkov as well, see Boterbloem 2004, 181; Khrushchev 2004, 249; Khlevniuk 2009, 185.

92. Service 2005, 329. Indeed, unlike nonpersonalist regimes, Stalin's regime resembles the assumptions of small-coalition systems in selectorate theory.

93. Boterbloem 2004, 289.

94. Montefiore 2004, 341.

95. Montefiore 2004, 297. Though see Haslam 2011, which argues that there were occasional limits to Molotov's obedience (65).

96. Admiral Kuznetsov, quoted in Boterbloem 2004, 191.

97. Glad 2002, 17.

98. Erickson [1962] 2001, 200; Shukman 1993, 313.

99. Volkogonov 1991, 219.

100. Bialer 1969, 106.

101. Bialer 1969, 461.

102. Shukman 1993, 6–7.

103. Van Dyke 1997, 207; see also Chubaryan and Shukman 2002, xxiv. This does not mean that Stalin never consulted with subordinates. The anecdote with General Rokossovsky provides at least one example of a subordinate airing his views. Stalin often remained above the fray, "encouraging others to argue the issues, and . . . vent longstanding frustrations, before taking a stand of his own." Haslam 1992, 109. This provided a way for him to gauge the views of others. Shukman also suggests by the middle of World War II Stalin "had acquired a good deal of strategic skill. At least now he was capable of listening to intelligent voices, well informed army men like Antonov, Shaposhnikov and Vasilevsky, who had the ability and the nerve to lay before him their frank assessment of the situation and to recommend what course of action he should adopt." Shukman 1993, 7. But most analyses stress the fear that pervaded discussions with Stalin.

104. Tanner 1957, 3.

105. Aspaturian 1984, 42.

106. Bialer 1969, 135; Bozek 1993, 30–36.

107. Haslam 1992, 118.

108. Bialer 1969, 89.

109. Aspaturian 1984, 24.

110. Montefiore 2004, 301.

111. Khrushchev 2004, 219–20. On the fact that Khrushchev was frequently not consulted on foreign policy and defense issues, see Aspaturian 1984, 26, 31, 32.

112. Montefiore 2004, 310.

113. Montefiore 2004, 377.

114. Volkogonov 1991, 541; Stueck 1997, 36. For a portrayal of Stalin that highlights his skill as a wartime leader, see Roberts 2006.

115. Stalin's fear of a two-front war and his desire to avoid it led to a cautious Soviet policy in the Far East. Garver 1988, 16–18; Haslam 1992, 92–95. Blumenson 1960 describes the Soviet action in 1938 at Changkufeng as "a gamble" that was "limited" and "shrewd" (250–51); some argue that the Changkufeng/Lake Khasan conflict played out with a tacit agreement between the two sides to prevent escalation. Tinch 1951, 179; Erickson [1962] 2001, 498.

Stalin's behavior in the Nomonhan conflict in 1939 was also cautious, according to some. Tinch 1951 argues that Soviet foreign policy was "grounded in an empirical realism as tough as it was pliable" (194). Sound intelligence (Whymant 1996, 109) allowed the Soviets to "practice 'brinkmanship' with the Japanese and derive full advantage from it." Erickson[1962] 2001, 745.

116. Service 2005 argues that by 1937, no one remained in the Politburo who would stand up to Stalin, and then a series of mass arrests and executions known as the Great Purge or Great Terror sealed the deal (349).

117. Quoted in Montefiore 2004, 301.

118. See Erickson [1962] 2001, 515; Haslam 1984, 214; Roberts 1992, 640–43; Pons 2002, 162; Montefiore 2004, 301.

119. Degras 1952, 395.

120. Tanner 1957, 3.

121. Tanner 1957, 9.

122. McSherry 1970, 25.

123. Van Dyke 1997, 19.

124. Tanner 1957; Van Dyke 1997, 18.

125. McSherry 1970, 32; see also Tanner 1957, 55.

126. Van Dyke 1997, 8.

127. Van Dyke 1997, 8.

128. Van Dyke 1997, 19. The Main Military Soviet consisted of Stalin, Voroshilov, Shapshnikov, Kuznetsov, and usually Meretskov in an unofficial capacity. Boterbloem 2004, 202.

129. Edwards 2006, 94.

130. Erickson [1962] 2001, 543; Medvedev 1989, 733. Shaposhnikov was not the only officer worried about the conflict. Artillery chief General Voronov thought they would be lucky to settle with Finland within two or three months. Even Meretskov complains in his memoirs how "the war was taken so lightly that they were not prepared when the order to cross the frontier came on 29 November." Spring 1986, 215.

131. Edwards 2006, 98. Some at high levels of government agreed with Stalin, though it is difficult to say to what extent these beliefs were genuine, as opposed to the product of fear of disagreeing once Stalin articulated his own viewpoint. Voroshilov supported Stalin's thinking, reporting to Stalin, "Most of the Finnish equipment consists of pre-war models of the old tsarist army. . . . The mood of their reservists is depressed. . . . The working masses of Finland . . . are threatening to mete out justice on those who pursue a policy hostile to the Soviet Union." Van Dyke 1997, 32.

132. Though importantly, he was not killed or imprisoned for standing up to Stalin.

133. This was probably a fabrication, but it was not necessarily a pretext for war. Rather, it might have well been one last chance to prove to Finland the seriousness of the matter and return them to the negotiating table. Spring 1986, 219.

134. Degras 1952, 402.

135. Edwards 2006, 125.

136. Sarkees and Wayman 2010, 143.

137. Khrushchev 2004, 254; Edwards 2006, 277.

138. Medvedev 1989, 734. Khrushchev also acknowledged the plausibility of such an argument in his memoirs. Khrushchev 2004, 254.

139. Baryshnikov 2000, 171.

140. Montefiore 2004, 391; Roberts 2006, 11.

141. Indeed, immediately after the war Stalin sought to contain tensions with the West. He also stayed out of the Korean War primarily out of fear of direct military engagement with the United States. Weathersby 1993, 29.

142. See, for example, Haslam 2011.

143. Roberts 2006, 346.

144. Roberts 2006, 361–62.

145. Roberts 2006, 331.

146. Roberts 2006, 350.

147. Adomeit 1984, 73.

148. Goncharov, Lewis, and Xue 1993, 207.

149. Goncharov, Lewis, and Xue 1993, 152; Weathersby 1993, 28; Stueck 1997, 36.

5. JUNTAS: USING THE ONLY LANGUAGE THEY UNDERSTAND

1. Freedman 2005a, 1–17.

2. A. Betts 1997, 81; Freedman 2005a, 8.

3. Calvert 1982, 90.

4. Calvert 1982, 95; Freedman 2005a, 17.

5. Hoffmann and Mingo Hoffmann 1984, 107, 110–12; Freedman and Gamba-Stonehouse 1991, 7–8.

6. Hoffmann and Mingo Hoffmann 1984, 129–30; Freedman and Gamba-Stonehouse 1991, 8.

7. Calvert 1982, 26–27; Dabat and Lorenzano 1984, 33; Vacs 1987, 21–22; Munck 1998, 55.

8. Munck 1998, 55; Arceneaux 2001, 111–15.

9. Hoffmann and Mingo Hoffmann 1984, 131–33; Freedman and Gamba-Stonehouse 1991, 9–10; Freedman 2005a, 153.

10. Büsser 1987, 42; Comisión Rattenbach 1988, no. 84; Freedman and Gamba-Stonehouse 1991, 23–24; Freedman 2005a, 153–54.

11. That is, the Northern summer or fall, which would be the Argentine winter or spring. Paul 1994, 153; Freedman 2005a, 166. See also the interview with Admiral Büsser in Charlton 1989, 111.

12. Paul 1994, 154; Munck 1998, 140; Freedman 2005, 168–83. There is some disagreement over whether there were really Argentine marines in the party. According to Freedman 2005a, there were, but earlier reports say that while such a plan (Project Alpha) existed, it was cancelled. Charlton 1989, 118–19.

13. Freedman and Gamba-Stonehouse 1990, 67.

14. Freedman and Gamba-Stonehouse 1990, 5–6; Freedman 2005a, 153.

15. Freedman and Gamba-Stonehouse 1990, 4.

16. Lai and Slater 2006.

17. Levy and Vakili 1992; Oakes 2006. For references to a number of other works advocating a diversionary interpretation, see Arquilla and Rasmussen 2001, 746n15; Oakes 2006, 449n55; Fravel 2010, 317.

18. For a helpful summary of the diversionary argument, see Oakes 2006.

19. Vacs, 1987, 25–27; Munck 1998, 123.

20. Munck 1998, 126.

21. Vacs, 1987, 27.

[201]

22. Oakes 2006, 449.

23. Jackson Diehl, "The Final Stage," *Washington Post*, January 28, 1982.

24. Munck 1998, 137.

25. Cardoso 1987, 79; Freedman and Gamba-Stonehouse 1991, 67.

26. Munck 1998, 142–43; Arquilla and Rasmussen 2001, 747; Fravel 2010, 324–25. These authors also point out that it is not clear why the regime would have repressed the demonstration on the 30th if it soon anticipated a rally effect. Arquilla and Rasmussen 2001, 748; Fravel 2010, 322.

27. Comisión Rattenbach 1988, no. 84.

28. Cardoso 1987; Comisión Rattenbach 1988; Costa Méndez 1993; Arquilla and Rasmussen 2001; Freedman 2005a, 153, 222.

29. Levy and Vakili 1992 suggests that the navy was particularly keen on the invasion, as it would increase the navy's position relative to the army (131).

30. Munck 1998, 139.

31. Büsser 1987, 42; Cardoso 1987, 4; Comisión Rattenbach 1988, no. 84; Freedman and Gamba-Stonehouse 1990, 3; Freedman 2005a, 153.

32. Büsser 1987, 42; Cardoso 1987, 3; Edward Schumacher, "Man of Hour in Argentina," *New York Times*, April 6, 1982.

33. Comisión Rattenbach 1988, 65; see also Charlton 1989, 110. Costa Méndez denied knowing any specifics of the invasion until later.

34. Freedman 2005a, 176.

35. Everett G. Martin, "Argentine Euphoria Already Wears Thin in Falklands Dispute," *Wall Street Journal*, April 9, 1982.

36. Freedman and Gamba-Stonehouse 1991, 73; Arquilla and Rasmussen 2001, 761.

37. Freedman and Gamba-Stonehouse 1991, 73–77.

38. Freedman 2005a, 187; see also Büsser 1987, 57.

39. Charlton 1989, 116.

40. Charlton 1989, 115; Freedman and Gamba-Stonehouse 1990, 68.

41. Freedman 2005a, 143; Fravel 2010, 330. Costa Méndez, Galtieri's (civilian) foreign minister, claimed that the British also sent "confusing" diplomatic signals by not clearly conveying their resolve to defend the islands. But his analysis is often self-contradictory or disingenuous. Costa Méndez 1987, 120.

42. Charlton 1989, 115–16.

43. Calvert 1982, 58.

44. Gamba-Stonehouse 1987, 136.

45. Freedman 2005a, 187; see also Büsser 1987, 42; Freedman and Gamba-Stonehouse 1991, 23.

46. See the later explanation of Argentine rear-admiral Carlos Büsser, reported in Charlton 1989, 115. Galtieri also appeared to believe that in the event of an invasion, U.S. President Reagan would restrain Thatcher from a military response, completely underestimating the strength of the NATO alliance. Charlton 1998, 115–16; Munck 1998, 142.

47. Comisión Rattenbach 1988, no. 94.

48. Comisión Rattenbach 1988, no. 93.

49. Munck 1998, 126–27.

50. "Argentine General Sworn In as Military Governor of Falklands," *Los Angeles Times*, April 7, 1982.

51. Jackson Diehl, "The Final Stage," *Washington Post*, January 28, 1982.

52. "Pro-Ongania Movement Seen Forming in Cordoba," *Daily Report Latin America*, November 18, 1975; "Retired Generals Forming 'National Unity' Group," *Daily Report Latin America*, November 18, 1977. Ongania was detained in his barracks for ten days in 1981, eleven years after losing power, but this was for vocally criticizing the Viola government. "Argentina Detains Former President," [Toronto] *Globe and Mail*, August 29, 1981; "Ongania Faction Criticizes Government Policies," *Daily Report Latin America*, August 18, 1981. He was also jailed for thirty days in 1982 "after saying that military attempts to run the country had run out of steam and that the junta should be replaced by a new power structure." "Ex-Junta Man in Argentina Is Imprisoned," [Toronto] *Globe and Mail*, January 21, 1982.

53. Levingston was arrested in October 1971 for attempting a coup of Lanusse six months *after* he himself had lost power, but I was unable to find any evidence that he was actually held. Juan de Oniss, "Lanusse Emerges Victor in Latest Argentine Crisis," *New York Times*, October 11, 1971. Moreover, there are multiple mentions of Levingston after his ouster, in which jail or other punishment are not mentioned and he instead seems to remain active in public life. Jonathan Kandell, "Moderate Stance by Peron Hailed." *New York Times*, June 26, 1973; "Ex-President Levingston Attacks Peronist Rule," *Buenos Aires La Nacion*, February 3, 1976.

Lanusse was briefly arrested at various points in 1976 and 1977, but the arrests do not appear to be related to his ouster and instead have to do with open criticism of the current military regime and shady financial dealings. "Ex-President Lanusse Arrested in Argentina," *Washington Post*, May 5, 1977; "General Lanusse Freed by Argentine Court," *Washington Post*, June 14, 1977; Lewis H. Diuguid, "Alejandro Lanusse Dies at 78; Ex-Military Ruler of Argentina," *Washington Post*, August 28, 1996.

54. Goemans, Gleditsch, and Chiozza 2009.

55. "Ex-Argentine Leaders Get Jail for War Fiasco," *Chicago Tribune*, May 16, 1986; "Argentine Ex-Rulers Lose in Appeal." *Chicago Tribune*, December 31, 1986; "Ex-Military President Goes Free in Argentina," *New York Times*, October 10, 1989.

56. Jansen 2000, 594.

57. Peattie 1975, 95; Seki 1984.

58. Peattie 1975, 49-83; Hata 1988, 294; Auer 2006, 52.

59. Peattie 1975, 92; Seki 1984, 143–44; Barnhart 1987, 31–32.

60. Weland 1994, 453; see also Jansen 2000, 583; Drea 2009, 129. Large cuts to military spending in 1921, 1923, and 1924 only exacerbated the distrust. Weland 1994, 448; Jansen 2000, 594.

61. Weland 1994, 448.

62. Ogata 1964, 4; Jansen 2000, 579; Auer 2006, 56.

63. Nish 1977, 155; see also Weland 1994, 453; Auer 2006, 56.

64. Royama 1941, 65–66; Nish 1977, 165; Jansen 2000, 594.

65. Seki 1984, 174; Weland 1994, 454.

66. Ogata 1964, 53–54; Crowley 1966, 113; Peattie 1975, 114; Seki 1984, 176.

67. Weland 1994, 456. A secret meeting bringing together the Kwantung commander-in-chief, the army vice chief of staff, and the vice minister of war was held to finalize the plot. Ogata 1964, 56.

68. Maxon 1957, 82–83; Ogata 1964, 58–59; Crowley 1966, 119–20; Seki 1984, 201–5; Weland 1994, 457.

69. Maxon 1957, 83; Ogata 1964, 58–59; Crowley 1966, 120; Beasley 1974, 245; Hata 1998, 295.

70. Royama 1941, 68; Maxon 1957, 85; Crowley 1966, 120–21; Beasley 1974, 245, 261; Shimada 1984, 251; Jansen 2000, 582, 596; Auer 2006, 57.

71. Ogata 1964, 62; Auer 2006, 56.

72. Seki 1984, 266–335; Barnhart 1987, 33.

73. Royama 1941, 69–71; Jansen 2000, 586–87; Drea 2009, 169. Jansen 2000 indicates that following the Manchurian Incident, "Civilian and diplomatic spokesmen sensed that acceptability to the army was gradually becoming a criterion for selection" (584). The international community did not agree with the Japanese public, unanimously condemning Japan in 1933 for its actions in Manchuria, which prompted Japan's exit from the League of Nations. Butow 1961, 154; Lu 1961, 155; 2002.

74. Maxon 1957, 108, 111; Toland 1970, 42; Pelz 1974, 10–12, 168; Nish 1977, 201; Drea 2009, 183.

75. Lu 1961, 12; Hata 1983, 254–55; Bix 2000, 317–18.

76. Peattie 1975, 269. Jansen 2000 cites "arrogance, avarice, and dishonesty," which "found shelter under the claims of crisis" (581).

77. Maxon 1957, 97; Butow 1961, 96.

78. Pelz 1974; Peattie 1975, 277; Barnhart 1987, 78.

79. Lu 1961, 12.

80. Maxon 1957, 103.

81. Nish 2002, 119–21.

82. Maxon 1957, 120; Bix 2000, 318.

83. Peattie 1975, 274–75; Barnhart 1987, 42–43; Hata 1988, 303; Auer 2006, 73, 75.

84. Crowley 1966, 282, 284; Toland 1970, 36.

85. Barnhart 1987, 144.

86. Shimada 1983, 229; Barnhart 1987, 82.

87. Lu 1961, 16; Crowley 1966, 324; Bix 2000, 317; Nish 2002, 120; Auer 2006, 73.

88. Butow 1961, 94–97; Hata 1983, 249; Bix 2000, 318; Drea 2009, 191–92.

89. Crowley 1966, 328; Barnhart 1987, 85; Bix 2000, 318; Nish 2002, 120.

90. Maxon 1957, 98; Beasley 1974, 263–64.

91. Peattie 1975, 303–4; Barnhart 1987, 90.

92. Barnhart 1987, 91; Coox 1988, 320.

93. Coox 1988, 320; Sarkees and Wayman 2010, 138.

94. Blumenson 1960, 253-253; Butow 1961, 126; Lu 1961, 37; Coox 1977. For an excellent summary of the broader background to the conflict, see Hata 1976.

95. Coox 1977, 22; Barnhart 1987, 112; Iriye 1987, 58-59; Kikuoka 1988, 44.

96. Coox 1977, 23.

97. Lu 1961, 38; Hata 1976, 144; Coox 1977, 36; Barnhart 1987, 112; Nish 2002, 131; Drea 2009, 202-203.

98. Blumenson 1960, 255–56; Hata 1976, 144–46; Kikuoka 1988, 44.

99. Blumenson 1960, 257; Lu 1961, 38; Hata 1976, 139–40; Kikuoka 1988, 82–83; Drea 2009, 201–2.

100. Hata 1976, 154–56; Coox 1977, 27; Kikuoka 1988, 87.

101. Coox 1977, 44.

102. Kikuoka 1988, 39.

103. Coox 1973, 103–8; Hata 1976, 146–49; Kikuoka 1988, 86; Nish 2002, 131; Drea 2009, 202.

104. Lu 1961, 38; Coox 1977, 178; Kikuoka 1988, 117.

105. Coox 1977, 182–83.

106. Blumenson 1960, 261–63.; Butow 1961, 126–27; Lu 1961, 38; Nish 2002, 131.

107. Blumenson 1960, 262; Coox 1977, 370. Lu estimates 1,200 (1961, 38), although General Staff records show that there were 900 wounded and 450 killed for a total of 1,350 casualties. Coox 1973, 53. Others have called this number too low. Blumenson 1960, 262.

108. Young 1967, 86, 92–93; Jansen 2000, 627–28.

109. Young 1967, 88; Coox 1969, 303; Hata 1976, 159; Nish 2002, 132; see also Coox 1985.

110. Coox 1969, 309.

111. Butow 1961, 127; Young 1967, 89; Hata 1976; Nish 2002, 132.

112. Young 1967, 90.

113. Young 1967, 90–92; Nish 2002, 132.

114. Hata 1976, 164.

115. Young 1967, 90; Coox 1969, 304; Hata 1976, 164–65.

116. Young 1967, 90–91; Coox 1969, 305.

117. Coox 1969, 305–6; Hata 1976, 171–72; Barnhart 1987, 143.

118. Young 1967, 92, 96; Nish 2002, 132.

119. Butow 1961, 128. Nish puts the number of dead at 17,500 (2002, 132), Coox at 15,000 (1969, 306), and Young at 11,000 (1967, 91).

120. Young 1967, 97; Coox 1969, 306; Drea 2009, 205.

121. Butow 1961, 128; Young 1967, 98.

122. Young 1967, 101.

123. Coox 1969, 305.

124. Coox 1969, 307.

125. Maxon 1957, 139; Lu 1961, 109; 2002, 155; Toland 1970, 59; Beasley 1974, 266; 2000, 199; Auer 2006, 87.

126. Butow 1961, 167; Lu 2002, 154.

127. Butow 1961, 139; Lu 1961, 154; 2002; Nish 1977, 237; Auer 2006, 89.

128. Lu 1961, 73; Toland 1970, 60, 64–65; Nish 2002, 237.

129. Beasley 1974; 2000, 267; Hata 1988, 310; Lu 2002, 154; Auer 2006, 89.

130. Butow 1961, 164; Toland 1970, 63; Pelz 1974, 214–15; Lu 2002, 157; Nish 2002, 139; Auer 2006, 88.

131. Butow 1961, 166–67; Nish 1977, 237; Barnhart 1987, 168; Lu 2002, 159.

132. Lu 1961, 111; Toland 1970, 63.

133. Lu 1961, 99; Pelz 1974, 215; Auer 2006, 94.

134. Maxon 1957, 144–45; Lu 1961, 76.

135. Butow 1961, 148; Lu 1961, 108; Toland 1970, 62; Auer 2006, 90.

136. Lu 1961, 106; Toland 1970, 60.

137. Butow 1961, 163, 166; Lu 1961, 106; 2002, 155; Toland 1970, 64; Hata 1988, 312.

138. Butow 1961, 169; Lu 1961, 116.

139. Butow 1961, 148; Toland 1970, 62; Auer 2006, 90. On September 4, Navy Minister Yoshida resigned due to ill health. His replacement Oikawa Koshirō was more amenable to an alliance and agreed on the pact provided that Japan could decide whether one of the contracting parties had been attacked before coming to their aid. Butow 1961, 160; Nish 1977, 237; Lu 2002, 159–66; Nish 2002, 140.

140. Ike 1967, 4–5, 9, 12.

141. Maxon 1957, 161; Ike 1967, 13; Lu 2002, 165.

142. Butow 1961, 181; Lu 1961, 114; Toland 1970, 63–64; Nish 1977, 238; Auer 2006, 87.

143. Schroeder 1958, 22–28; Iriye 1987, 117; Hata 1988, 313. After Japan signed the Tripartite Pact, the United States stepped up its economic sanctions on Japan. Barnhart 1987, 194–96.

144. Lu 1961, 118; Iriye 1987, 117.

145. Beasley 1974, 267–68; Nish 1977, 239; Hata 1030, 155–208; Barnhart 1987, 208–14; Coox 1988, 326.

146. Pelz 1974, 219.

147. Schroeder 1958, 48–52; Butow 1961, 234; Lu 1961, 188; Browne 1967, 91; Toland 1970, 86; Pelz 1974, 222–24; Beasley 1974, 269; 2000, 202; Nish 1977, 245; Barnhart 1987, 238; Tsunoda 1994, 159, 179; Bix 2000, 401; Miller 2007, 196.

148. Drea 2009, 219.

149. Worth 1995, 125–28.

150. Following the United States, Britain, India, Burma, Canada, and Holland had imposed freezes of their own. Nish 2002, 150.

151. Beasley 2000, 200–201, 240; Miller 2007, 165.

152. Barnhart 1987, 239–40; Coox 1988, 333. More recent estimates appear to concur. Record 2009 finds that the Japanese would indeed have been severely handicapped by their oil situation the longer they waited to initiate a war (24–25). In a review of contemporary and after-the-fact estimates, Worth 1995 also concludes that Japanese figures were correct. Moreover, if there were a war, the two-year figure dropped to only eighteen months (131–33).

153. Jansen 2000, 636.

154. Auer 2006, 115; Record 2009, 25.

155. Pelz 1974, 221.

156. Butow 1961, 247; Pelz 1974, 224; Barnhart 1987, 244–45.

157. Maxon 1957, 149–56; Butow 1961, 149. The Liaison Conferences were made up primarily of military officers; typical participants were the prime minister, the foreign minister, the war minister, the navy minister, and the army and navy chiefs and vice chiefs of staff, and sometimes some other ministers of state. Maxon 1957, 177; Butow 1961, 149; Record 2009, 32.

158. Maxon, 1957, 181.

159. Butow 1961, 314.

160. Butow 1961, 248–49; Toland 1970, 95.

161. Butow 1961, 248; Lu 1961, 201.

162. Quoted in Ike 1967, 131. See also Iriye 1987, 161.

163. Maxon 1957, 170; Butow 1961, 250; Toland 1970, 96.

164. Maxon 1957, 170–71; Butow 1961, 253–55; Browne 1967, 96; Toland 1970, 96; Bix 2000, 412.

165. Maxon 1957, 170; Butow 1961, 256; Lu 1961, 200; Browne 1967, 96; Toland 1970, 98; Barnhart 1987, 245; Bix 2000, 413; Nish 2002, 154. On the ceremonial nature of Imperial Conferences, see Worth 1995, 157–58.

166. Beasley 1974, 265; Coox 1988, 329; Hata 1988, 311; Auer 2006, 107.

167. Quoted in Ike 1967, 138.

168. Quoted in Ike 1967, 138–39.

169. Ike 1967, 141; Toland 1970, 96; Barnhart 1987, 249.

170. Maxon 1957, 170; Lu 1961, 201; Barnhart 1987, 245.

171. Tsunoda 1994, 212–14.

172. Maxon 1957, 173; Butow 1961, 270–72; Toland 1970, 109; Barnhart 1987, 252; Tsunoda 1994, 215–25.

173. Maxon 1957, 173.

174. Maxon 1957, 29, 173; Butow 1961, 273–74.

175. Quoted in Tsunoda 1994, 222–24. See also Iriye 1987, 165.

176. Butow 1961, 291; Browne 1967, 100; Toland 1970, 113; Beasley 1974, 270; Pelz 1974, 225; Barnhart 1987, 254; Bix 2000, 417; Nish 2002, 159.

177. Butow 1961, 302; Toland 1970, 119.

178. Maxon 1957, 176; Wetzler 1998, 46–47; Jansen 2000, 639; Drea 2009, 220. It has been suggested that the Tojo cabinet was already decided on war but that it feigned a reconsideration of policy in order to appease the emperor. Browne 1967, 111–12.

179. Trachtenberg 2006 suggests that the United States was intransigent because it wanted to provoke Japan into attacking the United States, as this would increase public support for a speedy U.S. entry into the European conflict. This argument does not, however, explain why the Japanese attacked when other options were available.

180. Beasley 2000, 200–201; Nish 2002, 162.

181. Coox 1988, 335; Titus 1994, xxviii–xxix, xxx–xxxi; Nish 2002, 160.

182. Maxon 1957, 177. The participants included Prime Minister/Home Minister/War Minister Tojo, the minister of the Navy, Foreign Minister Togo, Finance Minister Kaya, president of the Planning Board Suzuki, the army chief and vice chief of staff, the navy chief and vice chief of staff, the chief of the Military Affairs Bureau, the chief of the Naval Affairs Bureau, and the chief cabinet secretary.

183. Butow 1961, 319–20; Toland 1970, 124–25.

184. Lu 1961, 215; Toland 1970, 125.

185. Lu 1961, 215; Toland 1970, 124–25; Barnhart 1987, 258; Tsunoda 1994, 255–64.

186. Toland 1970, 124.

187. Ike 1967, 201–2, 203; Toland 1970, 124–25; Iriye 1987, 173–74.

188. Ike 1967, 203.

189. Maxon 1957, 177; Butow 1961, 324; Lu 1961, 215; Toland 1970, 124–29.

190. Maxon 1957, 176–77; Butow 1961, 321; Toland 1970, 126; Coox 1988, 335; Nish 2002, 160.

191. Butow 1961, 325; Lu 1961, 217; Browne 1967, 114; Toland 1970, 130; Beasley 1974, 270; Wetzler 1998, 39; Bix 2000, 424; Nish 2002, 160.

192. Maxon 1957, 178; Butow 1961, 343–44; Lu 1961, 231.

193. Maxon 1957, 179. Butow 1961, 345; Bix 2000, 430.

194. Quoted in Maxon 1957, 179. See also Tsunoda 1994, 324–26.

195. Maxon 1957, 180; Butow 1961, 359; Lu 1961, 231; Browne 1967, 123; Toland 1970, 181; Beasley 1974, 270; Coox 1988, 339; Bix 2000, 431; Barnhart 1987, 262.

196. Morley 1994 (xxx–xxxi) also discusses a "military mentality" that made compromise impossible, though he emphasizes the Japanese military's unwillingness to back down.

197. Bix 2000.

198. Titus 1994, xxiii.

199. Snyder 1991, 148.

200. On the issue of inevitability, see Titus 1994, xx–xxi.

6. Machines: Looking Before They Leap

1. Porter 1993, 101. Moreover, "although extrabureaucratic forces are excluded from formal policy-making processes, popular pressures in the form of economic resistance to existing policy and even active pursuit of an alternative model at local levels have, in practice, influenced the policy-making process" (101).

2. Gaussmann 1988, 102–28; Porter 1993, 66. This body was formally elected by the Central Committee, although because the Politburo was responsible for selecting and training the high-level party officials who ultimately became part of the Central Committee, the Central Committee was also "responsive" to the Politburo's "collective will." Porter 1993, 102. The flow of power in North Vietnam, as in other nonpersonalist communist systems, thus had a somewhat circular nature.

3. See, for example, Ang 2004.

4. Porter 1993, 103. Nguyen 2012 argues that after 1968, Le Duan consolidated power and was able to sideline top party officials who did not support his policies, intimidating their subordinates in the 1968 "Anti-Party Affair." But the evidence surrounding that interpretation is murky. For example, although Nguyen portrays Giap as Le Duan's bitter rival, Le Duan retained Giap as supreme commander of the armed forces until 1975, and Giap remained a top figure in the regime for decades. Pribbenow 2008, 24. There is also no evidence of purges of top officials anything like

that found in personalist regimes, or evidence of the sort of "personality cult" that personalist leaders typically develop as a way to hedge against coups.

5. Gausmann 1988, 10.

6. Porter 1993, 83. To control the army, the party used the Central Military Party Committee (CMPC), "with both military and nonmilitary members appointed by the Central Committee and operating under the direct leadership of the Political Bureau and the Secretariat." (ibid).

7. McNamara, Blight, and Brigham 1999, 69.

8. The United States needed French cooperation in NATO, and the Communists had just prevailed in China, coloring the Vietnamese nationalist cause in a Cold War light. McNamara, Blight, and Brigham 1999, 64–66.

9. For a description of the battle, see Duiker 1996, 168–70.

10. Duiker 1996, 171; SarDesai 2005, 67.

11. Duiker 1996, 172.

12. McNamara, Blight, and Brigham 1999, 68.

13. After an initial post-Geneva exodus of 50,000 to 90,000 Viet Minh cadres and supporters to the North, 5,000 to 10,000 cadres and many additional sympathizers remained in the South. SarDesai 2005, 80; Nguyen 2012, 31.

14. Duiker 1996, 196.

15. Duiker 1996, 187–88; Ang 2002, 16.

16. Duiker 1996, 189–90; Ang 2002, 15–18.

17. McNamara, Blight, and Brigham 1999, 92.

18. Porter 1993, 19; Duiker 1996, 194–95; Ang 2002, 16; Nguyen 2012, 42.

19. The Nam Bo Regional Committee, called the Southern Territorial Committee by some authors, was the Central Committee's Southern wing. In 1951 it was reorganized into the more powerful Central Office for South Vietnam (COSVN). In 1955, it reverted back to the Nam Bo Regional Committee. When the conflict intensified in 1961, it was reorganized into the COSVN again by the addition of members from the Central Committee who were "empowered to make decisions on the spot which formerly would have been referred to Hanoi." Race 1972, 29.

20. Duiker 1996, 189–90; Ang 2002, 15–16. Duiker argues that Le Duan's plan "although not recommending (as is sometimes asserted) a major shift toward a more military approach in the South, did appeal for an increased effort to promote reunification and, if necessary, to prepare for a possible revolutionary upsurge" (190).

21. Duiker 1996, 187–94; Ang 2002, 16.

22. Pribbenow 2002, 42.

23. Duiker 1996, 189. The meeting also featured a discussion of the errors of the Northern land reform campaign; Truong Chinh and other supporters of the land reform program were demoted but not removed from the Politburo.

24. Ang 2002, 19.

25. Duiker 1996, 189; Ang 2002, 19.

26. Duiker 1996, 190.

27. Porter 1993, 20.

28. Ang 2002, 20.

29. Ho Chi Minh had preferred Vo Nguyen Giap for the role, but Le Duan had the support of Le Duc Tho, the powerful head of the Party Organization Department. Duiker 1996, 194; Ang 2002, 21.

30. Nguyen 2012, 37–38.

31. Duiker 1996, 192; Pribbenow 2002, 21–22; Vinh 2009, 11.

32. Ang 2002, 25.

33. Ang 2002, 26.

34. Ang 2002, 27; see also Pribbenow 2002, 42.

35. Duiker 1996, 201; Pribbenow 2002, 49–50; Vinh 2009, 43–46.

36. According to Duiker, "knowledgeable sources in Vietnam now agree that a prime reason for the decision to shift to a strategy of revolutionary war was the anguished appeals from the leading members of the movement in the South to provide them with the means to defend themselves." Duiker 1996, 200. This differs in some ways from the interpretation in Nguyen 2012. Nguyen argues that on the one hand, a peasant revolt had already begun in the South before Hanoi's decision was transmitted, indicating that the preferences of Southern revolutionaries were sincere. On the other hand, she argues that something like a diversionary motive was at play: "Le Duan and his faction exploited the Party leadership's desire for a new cause that could rally the people behind the Party banner" (44). In my reading, however, Nguyen does not provide concrete evidence for this diversionary interpretation.

37. Porter 1993, 20; Ang 2002, 29–30; Vinh 2009, 43–44; Hunt 2010, 399.

38. Nguyen 2012, 45.

39. Ang 2002, 31–32.

40. Nguyen 2012, 46.

41. Nguyen 1976, 27; Pribbenow 2002, 49.

42. Ang 2002, 34, 42–43.

43. Duiker 1996, 207–8; Ang 2002, 52–54.

44. Duiker 1996, 207–9; Ang 2002, 54.

45. Duiker 1996, 207–8.

46. Duiker 1996, 209; Nguyen 2012, 58.

47. Duiker 1996, 213; Ang 2002, 55; SarDesai 2005, 77; Nguyen 2012, 52–53.

48. Duiker 1996, 209–10.

49. Tran Quang Co in June 1997, reported in McNamara, Blight, and Brigham 1999, 49.

50. Duiker 1996, 213.

51. Pike 1987, 93. An alternative interpretation can be found in Nguyen 2012, which suggests that the turn to a more militant strategy was in large part the product of Le Duan's personal hawkish views. But the evidence indicates that whatever Le Duan's views, there was a broad base of elite support for a more aggressive strategy and Le Duan had to win a majority in the Politburo in order to move forward.

52. Scholars remain unsure of the meaning of the North Vietnamese attempts. One possibility is that the Neutrality Offensive was Hanoi's attempt to entangle the United States in negotiations in order to delay the start of war and allow it to fight on better terms, rather than to reach a settlement and avoid war altogether. Alternatively, Hanoi's attempts at negotiation may have been a sincere attempt to avoid

war, but only if the settlement had a good prospect of allowing communists to take over politically in the South after some period of neutrality. Duiker 1996, 224; McNamara, Blight, and Brigham 1999, 120–23. Or perhaps negotiations were simply a public relations move designed to enlist external support. For analogous reasoning applied to later periods, see Asselin 2012, 553.

53. Emily Rauhala. "Madame Nhu," *Time*, May 16, 2011, available at www.time.com/time/magazine/article/0,9171,2069023,00.html#ixzz1OmtRNkY8, accessed January 10, 2014.

54. Ang 2002, 75.

55. Duiker 1996, 239; McNamara, Blight, and Brigham 1999, 182; Ang 2002, 73.

56. Ang 2002, 74.

57. Duiker 1996, 239.

58. Duiker 1996, 241–44.

59. Nguyen 2012, 63.

60. Duiker 1996, 244.

61. Indeed, by this point Ho Chi Minh himself was being criticized for his "two mistakes": compromising with the French in 1945, which led to the Franco–Viet Minh War, and compromising with the West again in Geneva in 1954, which led to the partition of Vietnam. Grossheim 2005, 454–55.

62. Ang 2002, 75.

63. This is Ang's implicit interpretation. Ang 2002, 73–75.

64. Bùi 1995.

65. Nguyen 2012, 66.

66. Grossheim 2005; Nguyen 2012, 69–70.

67. Nguyen 2012, 67. Grossheim 2005, drawing on Eastern European archives, argues that some of those who spoke out in 1963 were targeted four years later in the "Anti-Party Affair" around the time of the Tet Offensive, and Nguyen 2012 draws on Grossheim's evidence to draw a link between the 1967 Anti-Party Affair and the 1963 Ninth Plenum. But Quinn-Judge 2006 suggests that the evidence that the Anti-Party Affair was a punishment for views about escalation is rather sketchy. Certainly, even the Anti-Party Affair in no way approximates the kinds of threats and purges frequently seen in personalist regimes, and many of those who opposed escalation in 1963 enjoyed long political careers.

68. McNamara, Blight, and Brigham 1999, 167. Ang 2002 also indicates that the August 2 attack was authorized by a site commander (80). For the DRV version of events, see McNamara, Blight, and Brigham 1999, 184–85.

69. Ang 2002, 81. Rather, it appears that U.S. naval commanders misinterpreted radar signals and were themselves unsure. Nonetheless, U.S. authorities determined that the attacks probably had taken place and viewed them as a signal that North Vietnam intended to escalate the war. Johnson's reprisal bombing in turn was intended to signal that the United States would resist Northern aggression with force of its own. McNamara, Blight, and Brigham 1999, 167–70.

70. Ang 2002, 81.

71. Duiker 1996, 249.

72. Duiker 1996, 251–52; Ang 2002, 81.

73. Duiker 1996, 250; McNamara, Blight, and Brigham 1999, 185; Ang 2002, 81–82.

74. Duiker 1996, 250; Ang 2002, 83.

75. Duiker 1996, 252; McNamara, Blight, and Brigham 1999, 169, 172, 187; Ang 2002, 86.

76. McNamara, Blight, and Brigham 1999, 172, 188–89; Ang 2002, 86.

77. Sarkees and Wayman 2010, 155.

78. Asselin 2005, 439.

79. Porter 1993. Buttressed in large part by his success in the war against the United States, Le Duan stayed in power until his death in 1986. A recent book, Nguyen 2012, argues that over time Le Duan's regime became less collective. Nguyen points in particular to the Anti-Party Affair, a purge of about thirty high-level party officials who leaned toward the Soviet Union, in 1967; see also Grossheim 2005. However, while some scholars believe that Le Duan and Le Duc Tho, with support from Truong Chinh and Pham Hung, "dominated the decision-making process" in the DRV after 1968, they conceded that "it is still impossible to say just how total that domination was, how the party arrived at decisions, and who was behind each decision. Available documentary evidence does not allow us to discuss intra-party dynamics in a fully nuanced fashion." Asselin 2011, 102. Even Nguyen observes that "Le Duan recognized that the losses sustained in his drive to redeem his ambitious strategy in 1968 [i.e., the Tet Offensive] would mean that General Giap's moderating influence would be apparent in 1970. Le Duan's worst fears were realized in the plenum's Resolution 18, which promoted an 'economy of forces' strategy by elevating the political and diplomatic spheres of the war. . . . The first secretary's goal of fomenting a mass uprising in South Vietnam through large-scale attacks on its cities was put on hold indefinitely" (158). This is hardly the depiction of a leader unconstrained by his inner-regime peers. Moreover, even if one believes that Le Duan consolidated personal power over time, the nature of his rule comes nowhere near approximating the more personalistic regime structures of regimes such as Saddam's Iraq, Stalin's Soviet Union, the Kims' North Korea, or Gaddafi's Libya.

80. Many view the 1975 invasion as the continuation of the interstate war between North and South Vietnam. Sarkees and Wayman 2010. Since it came on the heels of a ceasefire and peace agreement, however, it could also be considered a new conflict.

81. Ang 2004, 102–7; Asselin 2011.

82. Taped conversation between President Nixon and Secretary of State Henry Kissinger, October 6, 1972, reproduced in Hunt 2010, 117.

83. Asselin 2002, 172, 188.

84. Duiker 1996, 325, 329; Ang 2004, 127.

85. Ang 2004, 125.

86. Ang 2004, 125–28. This is not to say that the ceasefire was observed; all Vietnamese parties violated the ceasefire soon after the accords were signed. Asselin 2002, 182.

87. Duiker 1996, 330.

88. Ang 2004, 129.

89. Duiker 1996, 331–35. For details of the countless meetings, see Ang 2004, 129–38. Many Southern cadres advocated a more aggressive approach.

90. Ang 2004, 130.

91. Ang 2004, 137, 147.

92. Ang 2004, 136.

93. Asselin 2002, 185–86. Or, according to Ang 2004, "Despite continued reservations by some sections of Hanoi leadership who were concerned that an expansion of fighting might overturn the Paris agreement and lead to the return of Americans to South Vietnam . . . the Politburo was able to issue Resolution 21 which tried to take into consideration the demands of all sides" (147).

94. Duiker 1996, 330.

95. Ang 2004, 152–58.

96. Duiker 1996, 333. The economic situation was an important factor in the decision to prepare for a military struggle and was taken up at key meetings on military strategy, including the Twenty-Second Plenary session in December and January; see also Ang 2004, 139.

97. Ang 2004, 148.

98. Pribbenow 1999, 59; Ang 2004, 152.

99. Ang 2004, 156.

100. Ang 2004, 156.

101. Ang 2004, 157.

102. Pribbenow 1999, 63; Ang 2004, 157. According to Asselin 2002, in November 1974 the Politburo ramped up its plans to launch a full-on campaign to conquer Saigon and the rest of the South (186).

103. Pribbenow 1999, 66; Ang 2004, 159; Vinh 2009, 268.

104. Ang 2004, 159; see also the assessment in Pribbenow 1999.

105. Ang 2004, 159–60.

106. Ang 2004, 159–60.

107. Duiker 1996, 339.

108. Duiker 1996, 343–44; Ang 2004, 162; Vinh 2009, 282.

109. Ang 2004, 162.

110. Ang 2004, 165.

111. Duiker 1996, 331.

112. Pribbenow 1999, 58.

113. Kiernan 2002, 456–63; Fawthorp and Jarvis 2004, 3–4. Even U.S. President Jimmy Carter, who later condemned the Vietnamese invasion and supported the Khmer Rouge in the UN General Assembly, said in 1979 that the Pol Pot regime was "the worst violator of human rights in the world." Jimmy Carter, "Human Rights Violations in Cambodia Statement by the President," April 21, 1978, available at www.presidency.ucsb.edu/ws/?pid=30693, accessed January 10, 2014.

114. Quinn-Judge 2006, 207. As Kissinger put it, "the North Vietnamese . . . were implacable revolutionaries, the terror of their neighbours, coming to claim the whole of the French colonial inheritance in Indochina by whatever force was necessary." Kissinger and Luce 1979, 1169; also cited in Quinn-Judge 2006, 207.

115. Malcolm W. Browne, "Third World and West Join to Assail Vietnam in U.N.," *New York Times*, January 14, 1979; Elizabeth Becker, "Soviets Block U.N. Demand for Withdrawal From Cambodia," *Washington Post*, January 16, 1979; "Phnom Penh Falls Again," *New York Times*, January 9, 1979; Joseph B. Treaster, "Peking Denounces Hanoi in U.N. Paper," *New York Times*, January 8, 1979.

116. Morris 1999, 16–18.

[213]

117. Western interpretations of Vietnamese motives were long influenced by the Cold War, including America's warming relations with China and bitter feelings about the costly Vietnam conflict, Chinese ambitions to stanch Soviet influence in Indochina, and Soviet desires to counterbalance China's growing power.

118. Kiernan 2002, 296, 389, 441–42, 458. Urban and rural deaths of ethnic Vietnamese come to 20,000.

119. Chanda 1986, 49–56.

120. Kiernan 2002, 25; Goscha 2006, 173.

121. Kiernan 2002, 63, 104.

122. Khoo 2011, 120; on emerging tensions, see also Chanda 1986, 66–67.

123. Chanda 1986, 68; Morris 1999, 55–68; Khoo 2011, 120.

124. Kiernan 2002, 101.

125. Chanda 1986, 72–73.

126. Chanda 1986, 73.

127. Chanda 1986, 72–73; Goscha 2006, 167; O'Dowd 2007, 34; Khoo 2011, 120.

128. Chanda 1986, 13–14; Kiernan 2002, 55–56.

129. Chanda 1986, 12–15; Kiernan 2002, 104–5; O'Dowd 2007, 34. In early June 1975, Le Duan and Pol Pot met in an attempt to resolve the maritime issues. While the meeting produced a brief break in conflict, the general negotiations over territory remained at a stalemate.

130. Kiernan 2002, 296; the remaining 20,000 were killed by late 1978 (458).

131. Chanda 1986, 81–83; Becker 1998, 265, 302; O'Dowd 2007, 35.

132. Chanda 1986, 83–84; Becker 1998, 302.

133. Chanda 1986, 83–85.

134. Chanda 1986, 133.

135. Chanda 1986, 181; Gilks 1992, 153; Thakur and Thayer 1992, 190, 194; Khoo 2011, 111–12, 118.

136. Khoo 2011, 119. Khoo also reports that at this point some pro-China elements in the Vietnamese leadership were replaced; according to Ross 1988, one Politburo member and four alternate members of the Central Committee who had been associated with Chinese relations were replaced (93).

137. Quinn-Judge 2006, 211; Khoo 2010, 347.

138. Chanda 1986, 92, 178; Khoo 2011, 112, 115. Even the Americans recognized Vietnam's quandary at the time. Chanda 1986, 150.

139. Chanda 1986, 159.

140. Chanda 1986, 184–91, 245; Khoo 2011, 111–12.

141. Chanda 1986, 240–47; Westad 2006, 6.

142. Kiernan 2002, 128–31, 132–39; O'Dowd 2007, 35.

143. O'Dowd 2007, 35–36; Khoo 2011, 120.

144. Chanda 1986, 91; Khoo 2011, 120–21; see also Kiernan 2002, 357–61.

145. Chanda 1986, 96; Kiernan 2006, 189. A 1977 article in the party journal asked, "Should we attack our enemies more fiercely, or should we be content with the results obtained. . . . We should attack them without respite on every terrain by

taking our own initiatives and by scrupulously following the directions of our party, both in the internal political field and in the field of foreign relations. . . . We must fight the enemy coming from the outside in all theatres of operations and in every form." The message would have been clear. Kiernan 2002, 359; Quinn-Judge 2006, 213.

146. Chanda 1986, 86–87; Chandler 1992, 141; Kiernan 2002, 296–98, 458–60.

147. Chanda 1986, 91–92; Chandler 1992, 141; Kiernan 2002, 359.

148. O'Dowd 2007, 35–36; Khoo 2011, 121.

149. Chanda 1986, 193; Chandler 1992, 141–42; Kiernan 2002, 361; O'Dowd 2007, 36.

150. Kiernan 2002, 362–63.

151. Chanda 1986, 194–95.

152. Chanda 1986, 196; Khoo 2011, 122.

153. Chanda 1986, 199.

154. Ross 1988, 159.

155. Kiernan 2006, 386. During 1977 and 1978, the Khmer Rouge also attacked Laos and Thailand. Kiernan 2006, 188.

156. Chandler 1992, 151; Khoo 2011, 124.

157. Chanda 1986, 207–9; Chandler 1992, 151.

158. Chandler 1992, 151.

159. Khoo 2011, 124.

160. Chanda 1986, 214.

161. Kiernan 2002, 388.

162. Chanda 1986, 217–19; Khoo 2010, 355; 2011, 124.

163. Duiker 1986, 73–74; Khoo 2010, 356.

164. Khoo 2010, 357.

165. Kiernan 2002, 389, 441–42. On its end, Vietnam was putting increasing pressure on ethnic Chinese, who were themselves fleeing Vietnam.

166. Khoo 2011, 126.

167. Pribbenow 2006, 459–60.

168. Kiernan 2002, 455.

169. For example, Khoo 2011 argues that "Hanoi's minimum security requirement in [the post–Vietnam War] period was to carve out secure borders. The establishment of a sphere of influence was a desirable but secondary goal" (131).

170. Kissinger and Luce 1979, 1169.

171. Westad 2006, 4; Khoo 2011, 131.

172. Quinn-Judge 2006, 213.

173. Westad 2006, 9–10.

174. Quinn-Judge 2006, 211.

175. Quinn-Judge 2006, 212, 214–15.

176. Khoo 2011, 120.

177. Chanda 1986, 91–92, 192–205.

178. Quinn-Judge 2006, 212.

179. Pribbenow 2006.

180. That is not to say that one should go to the opposite extreme and say that Vietnam overthrew Pol Pot primarily in order to stop his genocide against the Cambodian people. Goscha 2006, for example, argues that it is unlikely that "the Vietnamese Communists intervened in late 1978 to save the Khmer people from genocide (they were well aware of the [Khmer Rouge's] policies before 1978)" but that "there is no doubt that they put an end to the [Khmer Rouge's] butchery when other countries did nothing" (175).

181. Valenta 1979, 9; Shevchenko 1985, 71; Knight 1988, 48.

182. Triska and Finley 1968, 59–60, 77; Aspaturian 1971, 559; Gallagher and Spielmann 1972, 18; Valenta 1979, 9; Dallin 1981, 366; Simes 1984, 77; Ra'anan and Lukes 1990, 157, 171; Vertzberger 1998, 231. The number of full and candidate members has fluctuated slightly over time, but was usually around fifteen members. Gallagher and Spielmann 1972, 18.

183. In its investigation into the backgrounds of the top Soviet political officials, Triska and Finley 1968 describes three different career backgrounds of top foreign-affairs officials in the Politburo: "the Party 'line officer' who has achieved his status in domestic Party administration and, projected into the top decision-making echelon, necessarily assumes direct responsibility for foreign-policy decisions; secondly, the Party 'staff officer' whose specialization in foreign affairs has carried him up via the Party Central Apparatus and Secretariat to a seat in the Politburo, where he continues to be responsible for his field of technical competence and experience; thirdly, the 'production specialist,' successful in managing the Soviet economy and coopted into Party ranks at a relatively high level." Triska and Finley 1968, 81. The role of military officers in the Politburo was extremely limited; Marshal Zhukov was the minister of defense until he was dismissed by Khrushchev in 1957, but he was the last military official to serve on the Presidium until 1971. Triska and Finley 1968, 39; Aspaturian 1971, 518.

184. Hough and Fainsod 1979, 286.

185. Knight 1988, 49.

186. Valenta 1979, 9; Nogee and Donaldson 1981, 46. Zhores Medvedev credits Khrushchev with some of these changes: "By denouncing Stalin's crimes, and by rehabilitating many of his victims and adopting other practical measures, he brought about a change in the meaning of the term 'political crime.' This does not mean that the Soviet Union became a country in which a pluralism of ideas was allowed, or where there was democratic tolerance. Nonetheless, the scope of permitted criticism was increased enormously." Z. Medvedev 1983, 71.

187. Aspaturian 1971, 562. Although under Khrushchev, officials still faced political consequences for opposition to the leader, the consequences were substantially less dangerous under Khrushchev than they had been under Stalin. Aspaturian explains, "The blood purge was replaced with public condemnation and disgrace, demotion, or retirement but, since the execution of Beria in 1954, no fallen leader has been executed or even brought to trial. With the element of terror removed from the political process, however, the risks of opposition and dissent were considerably reduced" (570–71). Under Brezhnev, there was little opportunity to observe such purges because, heeding Khrushchev's fate, he was highly attuned to the importance of deliberation and consensus.

188. Valenta 1979, 140.

189. Valenta 1979, 18, 28.

190. Richter 1989, 71.

191. Valenta 1979, 27–28.

192. Sakwa 1998, 67.

193. Taubman 2003, 365–66.

194. Troyanovsky 2000, 218.

195. Fursenko and Naftali 2006, 202.

196. Taubman 2003, 366.

197. Taubman 2003, 582.

198. Shepilov, Bittner, and Austin 2007, 251. Note, however, that Shepilov's memoirs were written after his falling out with Khrushchev, so his "animus against his former patron is such that his testimony isn't always reliable." Taubman 2003, 661n3.

199. Dobrynin 1995, 47.

200. Dobrynin 1995, 130.

201. Fursenko and Naftali 2006, 537.

202. Ross 1984, 244.

203. Taubman 2003, 13.

204. Dobrynin 1995, 219. According to Tompson 2003, "Given that Khrushchev was removed in large part on account of what colleagues saw as his autocratic and high-handed treatment of them, Brezhnev had good reason to adopt a more consensus-oriented, collegial style of decision-making . . ." (17). Or, according to Ross 1984, "Brezhnev's commitment to consensus rule was probably no accident; by this I mean the lessons of Khrushchev's demise most certainly were not lost on Brezhnev and as a result he was more careful not to violate the norms or trappings of collective decision making" (240).

205. Simes 1984, 76; Dobrynin 1995, 219. Valenta 1979 also refers to the post-Khrushchev era under Brezhnev as a period of "collective leadership" and "coalition politics" (20).

206. Valenta 1979, 8.

207. Dobrynin 1995, 219.

208. Hough and Fainsod 1979, 475–76.

209. Hough and Fainsod 1979, 475–76; Tompson 2003, 20.

210. Richter 1989, 90–91.

211. Anderson 1989, 753.

212. Richter 1989, 720.

213. Anderson 1993.

214. Kramer 1998a, 186; Taubman 2003, 282, 298, 312–13, 317.

215. R. Medvedev 1983, 106.

216. R. Medvedev 1983, 106; Richter 1989, 294.

217. Kramer 1998a, 193–94; Cold War International History Project, "Protocol No. 58 of the Meeting of the Political Bureau of the CC of the RWP Which Adopted Some Measures to Ensure Order in Romania Given the Events Taking Place in Hungary." October 30, 1956.

218. Taubman 2003, 297.

219. Kramer 1998a, 189; Fursenko and Naftali 2006, 130.

220. Haslam 2011, 170.

221. Cold War International History Project, "Working Notes from the Session of the CPSU CC Presidium on 31 October 1956."

222. Cold War International History Project, "Working Notes from the Session of the CPSU CC Presidium on 1 November 1956." Mikoyan supported inaction because he believed that the situation had not yet deteriorated to the point of losing Hungary.

223. Mićunović and Kennan 1980, 134.

224. Saburov raised the issue at the October 31 meeting of the Presidium. Cold War International History Project, "Working Notes from the Session of the CPSU CC Presidium on 31 October 1956."

225. Cold War International History Project, "Working Notes from the Session of the CPSU CC Presidium on 30 October 1956."

226. Kramer 1998a, 188; Fursenko and Naftali 2006, 129.

227. Taubman 2003, 296.

228. Tompson 1995, 170.

229. Cold War International History Project, "Working Notes from the Session of the CPSU CC Presidium on 1 November 1956." Vladimir Malin was the head of the CPSU CC General Department during the entire Khrushchev period. See Kramer 1998a, 166.

230. Cold War International History Project, "Working Notes from the Session of the CPSU CC Presidium on 23 October 1956."

231. Breslauer 1982, 118.

232. Ross 1984, 244.

233. Richter 1994, 97. The anti-Party group had a majority in the Presidium, but Khrushchev was able to stay in power by bringing the matter to the full Central Committee, where he had more support. Khrushchev was ultimately able to rebuild his authority because there was a lack of unity regarding a policy strategy within the opposition group. Richter 1994, 92.

234. Troyanovsky 2000, 236, 241.

235. Adomeit 1984, 268.

236. Edmonds 1983, 26; Burlatskii 1991, 173.

237. Goldgeier 1990, 139–41; see also Burlatskii 1991, 171.

238. Garthoff 1988 also discusses Mikoyan's concerns (65).

239. Ross 1984, 244.

240. Tompson 1995, 253.

241. Sakwa 1998, 63.

242. Daniels 1998 argues that while "in foreign policy as in domestic, the early Brezhnev approach was cautious promotion of the status quo" (47), this changed in later years. Daniels argues that after 1975, Brezhnev and the Politburo took bold foreign policy initiatives in the Third World, and Brezhnev became an increasingly personalist and egotistical leader (49–50). Gelman 1984 also argues that foreign

policy became more aggressive during the 1970s but stresses the responsibility of the Politburo, instead of Brezhnev as an individual (105–73, esp. 115).

243. Dobrynin 1995, 130.

244. Vertzberger 1998, 253.

245. Adomeit 1984, 268.

246. Kelley 1987, 6.

247. Vertzberger 1998, 252. For more about the importance of Politburo consensus and compromise, see Kass 1978, 232; Valenta 1979, 17.

248. Ross 1984, 242.

249. Ross 1984, 245.

250. Brown 2008, 467.

251. Tompson 2003, 37; Brown 2008, 467–68; Haslam 2011, 245–46.

252. Kramer 1998b; 122; Tompson 2003, 37; Brown 2008, 468.

253. Tompson 2003, 37–38.

254. Coleman 1996, 84; Kramer 1998b, 122, 123, 125; Brown 2008, 468.

255. Tompson 2003, 37.

256. Kramer 1998b, 127, 129.

257. Kramer 1998b, 129.

258. Kramer 1998b, 126.

259. Kramer 1998b, 122–23, 130; Tompson 2003, 37–38.

260. Tompson 2003, 38.

261. Kramer 1998b, 134.

262. Vertzberger 1998, 247, 253.

263. Valenta 1979, 132; Ross 1984, 246.

264. Kramer 1998b, 134; Vertzberger 1998, 231–32.

265. Kramer 1998b, 145.

266. Valenta 1979; Valenta 1984, 144–45.

267. Kramer 1998b, 153.

268. Vertzberger 1998, 244; see also Kramer 1998b, 129.

269. Coleman 1996, 86.

270. It is also worth noting that Brezhnev did not attack Romania despite that country's increasingly independent policies, though of course Romania did not threaten to leave the Warsaw Pact or abandon communism.

Conclusion

1. Snyder 1984; Schweller 1994; Glaser 2010.

2. See, for example, Peceny, Beer, and Sanchez-Terry 2002. Among other questions, it would be interesting to see how regime type affects the emergence of trust between states (Kydd 2005).

3. See Pepinsky 2014 for an insightful analysis of the challenges that can arise when linking authoritarian institutions to behavioral outcomes.

4. Lake 2010.

5. Waltz 1959.

6. See also Byman and Pollack 2001; Saunders 2011.

7. Horowitz and Stam 2014.

8. Levitsky and Way 2010.

9. See, for example, Svolik 2012. As Pepinsky 2014 explains, it is particularly important to understand the origins of formal authoritarian institutions when one wishes to link them to behavioral outcomes, as institutions do not arise at random.

APPENDIX

1. Oren 1995.

Works Cited

Abrahamsson, Bengt. 1969. "Military Professionalization and Estimates on the Probability of War." In *Military Profession and Military Regimes: Commitments and Conflicts*, ed. Jacques Van Doorn, 35–51. The Hague: Mouton.

Adler, Emanuel. 1992. "The Emergence of Cooperation: National Epistemic Communities and the International Evolution of the Idea of Nuclear Arms Control." *International Organization* 46(1): 101–45.

Adomeit, Hannes. 1984. *Soviet Risk-Taking and Crisis Behavior: A Theoretical and Empirical Analysis*. London, Boston: Allen & Unwin.

al-Bazzaz, Sa'ad. 1995. "An Insider's View of Iraq." *Middle East Quarterly* 2(4): 67–75.

Al-Marashi, Ibrahim, and Sammy Salama. 2008. *Iraq's Armed Forces: An Analytical History*. London: Routledge.

Al-Samara'i, Wafiq. 1996. "Frontline: The Gulf War." *PBS*. Interview. January 9, 1996.

Anderson, Richard D. 1989. *Competitive Politics and Soviet Foreign Policy: Authority Building and Bargaining in the Brezhnev Politburo*. PhD dissertation, University of California at Berkeley.

——. 1993. *Public Politics in an Authoritarian State: Making Foreign Policy during the Brezhnev Years*. Ithaca: Cornell University Press.

Andreski, Stanislav. 1954. *Military Organization and Society*. London: Routledge & Kegan Paul.

——. 1992. *Wars, Revolutions, Dictatorships: Studies of Historical and Contemporary Problems from a Comparative Viewpoint*. London: Frank Cass.

Ang, Cheng G. 2002. *The Vietnam War from the Other Side: The Vietnamese Communists' Perspective*. London: RoutledgeCurzon.

——. 2004. *Ending the Vietnam War: The Vietnamese Communists' Perspective*. London: RoutledgeCurzon.

Angrist, Joshua D., and Jorn-Steffen Pischke. 2008. *Mostly Harmless Econometrics: An Empiricist's Companion*. Princeton, NJ: Princeton University Press.

Arceneaux, Craig L. 2001. *Bounded Missions: Military Regimes and Democratization in the Southern Cone and Brazil*. University Park: Pennsylvania State University Press.

Arendt, Hannah. 1951. *The Origins of Totalitarianism*. New York: Harcourt Brace.

Arquilla, John, and Maria Moyano Rasmussen. 2001. "The Origins of the South Atlantic War." *Journal of Latin American Studies* 33(4): 739–75.

Aspaturian, Vernon V. 1971. *Process and Power in Soviet Foreign Policy*. Boston: Little, Brown.

[221]

———. 1984. "The Stalinist Legacy in Soviet National Security Decision-Making." In *Soviet Decision-making for National Security*, ed. Jiri Valenta and William Potter, 23–73. Winchester, MA: Allen & Unwin.

Asselin, Pierre. 2002. *A Bitter Peace: Washington, Hanoi, and the Making of the Paris Agreement*. Chapel Hill: University of North Carolina Press.

———. 2005. "Hanoi and Americanization of the War in Vietnam." *Pacific Historical Review* 75(3): 427–40.

———. 2011. "The Democratic Republic of Vietnam and the 1954 Geneva Conference: A Revisionist Critique." *Cold War History* 11(2): 155–95.

———. 2012. " 'We Don't Want A Munich': Hanoi's Diplomatic Struggle during the American War, 1965–1968." *Diplomatic History* 36(3): 547–81.

Auer, James E., ed. 2006. *Who Was Responsible? From Marco Polo Bridge to Pearl Harbor*. Yomiuri Shimbun.

Aziz, Tariq. 1996. "The Gulf War." *Frontline*. PBS. Interview. January 9.

Banks, Arthur S. 2007. *Cross-national Time-Series Data Archive*. Jerusalem: Databanks International.

Baram, Amatzia. 2003. "Saddam's Power Structure: the Tikritis before, during, and after the War." *Adelphi Papers* 43(354): 93–114.

Baryshnikov, Vladimir N. 2000. "The USSR's Decision to begin the 'Winter War,' 1939–40." In *Mechanisms of Power in the Soviet Union*, ed. Niels E. Rosenfeldt, Bent Jensen, and Erik Kulavig. New York: St. Martin's.

Barnhart, Michael A. 1987. *Japan Prepares for Total War: The Search for Economic Security, 1919–1941*. Ithaca: Cornell University Press.

Beasley, W. G. 1974. *The Modern History of Japan*. New York: Praeger.

———. 2000. *The Rise of Modern Japan*. New York: St. Martin's.

Beck, Nathaniel, and Jonathan N. Katz. 2001. "Throwing Out the Baby with the Bathwater: A Comment on Green, Yoon, and Kim." *International Organization* 55(2): 487–95.

Becker, Elizabeth. 1998. *When the War Was Over: Cambodia and the Khmer Rouge Revolution*. New York: Public Affairs.

Bennett, Andrew, and Colin Elman. 2006. "Qualitative Research: Recent Developments in Case Study Methods." *Annual Review of Political Science* 9(1): 455–76.

———. 2007. "Case Study Methods in the International Relations Subfield." *Comparative Political Studies* 40(2): 170.

Betts, Alexander. 1997. *Malvinas: El Colonialismo Residual*. Buenos Aires: Grupo Editor Latinoamericano.

Betts, Richard K. 1977. *Soldiers, Statesmen, and Cold War Crises*. Cambridge, MA: Harvard University Press.

Bialer, Seweryn. 1969. *Stalin and His Generals*. New York: Pegasus.

Biddle, Stephen D. 2004. *Military Power: Explaining Victory and Defeat in Modern Battle*. Princeton, NJ: Princeton University Press.

Biddle, Stephen, and Robert Zirkle. 1996. "Technology, Civil-Military Relations, and Warfare in the Developing World." *Journal of Strategic Studies* 19(2): 171–212.

Biddle, Stephen, and Stephen Long. 2004. "Democracy and Military Effectiveness: A Deeper Look," *Journal of Conflict Resolution* 48(4): 525–46.

Bix, Herbert P. 2000. *Hirohito and the Making of Modern Japan*. New York: Harper Collins.

Blumenson, Martin. 1960. "The Soviet Power Play at Changkufeng." *World Politics* 12(2): 249–63.

Boterbloem, Kees. 2004. *The Life and Times of Andrei Zhdanov, 1896–1948*. Montreal: McGill-Queen's University Press.

Bozek, Gregory. 1993. *The Soviet-Finnish War, 1939–1940: Getting the Doctrine Right.* Fort Leavenworth, Kansas School of Advanced Military Studies, U.S. Army Command and General Staff College.

Brady, Henry E., and David Collier. 2004. *Rethinking Social Inquiry: Diverse Tools, Shared Standards.* Lanham, MD: Rowman & Littlefield.

Brady, Henry E., David Collier, and J. Seawright. 2006. "Toward a Pluralistic Vision of Methodology." *Political Analysis* 14(3): 353.

Brambor, Thomas, William R. Clark, and Matt Golder. 2006. "Understanding Interaction Models: Improving Empirical Analyses." *Political Analysis* 14(1): 63–82.

Bratton, Michael, and Nicholas Van de Walle. 1994. "Neopatrimonial Regimes and Political Transitions in Africa." *World Politics* 46(4): 453–89.

Brecher, Michael. 1996. "Crisis Escalation: Model and Findings." *International Political Science Review/Revue Internationale de Science Politique* 17(2): 215–30.

Breslauer, George W. 1982. *Khrushchev and Brezhnev as Leaders: Building Authority in Soviet Politics.* London, Boston: Allen & Unwin.

Brooker, Paul. 2000. *Non-Democratic Regimes: Theory, Government, and Politics.* New York: St. Martin's.

Brooks, Risa. 1998. *Political-Military Relations and the Stability of Arab Regimes.* Adelphi Paper 324. London: International Institute for Strategic Studies.

——. "Making Military Might: Why Do Some States Fail and Succeed? A Review Essay." *International Security* 28(2): 149–91.

Brown, Scott. 2008. "Socialism with a Slovak Face: Federalization, Democratization, and the Prague Spring." *East European Politics and Societies* 22(3): 467–95.

Browne, Courtney. 1967. *Tojo: The Last Banzai.* New York: Holt, Rinehart, & Winston.

Brownlee, Jason. 2007. *Authoritarianism in an Age of Democratization.* New York: Cambridge University Press.

Bueno de Mesquita, Bruce, Alastair Smith, Randolph M. Siverson, and James D. Morrow. 2003. *The Logic of Political Survival.* Cambridge, MA: MIT Press.

Bùi, Tín. 1995. *Following Ho Chi Minh: The Memoirs of a North Vietnamese Colonel.* Honolulu: University of Hawaii Press.

Burlatskii, Fedor. 1991. *Khrushchev and the First Russian Spring: The Era of Khrushchev through the Eyes of His Advisor.* New York: Scribner's Maxwell Macmillan International.

Büsser, Carlos. 1987. *Malvinas, la Guerra Inconclusa.* Buenos Aires: Ediciones Fernández Reguera.

Butow, Robert J. C. 1961. *Tojo and the Coming of War.* Princeton, NJ: Princeton University Press.

Byman, Daniel L., and Kenneth M. Pollack. 2001. "Let Us Now Praise Great Men: Bringing the Statesman Back In." *International Security* 25(4): 107–46.

Calvert, Peter. 1982. *The Falklands Crisis: The Rights and the Wrongs.* New York: St. Martin's.

Cardoso, Oscar. 1987. *Falklands, the Secret Plot.* East Molesey, U.K.: Preston Editions.

Carter, David B., and Curtis S. Signorino. 2010. "Back to the Future: Modeling Time Dependence in Binary Data." *Political Analysis* 18(3): 271–92.

Chanda, Nayan. 1986. *Brother Enemy: The War after the War.* San Diego: Harcourt Brace Jovanovich.

Chandler, David P. 1992. *Brother Number One: A Political Biography of Pol Pot.* Boulder, CO: Westview.

Charlton, Michael. 1989. *The Little Platoon: Diplomacy and the Falklands Dispute.* Oxford, U.K.: Basil Blackwell.

Chehabi, Houchang E., and Juan J. Linz. 1998. *Sultanistic Regimes*. Baltimore: Johns Hopkins University Press.

Cheibub, Jose A., Jennifer Gandhi, and James R. Vreeland. 2010. "Democracy and Dictatorship Revisited." *Public Choice* 143(1): 67–101.

Chiozza, Giacomo, and Hein E. Goemans. 2003. "Peace through Insecurity: Tenure and International Conflict." *Journal of Conflict Resolution* 47(4): 443–67.

——. 2004. "International Conflict and the Tenure of Leaders: Is War Still Ex Post Inefficient?" *American Journal of Political Science* 48(3): 604–19.

——. 2011. *Leaders and International Conflict*. New York: Cambridge University Press.

Choi, Ajin. 2004. "Democratic Synergy and Victory in War, 1816–1992." *International Studies Quarterly* 48(3): 663–82.

Chubaryan, Alexander O., and Harold Shukman. 2002. *Stalin and the Soviet-Finnish War, 1939–40*. London: Frank Cass.

Chubin, Shahram, and Charles Tripp. 1988. *Iran and Iraq at War*. Boulder, CO: Westview.

Clark, David H. 2003. "Can Strategic Interaction Divert Diversionary Behavior? A Model of U.S. Conflict Propensity." *Journal of Politics* 65(4): 1013–39.

Clarke, Kevin A., and Randall W. Stone. 2008. "Democracy and the Logic of Political Survival." *American Political Science Review* 102(3): 387–92.

Cockburn, Andrew, and Patrick Cockburn. 2002. *Saddam Hussein: An American Obsession*. London: Verso.

Coleman, Fred. 1996. *The Decline and Fall of the Soviet Empire: Forty Years That Shook the World, from Stalin to Yeltsin*. New York: St. Martin's.

Colgan, Jeff D. 2010. "Oil and Revolutionary Governments: Fuel for International Conflict." *International Organization* 64(4): 661–94.

——. 2013a. *Petro-Aggression: When Oil Causes War*. New York: Cambridge University Press.

——. 2013b. "Domestic Revolutionary Leaders and International Conflict." *World Politics* 65(4): 656–90.

Comisión Rattenbach. 1988. *Informe Rattenbach: el Drama de Malvinas*. Buenos Aires: Ediciones Espartaco.

Conquest, Robert. 1991. *Stalin: Breaker of Nations*. New York: Viking.

Coox, Alvin. 1969. "High Command and Field Army: The Kwantung Army and the Nomonhan Incident, 1939." *Military Affairs* 33(2): 302–12.

——. 1973. "The Lake Khasan Affair of 1938: Overview and Lessons." *Soviet Studies* 25(1): 51–65.

——. 1977. *The Anatomy of a Small War: the Soviet-Japanese Struggle of Changkufeng-Khasan, 1938*. Westport, CT: Greenwood Press.

——. 1985. *Nomonhan: Japan against Russia, 1939*. Stanford, CA: Stanford University Press.

——. 1988. "The Pacific War." In *The Cambridge History of Japan: The Twentieth Century*, ed. Peter Duus. New York: Cambridge University Press.

Costa Méndez, Nicanor. 1987. "Beyond Deterrence: The Malvinas Falklands Case." *Journal of Social Issues* 43(4): 119–22.

——. 1993. *Malvinas: Èsta es la Historia*. Buenos Aires: Editorial Sudamericana.

Coughlin, Con. 2005. *Saddam: His Rise and Fall*. New York: Harper Perennial.

Croco, Sarah E. 2011. "The Decider's Dilemma: Leader Culpability, Domestic Politics and War Termination." *American Political Science Review* 105(3): 457–77.

Croco, Sarah E., and Jessica L. P. Weeks. n.d. "The Effect of War Outcomes on Leader Tenure." (Working Paper).

Crowley, James. 1966. *Japan's Quest for Autonomy: National Security and Foreign Policy, 1930–1938*. Princeton, NJ: Princeton University Press.

Dabat, Alejandro, and Luis Lorenzano. 1984. *Argentina, the Malvinas, and the End of Military Rule*. London: Verso.

Dafoe, Allan, and Devin M. Caughey. 2011. "Honor and War: Using Southern Presidents to Identify Reputational Effects in International Conflict." Unpublished manuscript. University of California at Berkeley.

Dallin, Alexander. 1981. *German Rule in Russia, 1941–1945: A Study of Occupation Policies*. Boulder, CO: Westview.

Daniels, Robert V. 1998. *Russia's Transformation: Snapshots of a Crumbling System*. Lanham, MD: Rowman & Littlefield.

Debs, Alexandre, and Hein E. Goemans. 2010. "Regime Type, the Fate of Leaders, and War." *American Political Science Review* 104: 430–45.

Degras, Jane Tabrisky. 1952. *Soviet Documents On Foreign Policy: Volume 2*. London: Oxford University Press.

Desch, Michael C. 2002. "Democracy and Victory: Why Regime Type Hardly Matters." *International Security* 27(2): 5–47.

——. 2003. "Democracy and Victory: Fair Fights or Food Fights?" *International Security* 28(1): 180–94.

——. 2008. *Power and Military Effectiveness: The Fallacy of Democratic Triumphalism*. Baltimore: Johns Hopkins University Press.

Dixon, William J. 1994. "Democracy and the Peaceful Settlement of International Conflict." *American Political Science Review* 88(1): 14–32.

Dobrynin, Anatoly. 1995. *In Confidence: Moscow's Ambassador to America's Six Cold War Presidents (1962–1986)*. New York: Times Books, Random House.

Downes, Alexander B. 2008. *Targeting Civilians in War*. Ithaca: Cornell University Press.

——. 2009. "How Smart and Tough Are Democracies? Reassessing Theories of Democratic Victory in War." *International Security* 33(4): 9–51.

Downs, Anthony. 1957. *An Economic Theory of Democracy*. New York: Harper.

Downs, George W., and David M. Rocke. 1994. "Conflict, Agency, and Gambling for Resurrection: The Principal-Agent Problem Goes to War." *American Journal of Political Science* 38(2): 362–80.

Doyle, Michael W. 1986. "Liberalism and World Politics." *American Political Science Review* 80(4): 1151–69.

Drea, Edward. 2009. *Japan's Imperial Army: Its Rise and Fall, 1853–1945*. Lawrence: University Press of Kansas.

Duelfer, Charles, et al. 2005. *Comprehensive Report of the Special Advisor to the Director of Central Intelligence on Iraq's WMD, with Addendums*. Washington, DC: Government Printing Office.

Duiker, William J. 1986. *China and Vietnam: The Roots of Conflict*. Berkeley: Institute of East Asian Studies, University of California.

——. 1996. *The Communist Road to Power in Vietnam*. Boulder, CO: Westview.

Edmonds, Robin. 1983. *Soviet Foreign Policy—The Brezhnev Years*. Oxford, U.K., New York: Oxford University Press.

Edwards, Robert. 2006. *White Death: Russia's War with Finland 1939–1940*. London: Weidenfeld & Nicolson.

Egorov, Georgy, and Konstantin Sonin. 2011. "Dictators and Their Viziers: Endogenizing the Loyalty-Competence Trade-off." *Journal of the European Economic Association* 9(5): 903–30.

Elkins, David J., and Richard E. B. Simeon. 1979. "A Cause in Search of its Effect, or What Does Political Culture Explain?" *Comparative Politics* 11(2): 127–45.

Erickson, John. [1962] 2001. *The Soviet High Command: A Military-Political History, 1918–1941*. Reprint, London: Frank Cass.

Escribà-Folch, Abel, and Joseph Wright. 2010. "Dealing with Tyranny: International Sanctions and the Survival of Authoritarian Rulers." *International Studies Quarterly* 54(2): 335–59.

Ezrow, Natasha M., and Erica Frantz. 2011. *Dictators and Dictatorships: Understanding Authoritarian Regimes and Their Leaders*. New York: Continuum.

Fawthrop, Tom, and Helen Jarvis. 2004. *Getting Away with Genocide?: Elusive Justice and the Khmer Rouge Tribunal*. London: Pluto Press.

FBIS Daily Report. 1990. FBIS-NES-90-249, pp. 24–30.

Fearon, James D. 1994. "Domestic Political Audiences and the Escalation of International Disputes." *American Political Science Review* 88(3): 577–92.

——. 1995. "Rationalist Explanations for War." *International Organization* 49(3): 379–414.

——. 1999. "Electoral Accountability and the Control of Politicians: Selecting Good Types versus Sanctioning Poor Performance." In *Democracy, Accountability, and Representation*, ed. Bernard Manin, Adam Przeworski, and Susan Stokes, 55–97. Cambridge, U.K.: Cambridge University Press.

Feaver, Peter, and Christopher Gelpi. 2004. *Choosing Your Battles: American Civil-Military Relations and the Use of Force*. Princeton, NJ: Princeton University Press.

Finer, Samuel E. 1962. *The Man on Horseback*. London: Pall Mall.

Fink, Carole, Philipp Gassert, and Detlef Junker. 1998. *1968: The World Transformed*. Cambridge, U.K.: German Historical Institute; Cambridge University Press.

Finnemore, Martha. 1996. *National Interests in International Society*. Ithaca: Cornell University Press.

Fjelde, Hanne. 2010. "Generals, Dictators, and Kings." *Conflict Management and Peace Science* 27(3): 195.

Flores-Macías, Gustavo A., and Sarah E. Kreps. 2013. "Political Parties at War: A Study of American War Finance, 1789–2010." *American Political Science Review* 107(4): 833–48.

Frantz, Erica. 2008. "Tying the Dictator's Hands: Elite Coalitions in Authoritarian Regimes." PhD dissertation, University of California at Los Angeles.

Frantz, Erica, and Natasha M. Ezrow. 2009. " 'Yes Men' and the Likelihood of Foreign Policy Mistakes across Dictatorships." Presented at the Annual Meeting of the American Political Science Association, Toronto, Canada.

Fravel, M. Taylor. 2010. "The Limits of Diversion: Rethinking Internal and External Conflict." *Security Studies* 19(2): 307–41.

Freedman, Lawrence. 2005a. *The Origins of the Falklands War*, vol. 1 of *The Official History of the Falklands War*. London: Routledge, Taylor & Francis Group, 2005.

——. 2005b. *War and Diplomacy*, vol. 2 of *The Official History of the Falklands War*. London: Routledge, Taylor & Francis Group.

Freedman, Lawrence, and Virginia Gamba-Stonehouse. 1990. *Signals of War: The Falklands Conflict of 1982*. Princeton, NJ: Princeton University Press.

Frieden, Jeffry. 1999. "Actors And Preferences In International Relations." In *Strategic Choice and International Relations*, ed. David A Lake and Robert Powell, 39–76. Princeton, NJ: Princeton University Press.

Friedrich, Carl J., and Zbigniew K. Brzezinski. 1956. *Totalitarian Dictatorship and Autocracy*. Cambridge, MA: Harvard University Press.

Fursenko, A. A., and Timothy J. Naftali. 2006. *Khrushchev's Cold War: The Inside Story of an American Adversary*. New York: Norton.

Gallagher, Matthew, and Karl Spielmann. 1972. *Soviet Decision-Making for Defense: A Critique of U.S. Perspectives on the Arms Race*. New York: Praeger Publishers.

Gamba-Stonehouse, Virginia. 1987. *The Falklands/Malvinas War: A Model for North-South Crisis Prevention*. Boston: Allen & Unwin.

Gandhi, Jennifer. 2008. *Political Institutions under Dictatorship*. Cambridge, U.K.: Cambridge University Press.

Gandhi, Jennifer, and Adam Przeworski. 2006. "Cooperation, Cooptation, and Rebellion under Dictatorships." *Economics and Politics* 18(1): 1–26.

Garthoff, Raymond L. 1988. "Cuban Missile Crisis: The Soviet Story." *Foreign Policy* 72 (Fall): 61–80.

Gartzke, Erik. "Preferences and the Democratic Peace." *International Studies Quarterly* 44(2): 191–212.

Garver, John W. 1988. *Chinese-Soviet Relations, 1937–1945: The Diplomacy of Chinese Nationalism*. New York: Oxford University Press.

Gause, Gregory F., III. 2001. "Iraq and the Gulf War: Decision-Making in Baghdad." *Columbia International Affairs Online Series*. New York: Columbia University Press.

——. 2010. *The International Relations of the Persian Gulf*. Cambridge, U.K.: Cambridge University Press.

Gausmann, William C. 1988. *VWP-DRV Leadership, 1960–1973*. Saigon: United States Mission in Viet-Nam.

Geddes, Barbara. 1999. "What Do We Know about Democratization after Twenty Years?" *Annual Review of Political Science* 2: 115–44.

——. 2003. *Paradigms and Sand Castles: Theory Building and Research Design in Comparative Politics*. Ann Arbor: University of Michigan Press.

——. 2004. "Minimum Winning Coalitions and Personalization in Authoritarian Regimes." Paper presented at the annual meeting of the American Political Science Association.

Geddes, Barbara, Joseph Wright, and Erica Frantz. 2014. "Autocratic Breakdown and Regime Transitions: A New Data Set." *Perspectives on Politics*. Forthcoming.

Gelman, Andrew, and Jennifer Hill. 2006. *Data Analysis Using Regression and Multilevel/Hierarchical Models*. Cambridge University Press.

Gelman, Harry. 1984. *The Brezhnev Politburo and the Decline of Detente*. Ithaca: Cornell University Press.

Gelpi, Christopher. 1997. "Democratic Diversions: Governmental Structure and the Externalization of Domestic Conflict." *Journal of Conflict Resolution* 41(2): 255–82.

Gelpi, Christopher F., and Michael Griesdorf. 2001. "Winners or Losers? Democracies in International Crisis, 1918–94." *American Political Science Review* 95(3): 633–47.

George, Alexander L., and Andrew Bennett. 2005. *Case Studies and Theory Development in the Social Sciences*. Boston: MIT Press.

Gibler, Douglas. 2012. *The Territorial Peace: Borders, State Development, and International Conflict*. New York: Cambridge University Press.

Gilks, Anne. 1992. *The Breakdown of the Sino-Vietnamese Alliance, 1970–1979*. Berkeley: Institute of East Asian Studies, University of California, Center for Chinese Studies.

Glad, Betty. 2002. "Why Tyrants Go Too Far: Malignant Narcissism and Absolute Power." *Political Psychology* 23(1): 1–2.

Glaser, Charles L. 2010. *Rational Theory of International Politics: The Logic of Competition and Cooperation*. Princeton, NJ: Princeton University Press.

Gleditsch, Kristian Skrede. 2002. "Expanded Trade and GDP Data." *Journal of Conflict Resolution* 46(5): 712–24.

——. 2013. Modified Polity P4 and P4D Data, Version 4.0, http://privatewww. essex.ac.uk/~ksg/Polity.html.

Gleditsch, Kristian Skrede, Idean Salehyan, and Kenneth Schultz. 2008. "Fighting at Home, Fighting Abroad: How Civil Wars Lead to International Disputes." *Journal of Conflict Resolution* 52(4): 479–506.

Goemans, Hein E. 2000. *War and Punishment: The Causes of War Termination and the First World War*. Princeton, NJ: Princeton University Press.

——. 2008. "Which Way Out? The Manner and Consequences of Losing Office." *Journal of Conflict Resolution* 52(6): 771–94.

Goemans, Hein E., Kristian S. Gleditsch, and Giacomo Chiozza. 2009. "Introducing Archigos: A Dataset of Political Leaders." *Journal of Peace Research* 46(2): 269.

Goldgeier, James. 1990. *Soviet Leaders and International Crises: The Influence of Domestic Political Experiences on Foreign Policy Strategies*. PhD dissertation, University of California at Berkeley.

Goldstein, Judith, and Robert O. Keohane. 1993. *Ideas and Foreign Policy: Beliefs, Institutions, and Political Change*. Ithaca: Cornell University Press.

Goncharov, Sergei N., John Wilson Lewis, and Litai Xue. 1993. *Uncertain Partners: Stalin, Mao, and the Korean War*. Stanford, CA: Stanford University Press.

Goscha, Christopher. 2006. "Vietnam, the Third Indochina War and the Meltdown of Asian Internationalism." In *The Third Indochina War: Conflict between China, Vietnam, and Cambodia, 1972–79*, ed. Odd Westad and Sophie Quinn-Judge, 152–86. Abingdon, U.K.: Routledge.

Gowa, Joanne S. 1999. *Ballots and Bullets: The Elusive Democratic Peace*. Princeton, NJ: Princeton University Press.

Green, Donald P., Soo Yeon Kim, and David H. Yoon. 2001. "Dirty Pool." *International Organization* 55(2): 441–68.

Green, Jerrold D., Frederic M. Wehrey, and Charles Wolf. 2009. *Understanding Iran*. Rand Corporation.

Grossheim, Martin. 2005. " 'Revisionism' in the Democratic Republic of Vietnam: New Evidence from the East German Archives." *Cold War History* 5(4): 451–77.

Guisinger, Alexandra, and Alistair Smith. 2002. "Honest Threats: The Interaction of Reputation and Political Institutions in International Crises." *Journal of Conflict Resolution* 46(2): 175–200.

Gurr, Ted Robert. 1988. "War, Revolution, and the Growth of the Coercive State." *Comparative Political Studies* 21(1): 45–65.

Haber, Stephen. 2006. "Authoritarian Government." In *The Oxford Handbook of Political Economy*, ed. Barry R. Weingast and Donald A. Wittman, 693–707. Oxford: Oxford University Press.

Hadenius, Axel, and Jan Teorell. 2007. "Pathways from Authoritarianism." *Journal of Democracy* 18(1): 143–57.

Hao, Yufan, and Lin Su. 2005. *Chinese Foreign Policy Making: Societal Forces in Chinese American Policy Making*. London: Ashgate.

Hashim, Ahmed. 2003. "Saddam Husayn and Civil-Military Relations in Iraq: The Quest for Legitimacy and Power." *Middle East Journal* 57(1): 9–41.

Haslam, Jonathan. 1984. *The Soviet Union and the Struggle for Collective Security in Europe, 1933–1939*. New York: St. Martin's Press.

——. 1992. *The Soviet Union and the Threat From the East, 1933–1944*. Pittsburgh: University of Pittsburgh Press.

——. 2011. *Russia's Cold War: From the October Revolution to the Fall of the Wall*. New Haven, CT: Yale University Press.

Hata, Ikuhiko. 1976. "The Japanese-Soviet Confrontation, 1935–1939." In *Deterrent Diplomacy: Japan, Germany, and the USSR, 1935–1940*, ed. James William Morley. New York: Columbia University Press.

——. 1980. "The Army's Move into Northern Indochina." In *The Fateful Choice: Japan's Advance into Southeast Asia, 1939–41*, ed. James William Morley. New York: Columbia University Press.

——. 1983. "The Marco Polo Bridge Incident, 1937." In *The China Quagmire: Japan's Expansion on the Asian Continent, 1933–1941*, ed. James W. Morley, 233–88. New York: Columbia University Press.

——. 1988. "Continental Expansion, 1905–1941." In *The Cambridge History of Japan: The Twentieth Century*, ed. Peter Duus, 271–314. Cambridge, MA: Cambridge University Press.

Hoffmann, Fritz, and Olga Mingo Hoffmann. 1984. *Sovereignty in Dispute: The Falklands Malvinas, 1493–1982*. Boulder, CO: Westview.

Holsti, Kalevi J. 1991. *Peace and War: Armed Conflicts and International Order, 1648–1989*. Cambridge, U.K.: Cambridge University Press.

Holsti, Ole. 2004. *Public Opinion and American Foreign Policy*. Rev. ed. Ann Arbor: University of Michigan Press.

Horowitz, Michael C., and Allan C. Stam. 2014. "How Prior Military Experience Influences the Future Militarized Behavior of Leaders." Forthcoming. *International Organization*.

Hough, Jerry F., and Merle Fainsod. 1979. *How the Soviet Union is Governed*. Cambridge, MA: Harvard University Press.

Howell, William G., and Jon C. Pevehouse. 2007. *While Dangers Gather: Congressional Checks on Presidential War Powers*. Princeton, NJ: Princeton University Press.

Hunt, Michael H. 2010. *A Vietnam War Reader: A Documentary History from American and Vietnamese Perspectives*. Chapel Hill: University of North Carolina Press.

Huntington, Samuel P. 1957. *The Soldier and the State: The Theory and Politics of Civil-Military Relations*. Cambridge, MA: Belknap Press of Harvard University Press.

Ike, Nobutaka. 1967. *Japan's Decision for War: Records of the 1941 Policy Conferences*. Stanford, CA: Stanford University Press.

Iriye, Akira. 1987. *The Origins of the Second World War in the Pacific*. New York: Longman.

James, Patrick. 1987. "Conflict and Cohesion: A Review of the Literature and Recommendations for Future Research." *Cooperation and Conflict* 22(1): 21–33.

Janowitz, Morris. 1964. *The Military in the Political Development of New Nations: An Essay in Comparative Analysis*. Chicago: University of Chicago Press.

Jansen, Marius. 2000. *The Making of Modern Japan*. Cambridge, MA: Belknap Press of Harvard University Press.

Jervis, Robert. 1976. *Perception and Misperception in International Politics*. Princeton, NJ: Princeton University Press.

——. 1978. "Cooperation under the Security Dilemma." *World Politics* 30(2): 167–214.

Johns, Leslie. 2006. "Knowing the Unknown." *Journal of Conflict Resolution* 50(2): 228–52.

Johnson, Dominic. 2004. *Overconfidence and War: The Havoc and Glory of Positive Illusions*. Cambridge, MA: Harvard University Press.

Johnson, Dominic, and Dominic Tierney. 2006. *Failing to Win: Perceptions of Victory and Defeat in International Politics*. Cambridge, MA: Harvard University Press.

Johnston, Alastair Iain. 1995. "Thinking about Strategic Culture." *International Security* 19(4): 32–64.

Jones, Daniel M., Stuart A. Bremer, and J. David Singer. 1996. "Militarized Interstate Disputes, 1816–1992: Rationale, Coding Rules, and Empirical Patterns." *Conflict Management and Peace Science* 15(2): 163–213.

Kahl, Colin H. 1998. "Constructing a Separate Peace: Constructivism, Collective Liberal Identity, and Democratic Peace." *Security Studies* 8(2–3): 94–144.

Kant, Immanuel. [1795] 1991. *Kant's Political Writings*. Edited by Hans Reiss. 2nd ed. Cambridge, U.K.: Cambridge University Press.

Karsh, Efraim, and Inari Rautsi. 1991. *Saddam Hussein: A Political Biography*. New York: Free Press.

Kass, Ilana. 1978. *Soviet Involvement in the Middle East: Policy Formulation, 1966–1973*. Boulder, CO: Westview.

Katzenstein, Peter J., ed. 1996. *The Culture of National Security: Norms and Identity in World Politics*. New York: Columbia University Press.

Kaufmann, Chaim. 2004. "Threat Inflation and the Failure of the Marketplace of Ideas: The Selling of the Iraq War." *International Security* 29(1): 5–48.

Kelley, Donald. 1987. *Soviet Politics from Brezhnev to Gorbachev*. New York: Praeger.

Kennedy, Ryan. 2009. "Survival and Accountability: An Analysis of the Empirical Support for 'Selectorate Theory.'" *International Studies Quarterly* 53(3): 695–714.

Khlevniuk, Oleg. 2009. *Master of the House: Stalin and his Inner Circle*. New Haven, CT: Yale University Press.

Khoo, Nicholas. 2010. "Revisiting the Termination of the Sino–Vietnamese Alliance, 1975–1979." *European Journal of East Asian Studies* 9(2): 321–61.

——. 2011. *Collateral Damage: Sino-Soviet Rivalry and the Termination of the Sino-Vietnamese Alliance*. New York: Columbia University Press.

Khrushchev, Nikita. 2004. *Memoirs of Nikita Khrushchev: Volume 1: Commissar, 1918–1945*. University Park: Pennsylvania State University Press.

Kier, Elizabeth. 1997. *Imagining War: French and British Military Doctrine between the Wars*. Princeton, NJ: Princeton University Press.

Kiernan, Ben. 2002. *The Pol Pot Regime: Race, Power, and Genocide in Cambodia under the Khmer Rouge, 1975–79*. New Haven, CT: Yale University Press.

——. 2006. "External and Indigenous Sources of Khmer Rouge Ideology." In *The Third Indochina War: Conflict Between China, Vietnam, and Cambodia, 1972–79*, ed. Odd Westad and Sophie Quinn-Judge, 187–206. Abingdon, U.K.: Routledge.

Kikuoka, Michael. 1988. *The Changkufeng Incident: A Study in Soviet-Japanese Conflict, 1938*. Lanham, MD: University Press of America.

King, Gary, Robert O. Keohane, and Sidney Verba. 1994. *Designing Social Inquiry*. Princeton, NJ: Princeton University Press.

Kinne, Brandon J. 2005. "Decision Making in Autocratic Regimes: A Poliheuristic Perspective." *International Studies Perspectives* 6(1): 114–28.

Kirshner, Jonathan. 2007. *Appeasing Bankers: Financial Caution on the Road to War*. Princeton, NJ: Princeton University Press.

Kisangani, Emizet F., and Jeffrey Pickering. 2009. "The Dividends of Diversion: Mature Democracies' Proclivity to Use Diversionary Force and the Rewards They Reap from It." *British Journal of Political Science* 39(3): 483–515.

Kissinger, Henry, and Clare Boothe Luce. 1979. *White House Years*. Boston: Little, Brown.

Kleine-Ahlbrandt, Stephanie, and Andrew Small. 2008. "China's New Dictatorship Diplomacy." *Foreign Affairs*, June 1. Available at www.foreignaffairs.com/

articles/63045/stephanie-kleine-ahlbrandt-and-andrew-small/chinas-new-dictatorship-diplomacy. Accessed January 13, 2014.

Knight, Amy W. 1988. *The KGB: Police and Politics in the Soviet Union.* Boston: Unwin Hyman.

Kramer, Mark. 1998a. "The Soviet Union and the 1956 Crises in Hungary and Poland: Reassessments and New Findings." *Journal of Contemporary History* 33(2): 163–214.

———. 1998b. "The Czechoslovak Crisis and the Brezhnev Doctrine." In *1968: The World Transformed*, ed. Carole Fink, Philipp Gassert, and Detlef Junker, 111–72. Cambridge, U.K.: German Historical Institute; Cambridge University Press.

Kydd, Andrew H. 2005. *Trust and Mistrust in International Relations.* Princeton, N.J.: Princeton University Press.

Lai, Brian, and Dan Reiter. 2000. "Democracy, Political Similarity, and International Alliances, 1816–1992." *Journal of Conflict Resolution* 44(2): 203–27.

Lai, Brian, and Dan Slater. 2006. "Institutions of the Offensive: Domestic Sources of Dispute Initiation in Authoritarian Regimes, 1950–1992." *American Journal of Political Science* 50(1): 113–26.

Lake, David A. 1992. "Powerful Pacifists: Democratic States and War." *American Political Science Review* 86(1): 24–37.

———. 2010. "Two Cheers for Bargaining Theory: Assessing Rationalist Explanations of the Iraq War." *International Security* 35(3): 7–52.

Lando, Barry M. *Web of Deceit.* 2007. New York: Other Press.

Lee, Wayne E. 2011. *Barbarians and Brothers: Anglo-American Warfare, 1500–1865.* Oxford: Oxford University Press.

Leeds, Brett Ashley, and David R. Davis. 1997. "Domestic Political Vulnerability and International Disputes." *Journal of Conflict Resolution* 41(6): 814–34.

Leeds, Brett Ashley. 2003. "Alliance Reliability in Times of War: Explaining State Decisions to Violate Treaties." *International Organization* 57(4): 801–27.

Legro, Jeffrey W. 1996. "Culture and Preferences in the International Cooperation Two-Step." *American Political Science Review* 90(1): 118–37.

Levitsky, Steven, and Lucan A. Way. 2010. *Competitive Authoritarianism: Hybrid Regimes after the Cold War.* Cambridge, U.K.: Cambridge University Press.

Levy, Jack S. 1987. "Declining Power and the Preventive Motivation for War." *World Politics* 40(1): 82–107.

Levy, Jack S., and Lily I. Vakili. 1992. "Diversionary Action by Authoritarian Regimes: Argentina in the Falklands/Malvinas case." In *The Internationalization of Communal Strife*, ed. Manus I. Midlarsky, 118–46. New York: Routledge.

Lieberman, E. S. 2005. "Nested Analysis as a Mixed-Method Strategy for Comparative Research." *American Political Science Review* 99(3): 435–52.

Linz, Juan J. 2000. *Totalitarian and Authoritarian Regimes.* Boulder, CO: Lynne Rienner.

Lovell, John P. 1964. "The Professional Socialization of the West Point Cadet." In *The New Military: Changing Patterns of Organization*, ed. Morris Janowitz, 119–57. New York: Russell Sage Foundation.

Lu, David J. 1961. *From Marco Polo Bridge to Pearl Harbor.* New York: Public Affairs Press.

———. 2002. *Agony of Choice: Matsuoka Yosuke and the Rise and Fall of the Japanese Empire, 1880–1946.* Lanham, MD: Lexington Books.

Lustick, I. S. 1996. "History, Historiography, and Political Science: Multiple Historical Records and the Problem of Selection Bias." *American Political Science Review* 90(3): 605–18.

Magaloni, Beatriz. 2006. *Voting for Autocracy: Hegemonic Party Survival and Its Demise in Mexico*. Cambridge, U.K.: Cambridge University Press.
——. 2008. "Credible Power-sharing and the Longevity of Authoritarian Rule." *Comparative Political Studies* 41(4/5): 715–41.
Makiya, Kanan. 1989. *Republic of Fear*. Berkeley: University of California Press.
Mansfield, Peter. 1982. "Saddam Husain's Political Thinking." In *Iraq: The Contemporary State*, ed. Tim Niblock, 62–73. New York: St. Martin's.
Maoz, Zeev. 2005. *Dyadic Militarized Interstate Disputes Dataset Version 2.0*. Available at http://psfaculty.ucdavis.edu/zmaoz/dyadmid.html. Accessed January 31, 2011.
Maoz, Zeev, and Bruce Russett. 1993. "Normative and Structural Causes of Democratic Peace, 1946–1986." *American Political Science Review* 87(3): 624–38.
Marr, Phebe. 1985. *The Modern History of Iraq*. 1st ed. Boulder, CO: Westview.
——. 1988. "Iraq: Its Revolutionary Experience under the Ba'th." In *Ideology and Power in the Middle East*, ed. Peter J. Chelkowski and Robert J. Pranger, 185–209. Durham, NC: Duke University Press.
——. 2004. *The Modern History of Iraq*. 2nd ed. Boulder, CO: Westview.
Marshall, Monty G., and Keith Jaggers. 2002. *POLITY IV Project, Political Regime Characteristics and Transitions, 1800–2002, Dataset Users' Manual*. College Park: Center for International Development and Conflict Management, University of Maryland.
Mattes, Michaela and Mariana Rodriguez. 2014. "Autocracies and International Cooperation." *International Studies Quarterly*. Forthcoming.
Maxon, Yale C. 1957. *Control of Japanese Foreign Policy: A Study of Civil-Military Rivalry, 1930–1945*. Berkeley: University of California Press.
McGillivray, Fiona, and Alistair Smith. 2000, "Trust and Cooperation through Agent-Specific Punishments." *International Organization* 54(4): 809–25.
McNamara, Robert S., James G. Blight, and Robert K. Brigham. 1999. *Argument without End: In Search of Answers to the Vietnam Tragedy*. New York: Public Affairs.
McSherry, James. 1970. *Stalin, Hitler, and Europe*. Cleveland: World.
Medeiros, Evan S. 2009. "China's International Behavior: Activism, Opportunism, and Diversification." Rand Corporation Monograph Series.
Medeiros, Evan S., and M. Taylor Fravel. 2003. "China's New Diplomacy." *Foreign Affairs* 82(6): 22–35.
Medvedev, Roy. 1983. *Khrushchev*. Garden City, NY: Anchor Press/Doubleday.
——. 1989. *Let History Judge*. New York: Columbia University Press.
Medvedev, Zhores A. 1983. *Andropov*. New York: W. W. Norton.
Mercer, Jonathan. 1995. "Anarchy and Identity." *International Organization* 49(2): 229–52.
Mićunović, Veljko, and George Kennan. 1980. *Moscow Diary*. Garden City, NY: Doubleday.
Milani, Abbas. 2009. "Mullahs on the Verge: Iran's People, Iran's Pulpits." *World Affairs*, Fall 2009. Available at www.worldaffairsjournal.org/article/mullahs-verge-irans-people-irans-pulpits. Accessed January 13, 2014.
Miller, Edward S. 2007. *Bankrupting the Enemy: The U.S. Financial Siege of Japan before Pearl Harbor*. Annapolis, MD: Naval Institute Press.
Montefiore, Simon Sebag. 2004. *Stalin: The Court of the Red Tsar*. New York: Knopf.
Moravscik, Andrew. 1997. "Taking Preferences Seriously: A Liberal Theory of International Politics." *International Organization* 51(4): 513–53.
Morgan, T. Clifton, and Sally Howard Campbell. 1991. "Domestic Structure, Decisional Constraints, and War." *Journal of Conflict Resolution* 35(2): 187–211.

Works Cited

Morley, James William, ed. 1994. *The Final Confrontation: Japan's Negotiations with the United States, 1941.* New York: Columbia University Press.

Morris, Stephen J. 1999. *Why Vietnam Invaded Cambodia: Political Culture and the Causes of War.* Stanford, CA: Stanford University Press.

Most, Benjamin A., and Harvey Starr. 1989. *Inquiry, Logic, and International Politics.* Columbia: University of South Carolina Press.

Munck, Gerardo. 1998. *Authoritarianism and Democratization: Soldiers and Workers in Argentina, 1976–1983.* University Park: Pennsylvania State University Press.

Nguyễn, Thị Đ. 1976. *No Other Road to Take: Memoir of Mrs. Nguyễn Thị Định.* Ithaca: Southeast Asia Program, Dept. of Asian Studies, Cornell University.

Nguyen, Lien-Hang T. 2012. *Hanoi's War: An International History of the War for Peace in Vietnam.* Chapel Hill: University of North Carolina Press.

Nish, Ian. 1977. *Japanese Foreign Policy: 1869–1942.* London: Routledge & Kegan Paul.

———. 2002. *Japanese Foreign Policy in the Interwar Period.* Westport, CT: Praeger Publishers.

Nogee, Joseph L., and Robert H. Donaldson. 1981. *Soviet Foreign Policy since World War II.* New York: Pergamon Press.

Nordlinger, Eric A. 1977. *Soldiers in Politics: Military Coups and Governments.* Englewood Cliffs, NJ: Prentice-Hall.

O'Donnell, Guillermo A. 1973. *Modernization and Bureaucratic-Authoritarianism.* Berkeley: Institute of International Studies, University of California.

———. 1978. "Reflections on the Patterns of Change in the Bureaucratic-Authoritarian State." *Latin American Research Review* 13(1): 3–38.

O'Dowd, Edward C. 2007. *Chinese Military Strategy in the Third Indochina War: The Last Maoist War.* London: Routledge.

Oakes, Amy. 2006. "Diversionary War and Argentina's Invasion of the Falkland Islands." *Security Studies* 15(3): 431–63.

Ogata, Sadako N. 1964. *Defiance in Manchuria: The Making of Japanese Foreign Policy, 1931–1932.* Berkeley: University of California Press.

Oneal, John R., Bruce M. Russett, and Michael L. Berbaum. 2003. "Causes of Peace: Democracy, Interdependence, and International Organizations, 1885–1992." *International Studies Quarterly* 47(3): 371–93.

Oneal, John R., and Jaroslav Tir. 2006. "Does the Diversionary Use of Force Threaten the Democratic Peace? Assessing the Effect of Economic Growth on Interstate Conflict, 1921–2001." *International Studies Quarterly* 50(4): 755–79.

Oren, Ido. 1995. "The Subjectivity of the 'Democratic' Peace: Changing U.S. Perceptions of Imperial Germany." *International Security* 20(2): 147–84.

Oren, Ido, and Jude Hays. 1997. "Democracies May Rarely Fight One Another, but Developed Socialist States Rarely Fight at All." *Alternatives* 22: 493–521.

Paul, T. V. 1994. *Asymmetric Conflicts: War Initiation by Weaker Powers.* Cambridge, U.K.: Cambridge University Press.

Peattie, Mark R. 1975. *Ishiwara Kanji and Japan's Confrontation with the West.* Princeton, NJ: Princeton University Press.

Peceny, Mark, and Caroline C. Beer. 2003. "Peaceful Parties and Puzzling Personalists." *American Political Science Review* 97(2): 339–42.

Peceny, Mark, and Christopher K. Butler. 2004. "The Conflict Behavior of Authoritarian Regimes." *International Politics* 41(4): 565–81.

Peceny, Mark, Caroline C. Beer, and Shannon Sanchez-Terry. 2002. "Dictatorial Peace?" *American Political Science Review* 96(1): 15–26.

Pelz, Stephen E. 1974. *Race to Pearl Harbor: The Failure of the Second London Naval Conference and the Onset of World War II.* Cambridge: Harvard University Press.

Pepinsky, Thomas B. 2009. *Economic Crises and the Breakdown of Authoritarian Regimes: Indonesia and Malaysia in Comparative Perspective.* New York: Cambridge University Press.

Perlmutter, Amos. 1977. *Military and Politics in Modern Times: Professionals, Praetorians, and Revolutionary Soldiers.* New Haven, CT: Yale University Press.

Pickering, Jeffrey, and Emizet F. Kisangani. 2005. "Democracy and Diversionary Military Intervention: Reassessing Regime Type and the Diversionary Hypothesis." *International Studies Quarterly* 49(1): 23–44.

——. 2010. "Diversionary Despots? Comparing Autocracies' Propensities to Use and to Benefit from Military Force." *American Journal of Political Science* 54(2): 477–93.

Pike, Douglas. 1987. *Vietnam and the Soviet Union: Anatomy of an Alliance.* Boulder, CO: Westview.

Pons, Silvio. 2002. *Stalin and the Inevitable War: 1936–1941.* Portland, OR: Frank Cass.

Porter, Gareth. 1993. *Vietnam: The Politics of Bureaucratic Socialism.* Ithaca: Cornell University Press.

Posen, Barry. 1984. *The Sources of Military Doctrine: France, Britain, and Germany between the World Wars.* Ithaca: Cornell University Press.

Post, Jerrold M. 2004. *Leaders and Their Followers in a Dangerous World: The Psychology of Political Behavior.* Ithaca: Cornell University Press.

Powell, Robert. 1994. "Anarchy in International Relations Theory: The Neorealist-Neoliberal Debate." *International Organization* 48(2): 313–44.

——. 1999. *In the Shadow of Power: States and Strategies in International Politics.* Princeton, NJ: Princeton University Press.

——. 2002. "Bargaining Theory and International Conflict." *Annual Review of Political Science* 5: 1–30.

Pribbenow, Merle L. 1999. "North Vietnam's Final Offensive: Strategic Endgame Nonpareil." *Parameters,* Winter 1999–2000: 58–71.

——, trans. 2002. *Victory in Vietnam: The Official History of the People's Army of Vietnam, 1954–1975.* The Military History Institute of Vietnam. Lawrence: University Press of Kansas.

——. 2006. "A Tale of Five Generals: Vietnam's Invasion of Cambodia." *Journal of Military History* 70(2): 459–86.

——. 2008. "General Võ Nguyên Giáp and the Mysterious Evolution of the Plan for the 1968 Tết Offensive." *Journal of Vietnamese Studies* 3(2): 1–33.

Quinlivan, James T. 1999. "Coup-proofing: Its Practice and Consequences in the Middle East." *International Security* 24(2): 131–65.

Quinn-Judge, Sophie. 2006. "Victory on the Battlefield: Isolation in Asia: Vietnam's Cambodia Decade, 1979–1989." In *The Third Indochina War: Conflict Between China, Vietnam, and Cambodia, 1972–79,* ed. Odd Westad and Sophie Quinn-Judge, 207–30. Abingdon, U.K.: Routledge.

Ra'anan, Uri, and Igor Lukes. 1990. *Inside the Apparat: Perspectives on the Soviet System from Former Functionaries.* Lexington, MA: Lexington Books.

Race, Jeffrey. 1972. *War Comes to Long An: Revolutionary Conflict in a Vietnamese Province.* Berkeley: University of California Press.

Rahman, H. 1997. *The Making of the Gulf War.* Reading, U.K.: Garnet.

Record, Jeffrey. 2009. *Japan's Decision for War in 1941: Some Enduring Lessons.* Carlisle, PA: Army War College Strategic Studies Institute.

Reiter, Dan, and Allan C. Stam. 2002. *Democracies at War.* Princeton, NJ: Princeton University Press.

Reiter, Dan. 2003. "Exploring the Bargaining Model of War." *Perspectives on Politics* 1(1): 27–43.

Remmer, Karen L. 1989. *Military Rule in Latin America*. Boston: Unwin Hyman.

Renshon, Stanley A., ed. 1993. *The Political Psychology of the Gulf War: Leaders, Publics, and the Process of Conflict*. Pittsburgh: University of Pittsburgh Press.

Rezun, Miron. 1992. *Saddam Hussein's Gulf Wars: Ambivalent Stakes in the Middle East*. Westport, CT: Praeger.

Richards, Diana, T. Morgan, Clifton, Rick K. Wilson, Valerie L. Schwebach, and Garry Y. Young. 1993. "Good Times, Bad Times, and the Diversionary Use of Force: A Tale of Some Not-So-Free Agents." *Journal of Conflict Resolution* 37(3): 504–35.

Richter, James G. 1989. "Action and Reaction in Khrushchev's Foreign Policy: How Leadership Politics Affect Soviet Responses to the International Environment." PhD dissertation, University of California at Berkeley.

——. 1994. *Khrushchev's Double Bind: International Pressures and Domestic Coalition Politics*. Baltimore: Johns Hopkins University Press.

Risse-Kappen, Thomas. 1995. "Democratic Peace—Warlike Democracies? A Social Constructivist Interpretation of the Liberal Argument." *European Journal of International Relations* 1(4): 491–517.

Roberts, Geoffrey. 1992. "The Fall of Litvinov: A Revisionist View." *Journal of Contemporary History* 27(4): 639–57.

——. 2006. *Stalin's Wars: From World War to Cold War, 1939–1953*. New Haven, CT: Yale University Press.

Rosen, Stephen Peter. 2005. *War and Human Nature*. Princeton, NJ: Princeton University Press.

Rosenfeldt, Niels E., Bent Jensen, and Erik Kulavig. 2000. *Mechanisms of Power in the Soviet Union*. New York: St. Martin's.

Ross, Dennis. 1984. "Risk Aversion in Soviet Decisionmaking." In *Soviet Decision-making for National Security*, ed. Jiri Valenta and William Potter, 237–51. London: G. Allen & Unwin.

Ross, Robert S. 1988. *The Indochina Tangle: China's Vietnam Policy, 1975–1979*. New York: Columbia University Press.

——. 2009. *Chinese Security Policy: Structure, Power, and Politics*. New York: Routledge.

Roy, Denny. 2009. "China's Democratised Foreign Policy." *Survival* 51(2): 25–40.

Royama, Masamichi. 1941. *Foreign Policy of Japan: 1913–1939*. Japan: Kenkyusha.

Russett, Bruce M., and John R. Oneal. 2001. *Triangulating Peace: Democracy, Interdependence, and International Organizations*. New York: Norton.

Sagan, Scott. 2000. *Planning the Unthinkable: How New Powers Will Use Nuclear, Biological, and Chemical Weapons*. Ithaca: Cornell University Press.

Sakwa, Richard. 1998. *Soviet Politics in Perspective*. London: Routledge.

SarDesai, D. R. 2005. *Vietnam, Past and Present*. Boulder, CO: Westview.

Sarkees, Meredith Reid, and Frank Whelon Wayman. 2010. *Resort to War: A Data Guide to Inter-State, Extra-State, Intra-State, and Non-State Wars, 1816–2007*. Washington, DC: CQ Press.

Sassoon, Joseph. 2011. *Saddam Hussein's Ba'th Party: Inside an Authoritarian Regime*. Cambridge, U.K.: Cambridge University Press.

Saunders, Elizabeth N. 2009. "Transformative Choices: Leaders and the Origins of Intervention Strategy." *International Security* 34(2): 119–61.

——. 2011. *Leaders at War: How Presidents Shape Military Interventions*. Ithaca: Cornell University Press.

Schroeder, Paul W. 1958. *The Axis Alliance and Japanese-American Relations*. Ithaca: Cornell University Press.

Schultz, Kenneth A. 1999. "Do Democratic Institutions Constrain or Inform? Contrasting Two Institutional Perspectives on Democracy and War." *International Organization* 53(2): 233–66.

——. 2001a. *Democracy and Coercive Diplomacy*. New York: Cambridge University Press.

——. 2001b. "Looking for Audience Costs." *Journal of Conflict Resolution* 45(1): 32.

Schweller, Randall L. 1994. "Bandwagoning for Profit: Bringing the Revisionist State Back In." *International Security* 19(1): 72–107.

——. 1998. *Deadly Imbalances: Tripolarity and Hitler's Strategy of World Conquest*. New York: Columbia University Press.

Seawright, Jason, and John Gerring. 2008. "Case Selection Techniques in Case Study Research: A Menu of Qualitative and Quantitative Options." *Political Research Quarterly* 61(2): 294.

Sechser, Todd S. 2004. "Are Soldiers Less War-prone than Statesmen?" *Journal of Conflict Resolution* 48(5): 746–74.

Seki, Hiroharu. 1984. "The Manchurian Incident." In *Japan Erupts: The London Naval Conference and the Manchurian Incident, 1928–1932*, ed. James Morley, 139–230. New York: Columbia University Press.

Service, Robert. 2005. *Stalin: A Biography*. Cambridge, MA: Belknap Press of Harvard University Press.

Shepilov, D. T., Stephen V. Bittner, and Anthony Austin. 2007. *The Kremlin's Scholar: A Memoir of Soviet Politics under Stalin and Khrushchev*. New Haven, CT: Yale University Press.

Shevchenko, Arkady N. 1985. *Breaking with Moscow*. New York: Knopf.

Shimada, Toshihiko. 1983. "Designs on North China, 1933–1937." In *The China Quagmire: Japan's Expansion on the Asian Continent, 1933–1941*, ed. James W. Morley, 11–232. New York: Columbia University Press.

——. 1984. "The Extension of Hostilities, 1931–1932." In *Japan Erupts: The London Naval Conference and the Manchurian Incident, 1928–1932*, ed. James Morley. New York: Columbia University Press.

Shirk, Susan L. 2007. *China: Fragile Superpower*. New York: Oxford University Press.

Shukman, Harold. 1993. *Stalin's Generals*. New York: Grove Press.

Simes, Dimitri. 1984. "The Politics of Defense in the Soviet Union: Brezhnev's Era." In *Soviet Decisionmaking for National Security*, ed. Jiri Valenta and William Potter, 74–84. London and Boston: G. Allen & Unwin.

Simpson, John. 2003. *The Wars against Saddam*. London: Macmillan.

Singer, J. David, Stuart Bremer, and John Stuckey. 1972. "Capability Distribution, Uncertainty, and Major Power War, 1820–1965." In *Peace, War, and Numbers*, ed. Bruce Russett, 19–48. Beverly Hills, CA: Sage.

Slantchev, Branislav. 2003. "The Power to Hurt: Costly Conflict with Completely Informed States." *American Political Science Review* 97(1): 123–33.

Slater, Dan. 2003. "Iron Cage in an Iron Fist: Authoritarian Institutions and the Personalization of Power in Malaysia." *Comparative Politics* 36(1): 81–101.

Smith, Alastair. 1996. "Diversionary Foreign Policy in Democratic Systems." *International Studies Quarterly* 40(1): 133–53.

——. 1998. "International Crises and Domestic Politics." *American Political Science Review* 92(3): 623–38.

Snyder, Jack L. 1984. *The Ideology of the Offensive: Military Decision Making and the Disasters of 1914*. Ithaca: Cornell University Press.

———. 1991. *Myths of Empire: Domestic Politics and International Ambition*. Ithaca: Cornell University Press.

Sobek, David. 2005. "Machiavelli's Legacy: Domestic Politics and International Conflict." *International Studies Quarterly* 49(2): 179–204.

Spring, D. W. 1986. "The Soviet Decision for War against Finland, 30 November 1939." *Soviet Studies* 38(2): 207–26.

Stepan, Alfred. 1988. *Rethinking Military Politics: Brazil and the Southern Cone*. Princeton, NJ: Princeton University Press.

Stewart, Brandon M., and Yuri M. Zhukov. 2009. "Use of Force and Civil–Military Relations in Russia: An Automated Content Analysis." *Small Wars and Insurgencies* 20(2): 319–43.

Stinnett, Douglas M., Jaroslav Tir, Philip Schafer, Paul F. Diehl, and Charles Gochman. 2002. "The Correlates of War (COW) Project Direct Contiguity Data, Version 3.0." *Conflict Management and Peace Science* 19(2): 59–68.

Stueck, William. 1997. *The Korean War: An International History*. Princeton, NJ: Princeton University Press.

Svolik, Milan W. 2009. "Power Sharing and Leadership Dynamics in Authoritarian Regimes." *American Journal of Political Science* 53(2): 477–94.

———. 2012. *The Politics of Authoritarian Rule*. Cambridge, U.K.: Cambridge University Press.

———. Forthcoming. "Contracting on Violence: Moral Hazard in Authoritarian Repression and Military Intervention in Politics." *Journal of Conflict Resolution*.

Talmadge, Caitlin. 2013. "The Puzzle of Personalist Performance: Iraqi Battlefield Effectiveness in the Iran-Iraq War." *Security Studies* 22(2): 180–221.

Tangerås, Thomas. 2009. "Democracy, Autocracy, and the Likelihood of International Conflict." *Economics of Governance* 10(2): 99–117.

Tanner, Väinö. 1957. *The Winter War: Finland against Russia, 1939–1940*. Stanford, CA: Stanford University Press.

Taubman, William. 2003. *Khrushchev: The Man and His Era*. New York: Norton.

Thakur, Ramesh C., and Carlyle A. Thayer. 1992. *Soviet Relations with India and Vietnam*. New York: St. Martin's.

Tinch, Clark. 1951. "War Between Japan and the U.S.S.R, 1937–1939." *Quasi-W World Politics* 3(2): 174–99.

Tir, Jaroslav. 2010. "Territorial Diversion: Diversionary Theory of War and Territorial Conflict." *Journal of Politics* 72(2): 413–25.

Titus, David A. 1994. "Introduction." In *Japan's Road to the Pacific War: The Final Confrontation*, ed. James William Morley, New York: Columbia University Press.

Toland, John. 1970. *The Rising Sun: The Decline and Fall of the Japanese Empire, 1936–1945*. New York: Random House.

Tompson, William. 1995. *Khrushchev—A Political Life*. New York: St. Martin's.

———. 2003. *The Soviet Union under Brezhnev*. Harlow, U.K.: Pearson/Longman.

Tomz, Michael, and Jessica Weeks. 2013. "Public Opinion and the Democratic Peace." *American Political Science Review* 107(4): 849–65.

Tomz, Michael, Jason Wittenberg, and Gary King. 2003. "Clarify: Software for Interpreting and Presenting Statistical Results." *Journal of Statistical Software* 8(1): 1–30.

Trachtenberg, Marc. 2006. *The Craft of International History: A Guide to Method*. Princeton, NJ: Princeton University Press.

Tripp, Charles. 1987. "The Consequences of the Iran-Iraq War for Iraqi Politics." In *The Iran-Iraq War*, ed. Efraim Karsh, 58–77. London: Macmillan.

Triska, Jan, and David D. Finley. 1968. *Soviet Foreign Policy*. New York: Macmillan.

Troyanovsky, Oleg. 2000. "The Making of Soviet Foreign Policy." In *Nikita Khrush-chev*, ed. W. Taubman, S. Khrushchev, and A. Gleason, 209–41. New Haven, CT: Yale University Press.

Tsunoda, Jun. 1994. "Leaning Toward War" and "Decision for War" in *The Final Confrontation: Japan's Negotiations with the United States, 1941*, ed. James William Morley. New York: Columbia University Press.

Tucker, Robert C. 1990. *Stalin in Power: The Revolution from Above, 1928–1941*. New York: Norton.

Vagts, Alfred. 1956. *Defense and Diplomacy: The Soldier and the Conduct of Foreign Relations*. New York: King's Crown Press.

Valenta, Jiri. 1979. *Soviet Intervention in Czechoslovakia, 1968: Anatomy of a Decision*. Baltimore: Johns Hopkins University Press.

——. 1984. "Soviet Decisionmaking on Afghanistan, 1979." In *Soviet Decisionmaking for National Security*, ed. Jiri Valenta and William Potter, 218–36. London, Boston: G. Allen & Unwin.

Valentino, Benjamin A., Paul K. Huth, and Sarah Croco. 2006. "Covenants without the Sword: International Law and the Protection of Civilians in Times of War." *World Politics* 58(3): 339–77.

——. 2010. "Bear Any Burden? How Democracies Minimize the Costs of War." *Journal of Politics* 72(2): 528–44.

Van Dyke, Carl. 1997. *The Soviet Invasion of Finland 1939–1940*. Portland, OR: Frank Cass.

Van Evera, Stephen. 1984a. *Causes of War*. PhD dissertation, University of California at Berkeley.

——. 1984b. "The Cult of the Offensive and the Origins of the First World War." *International Security* 9(1): 58–107.

——. 1997. *Guide to Methods for Students of Political Science*. Ithaca: Cornell University Press.

Vertzberger, Yaacov. 1998. *Risk Taking and Decisionmaking: Foreign Military Intervention Decisions*. Stanford, CA: Stanford University Press.

Vinh, Dong, ed. 2009. *The 30-Year War, 1945–1975*. Hanoi: Thê Gió'i Publishers.

Volkogonov, Dmitri. 1988. *The Soviet Army*. Moscow: Planeta Publishers.

——. 1991. *Stalin: Triumph and Tragedy*. London: George Weidenfeld & Nicholson.

Wahman, Michael, Jan Teorell, and Axel Hadenius. 2013. "Authoritarian Regime Types Revisited: Updated Data in Comparative Perspective." *Contemporary Politics* 19(1): 19–34.

Wallace, Geoffrey. 2010. "Surrendering the Higher Ground: The Abuse of Combatants during War." PhD dissertation, Cornell University.

Walt, Stephen M. 1996. *Revolution and War*. Ithaca: Cornell University Press.

Waltz, Kenneth N. 1959. *Man, the State, and War: A Theoretical Analysis*. New York: Columbia University Press.

Watson, Derek. 2004. "Molotov, Foreign Policy and the Politburo 1926–1939." In *The Nature of Stalin's Dictatorship: the Politburo 1924–1953*, ed. E.A. Rees, New York: Palgrave Macmillan.

Way, Christopher, and Jessica Weeks. Forthcoming. "Making it Personal: Regime Type and Nuclear Proliferation." *American Journal of Political Science*.

Weart, Spencer R. 1994. "Peace among Democratic and Oligarchic Republics." *Journal of Peace Research* 31(3): 299–316.

Weathersby, Kathryn. 1993. *Soviet Aims in Korea and the Origins of the Korean War, 1945–1950: New Evidence from Russian Archives*. Washington, DC: Cold War

Works Cited

International History Project, Woodrow Wilson International Center for Scholars.

Weber, Max. [1947] 1997. *The Theory of Social and Economic Organization*. Glencoe, IL: Free Press.

Weeks, Jessica L. 2008. "Autocratic Audience Costs: Regime Type and Signaling Resolve." *International Organization* 62(1): 35–64.

——. 2012. "Strongmen and Straw Men: Authoritarian Regimes and the Initiation of International Conflict." *American Political Science Review* 106(2): 326–47.

Weiss, Jessica Chen. 2013. "Autocratic Signaling, Mass Audiences, and Nationalist Protest in China." *International Organization* 67(1): 1–35.

——. 2014. *Powerful Patriots: Nationalist Protest in China's Foreign Relations*. New York: Oxford University Press.

Weland, James. 1994. "Misguided Intelligence: Japanese Military Intelligence Officers in the Manchurian Incident, September 1931." *Journal of Military History* 53(3): 445–60.

Wendt, Alexander. 1992. "Anarchy Is What States Make of It: The Social Construction of Power Politics." *International Organization* 46(2): 391–425.

Westad, Odd Arne. 2006. "From War to Peace to War in Indochina." In *The Third Indochina War: Conflict Between China, Vietnam, and Cambodia*, ed. Odd Westad and Sophie Quinn-Judge, 1–11. Abingdon, U.K.: Routledge.

Wetzler, Peter M. 1998. *Hirohito and War: Imperial Tradition and Military Decision Making in Prewar Japan*. Berkeley, CA: University of Hawai'i Press.

Whymant, Robert. 1996. *Stalin's Spy: Richard Sorge and the Tokyo Espionage Ring*. London: I.B. Tauris.

Wintrobe, Ronald. 2000. *The Political Economy of Dictatorship*. New York: Cambridge University Press.

Woods, Kevin M. 2008. *The Mother of All Battles: Saddam Hussein's Strategic Plan for the Persian Gulf War*. Annapolis, MD: Naval Institute Press.

Woods, Kevin M., Michael R. Pease, Mark E. Stout, Williamson Murray, and James G. Lacey. 2006. *Iraqi Perspectives Project: A View of Operation Iraqi Freedom from Saddam's Senior Leadership*. Norfolk, VA: United States Joint Forces Command, Joint Center for Operational Analysis.

Worth, Roland H. 1995. *No Choice But War: The United States Embargo against Japan and the Eruption of War in the Pacific*. Jefferson, NC: McFarland.

Wright, Joseph. 2008. "Do Authoritarian Institutions Constrain? How Legislatures Affect Economic Growth and Investment." *American Journal of Political Science* 52(2): 322–43.

——. 2009. "How Foreign Aid Can Foster Democratization in Authoritarian Regimes." *American Journal of Political Science* 53(3): 552–71.

——. 2010. "Aid Effectiveness and the Politics of Personalism." *Comparative Political Studies* 43(6): 735–62.

Young, Katsu H. 1967. "The Nomonhan Incident: Imperial Japan and the Soviet Union." *Monumenta Nipponica* 22(1/2): 82–102.

Index

Note: Page numbers followed by *t* indicate tables and page numbers followed by *f* indicate figures.